Knowledge Innovation

To My Family

Knowledge Innovation

Strategic Management as Practice

Mitsuru Kodama

Professor of Information and Management, College of Commerce and Graduate School of Business Administration, Nihon University at Tokyo, Japan

Edward Elgar
Cheltenham, UK • Northampton, MA, USA

Published by
Edward Elgar Publishing Limited
Glensanda House
Montpellier Parade
Cheltenham
Glos GL50 1UA
UK

Edward Elgar Publishing, Inc.
William Pratt House
9 Dewey Court
Northampton
Massachusetts 01060
USA

A catalogue record for this book
is available from the British Library

ISBN 978 1 84542 929 4

Printed and bound in Great Britain by MPG Books Ltd, Bodmin, Cornwall

Contents

List of figures

List of tables

Preface and acknowledgements

This book deals with activities related to corporate strategic management from the viewpoint of the knowledge possessed by individuals and groups. I have based the book's contents on many years of close observation and analysis in the workplace. My research has mainly targeted the ICT (Information and Communications Technology) industry. I chose this industry, and especially the area of telecommunications carriers, because it has seen the greatest shifts in business models of all industries over the past decade.

The world's telecommunications carriers constantly face strategic and organizational upheaval aimed at creating markets for broadband and wireless communication businesses under dramatically changing conditions of evolving markets and technologies, deregulation and global competition. Over the last ten years, the telecommunications industry has developed enormously. Content-centered broadband business arose from the static phone-centered business model. Now Japan is leading the world in terms of technology and markets for content-centered mobile phone services, and players in various industries and business environments are participating in this industry and targeting new business opportunities.

Until recently, I was involved in the exciting business of new product and service development, new business development and internal corporate ventures in the dramatically changing field of ICT. Through this business experience, I have come to feel that the driving forces supporting corporate learning and innovation have as their starting point the structures of knowledge possessed by individuals and groups, top and middlemanagement leadership and the processes by which actual business is implemented. This knowledge, leadership and process leads to the formulation and implementation of dynamic strategy in the company (or organization). The network is an especially important focal point. On a microlevel, the dynamic knowledge networks consciously implemented by the actors during the process give rise to new knowledge and innovation.

The purpose of this book is to ascertain the constantly changing strategies and organizational dynamics and processes, in real-time and on a temporal axis, in the ICT and other fields in fast-changing industries, and then to derive a micro-level theoretical framework for the new knowledge and innovation that companies should create. As a practitioner and researcher in the field of management studies, my focus in this book is how to bridge theory and practice. In order to achieve this, I have observed and analyzed in detail the thoughts and behavior processes of a large number of actors, including customers and partner ventures deeply involved with a company's internal organization.

I have also undertaken in-depth qualitative studies from my own observations and experience concerning the way actors in reality dynamically formulate and implement strategies within and outside the company, and pursued the research topic of how companies reorganize and acquire new competences. Accordingly, the research methods focus on participant observation and ethnography. I myself have collected detailed raw data relating to management generally from the daily comments and meeting patterns of top management, middle management and staff at the workplace, and from daily work styles, informal discussion and in-depth interviews. I have also collected a large amount of data from formal and informal meetings and discussions with customers and external partners. The important axis acquired from data includes, in particular, shared vision and strategic aims, shared values, knowledge, boundaries, teamwork, community, collaboration, network, motivation, trust, leadership, conflict and discord. I then derived many of the core concepts of this book by means of grounded theory arising from the data categorized around the important axes.

Many years of field research into the practical activities of actors living various lifestyles, and aiming to create the future and achieve their visions in lively workplaces, have provided me with valuable insights and courage. Any business activity (macro or micro, instance of success or instance of failure) contains drama, and the actors' subjectivity and values in the forms of conviction and feelings go into achieving strategies and acquiring competences. Put in another way, management theory that rejects subjectivity cannot be realistic. In daily business activities, practitioners face a barrage of issues and questions, such as 'What should I think and do when facing difficulty?' 'What relations should I have with my superiors, colleagues, juniors, partners and customers?' 'How can I overcome discord and conflict?' The thinking of scientific, objective, theoretical analysis cannot solve all the problems facing the practitioners in the practical arena of the workplace.

This book could not have been completed without the thorough and demanding interaction that I have had with many practitioners. I would like to extend my gratitude to these practitioners, who are of a number too great to count. Among them, I would like to express my deep gratitude to Mr

Shigeru Ikeda, former senior executive vice president of NTT and former president of CIAJ. I learned a great deal about methods of change management from Mr Ikeda. I would also like to accord deep thanks to the late Mr Norioki Morinaga (former NTT DoCoMo vice-president) and Mr Shiro Tsuda (a former vice-president of NTT DoCoMo and former CEO of Vodafone K.K.). Both these people were my immediate superiors at head office at the time I joined NTT. They also warmly welcomed me when I was transferred from NTT East to NTT DoCoMo. I also wish to thank my family, who supported me when I made the transition from the business to the academic world. Concerning the publication of this book, I wish to extend my appreciation to Ms Francine O'Sullivan, Senior Commissioning Editor, Mr Jo Betteridege, Editor, and Ms Emma Gorden-Walker, Editorial Assistant in Edward Elgar, who provided tremendous support.

Finally, I have used fragments of material I have previously published. These are refereed papers cited below. I am deeply appreciative to the following publishers for their permission to reuse this material.

Permission has been received from Elsevier Science to use the following papers:
Kodama, M. (1999), 'Customer Value Creation through Community-Based Information Networks', *International Journal of Information Management*, Vol. 19, No. 6.
Kodama, M. (2002), 'Transforming the Old Economy Company to New Economy', *Long Range Planning*, Vol. 35, No. 4.
Kodama, M. (2004), 'Business innovation through strategic community creation: a case study of multimedia business field in Japan', *Journal of Engineering and Technology Management*, Vol. 21, No. 3.

Permission has been received from Taylor & Francis to use the following paper:
Kodama, M. (2001), 'New Business Through Strategic Community Management', *International Journal of Human Resource Management*, Vol. 11, No. 6.

Permission has been received from Blackwell to use the following paper:
Kodama, M. (2001), 'Innovation through Strategic Community Management – A Case Study Involving Regional Electric Networking Promotion in Japan', *Creativity and Innovation Management*, Vol. 9, No. 2.

Permission has been received from Emerald to use the following papers:

Kodama, M. (1999), 'Business Innovation through Joint Ventures Supported by Major Businesses: Case Study on US–Japan Joint Venture Businesses', *Journal of Management Development*, Vol. 18, No. 7.

Kodama, M. (2005), 'New Knowledge Creation through Dialectical Leadership – A Case of IT and Multimedia Business in Japan', *European Journal of Innovation Management*, Vol. 8, No 1.

Permission has been received from Springer to use the following papers:

Kodama, M. (2002), 'Strategic Community Management with Customers – Case Study on Innovation Using IT and Multimedia Technology in Education, Medical and Welfare Fields', *International Journal of Value-Based Management*, Vol. 15, No. 3.

Mitsuru Kodama

1. Knowledge innovation

1.1 INNOVATION IN A NETWORK ECONOMY

The shape of business is changing rapidly with the expansion of ICT (Information and Communication Technology) and transformation of the structure of industry and the business environment. Companies are increasingly focusing on strategic business approaches that look beyond the resources of existing business units within the corporation to take in strategic alliances with external partners, mergers and acquisitions (M&As) and strategic outsourcing, as well as external knowledge and human resources. In particular, superior core technologies and diverse business models in such cutting-edge business fields as IT, e-business, content provision, electronics and biotechnology are being transformed and spreading around the globe. In this age of mass production, companies are finding it harder to control innovation fully under closed, autonomous system conditions within the existing hierarchical organization.

Examples of new approaches include open innovation (Chesbrough, 2003) and distributed innovation (Haour, 2004), which emphasize engendering new innovation by managing a wide range of knowledge from both internal and external perspectives. Another approach is to focus on an edge-of-chaos model called 'Community of creation' (Sawhney and Prandelli, 2000) as a new mechanism of governance managing distributed innovation, which lies somewhere between control and chaos. Thus corporations are focusing on management models that synthesize advanced knowledge from a wide area within and outside the corporation (including customers) in an open, networked system in their drive to enhance competitive advantage in a knowledge economy (Kodama, 2005a).

First of all, I would like to introduce some case studies. The first case concerns the communications industry. In the business model centered on telephone services prior to the advent of the Internet, the field of technology was clear, and corporations possessed core technologies and knowledge in a closed system within the corporation (such as *keiretsu* networks that included suppliers). Periods for developing products and services were relatively long, and it was an age when corporations could provide their own

1

vertically-integrated services. Then came the 1990s, when dramatic technological innovations accompanying the advent of the Internet were followed by broadband, and then the mobile Internet rapidly transformed conventional business models. As shown in Figure 1.1, the vertically-integrated business model centered on telephone services has crumbled in the age of IP (Internet Protocol), and the players have engaged in fierce one-to-one competition over multiple layers, including: terminals (telephone sets, PCs, PDAs, mobile phones, iPods and other portable information terminals); networks (broadband, mobile and other types); platforms performing functions such as content authentication (for music, video, game software, e-commerce and other areas); billing; content distribution; copyright management; and content and applications providing services to end users with various types of terminals. These trends indicate a shift from vertically-integrated to horizontally-dispersed business models. In the real world, individual players in individual layers compete with one another while promoting strategic alliances with players in adjacent layers or expanding business opportunities through M&As.

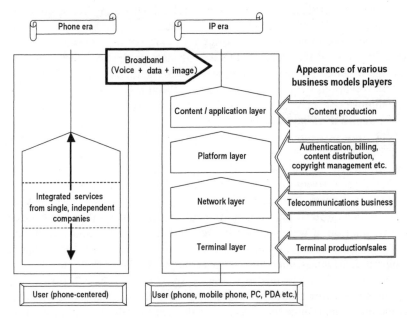

Figure 1.1   The value chain revolution in the communications industry

The primary business strategy of NTT DoCoMo, KDDI and other mobile phone carriers in Japan is to propagate and expand 3G mobile phone services. DoCoMo pursued strategic alliances with leading communications device manufacturers, computer makers and software vendors to develop a technical platform for hardware and software and create new services, and at the same time actively pursued collaborations with various industries and organizations to realize electronic payment services. DoCoMo has also been pursuing joint development of mobile e-cash and e-credit services through strategic alliances with companies such as Sony, which has electronic money card technology; Japan Railway (JR), Japan's largest railway company, which has prepaid card service know-how; and Mitsui Sumitomo VISA card, which is a member company of a major finance group in Japan. DoCoMo launched its mobile e-cash service in October 2004, and followed it up by launching the world's first mobile credit card service in December 2005 (Figure 1.2). In the search for new business models, players are striving to acquire knowledge that transcends the boundaries of their own company at each level.

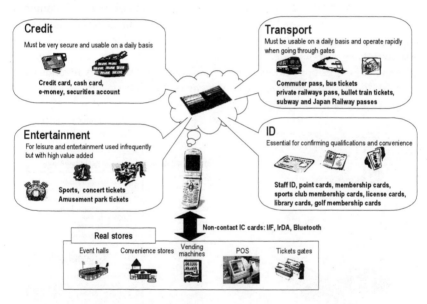

Figure 1.2 Mobile wallet service from mobile phones

The second case study involves a situation that is causing major change in the automobile industry. The mass-production business model pioneered by Ford is changing as market conditions require smaller quantities of a larger number of types to handle greater diversification in models and shorter development times. Automobile manufacturers are also facing new challenges, such as greater cabin comfort for customers, safety and protecting the environment.

One major issue automobile manufacturers are facing involves how to respond to the growing need for information in the car. As well as communication functions like voice or email that they would expect from a mobile phone or computer, customers require multimedia functions, such as the ability to download text, music and video content, or even to make e-commerce transactions from the car. Automakers need to develop these functions, and are therefore creating strategic alliances for joint development with mobile phone carriers (Toyota has an alliance with KDDI and Nissan with NTT DoCoMo). Automobile manufacturers are also teaming up with Apple Computer to improve in-car music distribution services for the iPod, and developing other communication content functions with various software and IT vendors. In addition, automakers are working with influential content providers to include wireless telematics services (interactive information transmission systems) in the cabin (Toyota's brand is called G-BOOK, Nissan's is CARWINGS, and Honda's is Premium Club). Automakers are also looking for new content businesses with providers. A collaboration with Microsoft has resulted in the installation of the Windows Automobile 5.0 operating system (OS) in car navigation systems. This OS not only enhances conventional navigation functions but also facilitates the development of the car navigation system as a PC that supports telematics services (Figure 1.3).

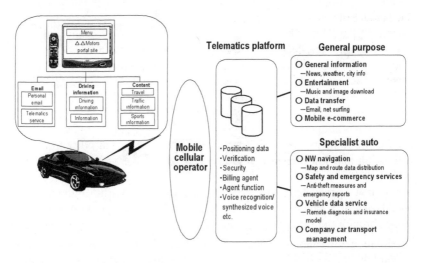

Figure 1.3   Telematics services

Another issue involves the need to respond to safety and environmental concerns. Faced with recent environmental regulations and the rapid increase in oil prices, automobile manufacturers are under pressure to develop cars that are both clean and affordable to run. To develop hybrid cars, which are enjoying increasingly strong demand, automobile manufacturers need to strengthen their relationships with Denso, Aisin Seiki and other parts manufacturers, while collaborating with electrical machinery manufacturers such as Hitachi, Mitsubishi, Toshiba, Matsushita, NEC, Fujitsu and Sharp. Automakers also need to respond urgently to information, safety and environmental demands by developing dedicated semiconductor chips (Large Scale Integrated Circuit (LSIs)). To this end, they are strengthening collaborative relationships with leading semiconductor vendors in Japan and around the world, including Motorola and Freescale Semiconductor in the United States. Finally, automakers are aiming to make their future cars lighter by pursuing strategic ties with General Electric, Du Pont and other manufacturers that develop resins and aluminum materials.

As well as promoting strategic alliances among disparate industries, automakers are collaborating with other players in their own industry. Sony has already formed a joint venture with Ericsson to develop and manufacture mobile phones, while in February 2006 Sanyo Electric, a Japanese home appliance manufacturer, issued a press release announcing a similar joint venture with Nokia. In the field of digital home appliances, Sony and Samsung have formed a joint venture to produce flat-panel liquid crystal display televisions, and Canon and Toshiba have established one to produce flat-panel SED (surface electric display) televisions. In the area of digital cameras, Matsushita Electric and Olympus have announced plans to develop jointly digital single lens reflex (SLR) cameras. In the automobile industry, Honda announced an agreement in August 2005 whereby it would jointly develop fuel cell vehicles with General Motors of the United States and BMW of Germany. In September 2002, a Nissan–Toyota venture was announced that involved Toyota supplying hybrid systems to Nissan. Inter-rival collaboration is also gaining momentum in the globally-competitive automobile industry, as rivals form flexible ties with each other to acquire new skills and knowledge and enhance competitiveness (Hamel, Doz and Prahalad, 1989).

So new products and services that transcend the organizational boundaries of a range of industries are continuing to appear in the Asian arena through the integration of knowledge in the automobile industry and in digital appliances such as mobile phones. This integration is forming value chains that become the basis for new strategic frameworks.

1.2   INNOVATION RESULTING FROM DYNAMIC STRATEGY

Traditional innovation in mature industries was entirely controlled by the corporation through hierarchical, closed, autonomous systems such as research laboratories, with the corporation retaining the intellectual property rights (Sawhney and Prandelli, 2000). The governance mechanism of this type of innovation created a corporation's unique core competences and was the source of competitive advantage (Hamel and Prahalad, 1994).

Meanwhile, by outsourcing areas where it lacked resources, a company could expand horizontal boundaries, boost economies of scope, and improve the efficiency of the overall organization (Teece, 1982). In a slowly changing environment, this was best achieved by building tight-coupled, vertically integrated business models, either within the company or within *keiretsu*-style business groupings, by means of close interdependency of technological resources and vertical boundaries among business units.

The creation of industry value chains had become crucial (Porter, 1985) (the established telecommunications services in Figure 1.1 relate to this). However, although path-dependent, tight internal linkage is a strength, a weakness in this model was that major problems tended to occur as a result of the changing environment (Siggelkow, 2001; Hargadon and Sutton, 1997; Henderson and Clark, 1990). Moreover, it is clear that changing markets and disruptive technology (Christensen, 1997) were turning the strength of original technology and value chains to weakness (Levitt and March, 1988; Martines and Kambil, 1999; Leonard-Barton, 1992, 1995).

Moreover, faster changes in the market environment (Eisenhardt, 1989; Brown and Eisenhardt, 1998; D'Aveni, 1994, 1995; Chakravarthy, 1997; Eisenhardt and Sull, 2001) have underlined the importance of 'dynamic capabilities' – the process of responding flexibly to changing environments by aggressively adopting resources external to the company – although companies continue to strengthen and maintain core competences using traditional 'focus and choose' methods. Dynamic capabilities have been defined as organizational processes by which members manipulate resources to develop new value-creating strategies (Teece *et al.*, 1997; Eisenhardt and Martine, 2000). Thus it is important for a company to integrate its resources and build new product and service business models by refining and deepening its in-house core competences (path-dependent resources) while dynamically adopting external core competences (including path-breaking resources). To achieve this requires the integration of internally and externally distributed knowledge (resources) and dynamic processes of remodeling in response to conditions.

This means that the vertical and horizontal boundaries formed by corporate business models must always be revamped in response to changing environments, or when a company intentionally changes its own environment (Eisenhardt and Bingham, 2005). From now on, companies must look beyond the growth of their existing businesses to the acquisition of new business opportunities. They must have the capability to acquire knowledge ambitiously and tenaciously through smart combinations of path-dependent and path-breaking resources such as strategic alliances and M&As, which can be forged within the corporate group, within the same industry or across industry boundaries (see, for example, Karmin and Mitchell, 2000; Graebner, 2004).

To take a recent example, in the field of digital appliances including flat-screen TVs, DVD recorders and digital cameras, where Asian companies excel (Matsushita Electric Industrial Co., Sharp, Canon, SONY and Toshiba in Japan, and Samsung, LG Industries and others in South Korea), companies are constantly reviewing and remodeling their vertical boundaries (including R&D, components development, equipment development, manufacturing, marketing, distribution and services) and their horizontal boundaries (including sales, outsourcing and OEM). Matsushita Electric Industrial Co. and Sharp have a 'black box' of original technology for R&D, components development, equipment development and manufacturing, combined with procurement from other companies for old technology, outsourcing of established manufacturing methods (copiable technology) to other countries, and flexible promotion of other-brand original equipment manufacturers (OEMs).

At the same time, strategic alliances and M&As are expanding horizontal boundaries and propelling joint development and service and sales tie-ups (see, for example, Kodama 2007). This flexible combination of commitment to original development alongside joint development with other companies is progressing especially for System LSI development, which lies at the heart of digital appliances and where each company ruthlessly competes with a 'winner takes all' mentality.

As Philips' CEO, Mr Gerard Kleisterlee, describes:

> We used to start by identifying our core competences and then looking for market opportunities. Now we ask what is required to capture an opportunity and then either try to get those skills via alliances or develop them internally to fit. (*The Economist*, 9 February 2002)

Akinobu Kanasugi, the CEO of NEC, a company at the heart of mobile phone manufacturing, has this to say about corporate activities in the ubiquitous age:

Business in the high economic growth period focused on the 'integration principle' required by the expansion of business models based on a company's own resources. When the recession came, outsourcing activity began whereby non-core business was aggressively transferred outside the company, leaving the company to 'select and focus' its core competences. Business processes that were difficult to differentiate also began to be outsourced. Now, as competition among companies intensifies, companies are stepping up this select and focus approach, and are dynamically searching for new business development models through collaborating with strategic combinations that exploit the strengths of their own company and the outsource companies. Through flexible collaboration with the client companies, especially buyers, this new business model combines multiple strengths to create new corporate value and raise competitiveness. The new model requires the ability to respond to sharp changes in the business environment and to adjust partnerships. A company aims to optimize its valuation at all times during the switch to this model. NEC calls this process 'dynamic collaboration'. (*Nihon Keizai Shimbun*, 2003, 'Dynamic Collaboration', 25 August, p. 8)

The mobile phone, digital appliance and automaker industries go beyond the deepening and refining of core competences (path-dependent resources) to transcend industry boundaries and acquire new, differentiated knowledge (including path-breaking resources). Thus they hold dynamic views of strategy (see, for example, Markides, 1997; Eisenhardt and Sull, 2001) that are constantly and deliberately built around new market positions such as new products, services and business models.

Just how do companies acquire dynamic capability with a dynamic view of strategy in the face of rapid changes of environment? Company practitioners (managers and administrators) dealing with real-life problems face the following kinds of specific questions on a daily basis:

- How should we acquire new knowledge, and how should we formulate and implement strategy on the basis of that knowledge?
- How should actors go about scaling the walls between organizations and companies to share and integrate knowledge?
- What kind of leadership should the actors display to explore and implement new business?
- What shape should an organization have in order to implement new business?
- How should business-driven actors acquire and apply knowledge and skills?

Concerning agendas like these, the purpose of this book is to show the actors' thinking and behavior patterns in detail from a knowledge creation and practice-based view of strategic management founded on fieldwork analysis and consideration over a long period. In the following section, I will describe the integration of knowledge and the thinking, behavior and organization of the actors that should give birth to new innovations.

1.3 STRATEGIC COMMUNITIES ENGENDERING DYNAMIC KNOWLEDGE

The creativity or innovation of new organizations has a strong tendency to create boundaries between disciplines and specializations (Leonard-Barton, 1995). Companies are divisible into various functional and specialist areas and possess multiple boundaries, stretching from visible to invisible. These boundaries can be geographic (globalization), strategic (industry type), organizational (theory of the firm) and cognitive (bounded rationality).

As mentioned above, in the harsh business world subject to changing conditions and strong competition, many companies cross internal and external boundaries (including clients) in the search for the creation of new knowledge and innovation, and the actors integrate various kinds of knowledge and implement strategies. While knowledge is certainly the source of competitive edge (Kogut and Zander, 1992; Nonaka and Takeuchi, 1995; Leonard-Barton, 1995), the fixed mental models (Spender, 1990; Grinyer and McKiernan, 1994) and path-dependent knowledge held by each actor can also be a barrier to innovation (Carlile, 2002), as actors are constrained within organizational boundaries (sectionalism) and retain their individual values, background and specialties within knowledge boundaries (Brown and Duguid, 2001).

During my many years of business experience in numerous companies, I have often heard the following comments from business practitioners:

- I cannot make the appropriate adjustments to the division, and so cannot solve the outstanding problem.
- The customer has an urgent issue, but I can't get support from within the company.
- Another company has better, cheaper technology for product development, but our engineers are not trying positively to use it.
- There is a product development duplication in the business division. We are unable to adjust for the effective use of resources.
- Nobody is listening to other divisions' views on product development.
- We cannot meet the deadline because the design is difficult to assemble.

• Management always develops products that are difficult to explain to the customer.

Thus many practitioners acknowledge the invisible barriers between divisions within a company. I have also come across a large number of extended, difficult-to-define problems. The more trivial the problem, the greater the backbiting and blame passing. But the problem points and issues arising from relations with external partners and customers engender far greater tension and complexity. So how can we transcend organizational and knowledge boundaries to manage actors' knowledge and create new knowledge?

I am certain that the actors who have always shared knowledge from in-depth fieldwork and used it to create new knowledge have a network-minded behavior pattern. Such networks comprise person-to-person and knowledge networks on a micro scale, and group, organizational and corporate networks on a more macro scale. The macro networks can cross corporate (including client) internal and external boundaries, various management layers and different functional areas. A large number of scientific research reports (examples include Powell and Brantley, 1992; Powell, Koput and Smith-Doerr, 1996; and Rosenkopf and Tushman, 1998) have been written on the relation between the corporate network and innovation, but most of them have focused on analysis of the corporate or inter-corporate macro units.

In this book, I will analyze and study micro-network dynamism from a micro-strategy, strategizing and organizing (explained in Chapter 2) viewpoint focusing on corporate-driven actors, and then provide the reader with the research and managerial implications arising from the new theoretical frameworks. The focal concepts of the book deriving from in-depth observation and analysis of my business arena are those of the strategic community (SC) – a dynamic network of actors promoting knowledge sharing, knowledge integration and innovation – and the networked strategic community (Networked SC or NSC). Next, I would like to describe specifically the SC and NSC concepts and present two relevant cases, the first American and the second Japanese.

1.3.1 Buckman Laboratories

Buckman Laboratories has 1300 employees operating in research laboratories and bases in 21 countries, with headquarters in Memphis, Tennessee (see www.buckman.com). It mainly undertakes research contracts from paper manufacturing companies. Buckman Laboratories' technology forum (comprising 24 subcommittees and organized around paper pulp, leather, and other industries) is a network for knowledge sharing and knowledge creation that is essentially employee-driven. This forum, known as 'Techforum' on the K'Netix network, is always accessed through a single website from each employee's PC when floating new product concepts or experiencing deadlock (see Figure 1.4).

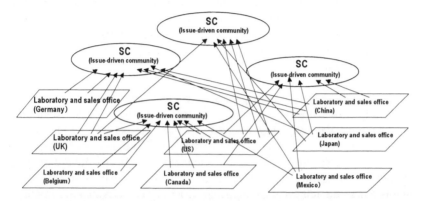

Figure 1.4   Techforum SC structure

Employees in every country can access Techforum, and requests are sent out for those with similar knowledge or interests to participate. The Techforum project is set up to function independently so that large numbers of employees can collaborate to transcend national, specialty, section and organizational boundaries. Employees can drive successive projects along by pooling knowledge and debating on the network. Every year more than 20 new technologies are created through this type of project, especially in the specialist field of paper products.

To illustrate how employees combined and produced results through Techforum, I will introduce an exchange about a cardboard product development case (Mizukoshi, 2002; Stepanek, 2000).

An English sales representative submitted a problem to Techforum, arising at his client's paper products company: the starch was not functioning properly to strengthen the paper during development. Numerous comments and suggestions on the cause and substitution methods arrived from Canada's vice-president of research and sales officials. An American engineer wrote that it indicated a problem with the starch itself, and then suggested a new project to solve the problem. Why wasn't the starch functioning as it should to strengthen the paper? Just when the discussion seemed to have reached a dead end, a German sales representative unexpectedly pointed out that the starch was being broken down by micro-organisms. Inspired by this new knowledge, members from other countries participated in a positive debate, creating a thread that led to a solution.

Micro-organisms appeared to be the cause of the problem. This hint led to pharmaceutical development on the activities of micro-organisms, propelled by the Techforum project. Around one month after the posting of the initial question a prototype robust paper used in cardboard was produced, thanks to this project in which eight people from five countries (including sales representatives, researchers, and a vice-president) participated.

Daniel Glover (Bubble section engineer), one of the project participants, said the following:

> The feeling I had on discovering the answer to the problem was just the same as when I discovered a five-dollar bill in the pocket of a coat I hadn't worn for a long time. It was a very happy feeling.

Today, Techforum is driven by an annual budget of 40 billion yen. Within the company, a result achieved by a project team is valued more highly than one achieved through individual effort. Buckman Laboratories has adopted the thinking that its power lies in the dissemination of individual knowledge to all.

Employees are now driven by desire for peer approval rather than for promotion or better working conditions, and Techforum members participate of their own volition rather than on request. Employees gain a sense of purpose and motivation by helping others and adding to each other's knowledge. Employees with good ideas earn the respect of their peers, creating positive feedback that confers a still greater sense of purpose. This has become Buckman Laboratories' corporate culture.

Through the knowledge creation processes, Techforum's 'issue-driven community' (Buckman Laboratories' president named it thus – Buckman, 2003), each employee's tacit knowledge is shared and inspired with positive dialog and thinking to constantly create new knowledge (new product development). In this way, Buckman Laboratories' Techforum has become a source of knowledge sharing and creation of new knowledge. Another feature is the participation of company president Bob Buckman himself in this virtual issue-driven community right from the start.

1.3.2 The NTT DoCoMo i-mode Revolution

The following case study is one of Japanese-pioneered innovation that is being studied in business schools the world over (see, for example, Kodama, 2002b). The story of i-mode, from development to product stage, is a classic example of SCs and NSCs.

At present, DoCoMo's corporate activities are supported by a solid knowledge vision that aims to create a new culture of communication based on mobile communications in the 21st century, realize a new knowledge-based society over the long term, and pursue the creation of absolute value. DoCoMo is constantly engaged in knowledge creation activities that are aimed at realizing the corporate mission and business domain based on this knowledge vision.

Data communication over mobile phones has expanded the possibilities of mobile computing and made it dramatically easier to perform. DoCoMo's i-mode Internet access technology for mobile phones has enabled the mobile handset to evolve from a simple mobile phone device into an information terminal. Studies have shown that Japan leads Europe and the United States in the area of mobile Internet use by at least two to three years. American journalists have also suggested that the wireless Internet services that have taken Japan by storm will capture the world.

Koji Oboshi, who was president of DoCoMo in 1997, predicted that the growth curve of subscribers using mobile phones for voice communications would soon reach market saturation point. As a result, he said, DoCoMo's profits would begin to fall and its growth would be threatened. Oboshi therefore turned his focus toward the market for data communications, a new market that could become an alternative to voice communications:

> When DoCoMo was founded, I projected that the mobile phone market in Japan would grow to about 10% of the country's population, or 12 million units, by 1999. At the time, I was told my projection was quite exaggerated. As it turned out, however, the speed of growth was much faster than that, and the 12 million level was reached in mid-1996, about three years earlier than projected. Seeing this excessively fast growth rate, I believed it wouldn't be long before the market would reach the saturation point, and I felt the need to create a new market outside the area of voice communications. I therefore decided to focus our energies on creating and improving non-voice services for the general market based on a direction moving from 'volume' to 'value', as I believed the business market for mobile computing or text and data communications could effectively expand to become a universal market.

Oboshi at the top acted alone in forming a new organization that would plan the new services for the launch of this new market. In January 1997, he issued a directive to Keiichi Enoki (currently director of the i-mode Business Division and an executive director of DoCoMo), who was then manager of the Corporate Sales Department, to develop non-voice services for mobile phones geared toward general users. Oboshi also instructed Enoki to build a new organization comprised of human resources he would recruit from outside the company as well as personnel from within DoCoMo. Enoki was given full authority in the areas of human resources and capital to prepare for the launch of the new services.

Oboshi reflects:

> I learned through the experience of direct dialogs with many employees in the past that this new area of business was enabled not so much by an organization as by the abilities of individuals. Thus it was of utmost importance to decide who would generate the ideas, and plan and develop the new products. Most of the novel, innovative ideas come from the minds of individuals. It is then the competences of the organization that nurture, manufacture and refine these ideas for the market.

Enoki gathered varied and capable personnel from both inside and outside the company and started work on the project (in charge of gateways). There were 10 people at the beginning, including Mari Matsunaga from Recruit, Inc., who was in charge of content strategies, and Takeshi Natsuno from IT Venture, Inc., who was in charge of overall business strategies, and in August 1997 a new organization, the Gateway Business Department (GBD), consisting of 70 people, was launched. GBD, with Enoki as leader, worked toward the development of a new service known as i-mode.

To create a business model dedicated to making the i-mode service a success, content providers (CPs) needed to provide attractive digital content continually to end users using i-mode-compliant mobile phones, which in turn would boost the number of end users. They also needed to receive positive feedback, leading to further improvements in CP content. The first issue to be addressed was hardware-related – how to develop a user-friendly i-mode-compliant mobile handset and a network system (including servers) that could distribute the content. The second issue was software-related – how to secure CPs in possession of attractive content.

To resolve these two major issues and realize the new service, Enoki, Matsunaga and Natsuno needed to merge and integrate intellectual assets, such as the knowledge and new ideas of different people in the GBD, the excellent technologies and sales expertise nurtured over many years in DoCoMo's traditional organizations (existing line organizations other than GBD), and content and other intellectual assets among CPs comprising customers external to DoCoMo. In other words, they had to merge and integrate knowledge from a range of organizations at multiple organizational boundaries (strategic communities). This merged and integrated knowledge (new knowledge resulting from the integration of networked strategic communities) then became a valuable element capable of building the new business model known as i-mode.

As a community leader, Enoki acted positively to build strategic communities (Figure 1.5) with the following:

- Traditional internal organizations centered on GBD (SC-a)
- CP clients (SC-b)
- Mobile phone manufacturers realizing i-mode services (SC-c)
- Music, image distribution, games, positioning data, mobile e-commerce and other manufacturers developing technology platforms realizing mobile telephony (SC-d)
- Overseas carriers for global distribution of i-mode services (SC-e)
- Tie-ups with other industries (distribution, finance, insurance, manufacturing, physical distribution, entertainment, education, medicine, welfare and others) to enable the use of mobile commerce in various daily life scenarios (see Figure 1.2) and to create new business models merging mobile telephony and broadcasting (SC-f).

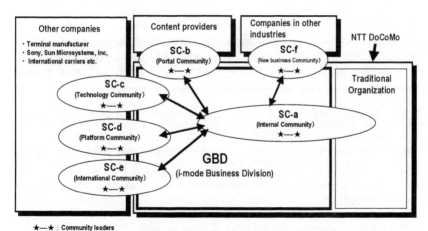

★----★ : Community leaders

Notes:

SC-a: Internal Community with GBD and traditional organization
SC-b: Portal Community with contents provider (CP)
SC-c: Technology Community with terminal manufacturer
SC-d: Platform Community with platform vendor and heterogeneous businesses
SC-e: International Community with international telecommunication carriers
SC-f: New Business Community with companies from other industries targeting mobile e-commerce, mobile phones, and broadcast integration services

Figure 1.5 Networked strategic communities – case of NTT DoCoMo

Next, the GBD had to overcome the two above-mentioned issues (hardware- and software- related) arising from consolidating, uniting and

creating a range of new knowledge engendered by these strategic
communities. It had also created and established an i-mode service business
model that enabled positive feedback. The number of i-mode subscribers
reached 45 million by the end of 2005, and DoCoMo is now aiming to
spread and expand the i-mode business model on a global level, mainly
through the i-mode business division creating SC tie-ups with overseas
carriers. Services are currently provided by 13 operators in 21 countries and
regions throughout the world, including Japan.

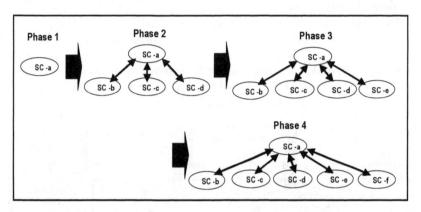

Phase 1: Creating SC with DoCoMo in-house (establishing i-mode business models)
Phase 2: Networking SC with DoCoMo, mobile phone manufacturers, platform vendors and content
         providers (realizing i-mode services)
Phase 3: Networking SC with DoCoMo, mobile phone manufacturers, platform vendors, content
         providers and overseas operators (i-mode overseas development)
Phase 4: Networking SC with DoCoMo, mobile phone manufacturers, platform vendors, content
         providers, overseas operators and other-industry companies (realizing new business
         models)

Figure 1.6   Dynamics of networked SCs at DoCoMo

SCs and NSCs have dynamic process structures. In Figure 1.5, various
areas of context and knowledge are networked in five SCs (SC-b to SC-f),
mainly within DoCoMo's internal SC (SC-a). The i-mode service itself is
implemented from integration of context and knowledge that crosses
different technologies and industries. These SCs have not suddenly become
networked. Instead, actors' autonomous implementation of strategy has
resulted in specific behavior aimed at integration of different contexts and
knowledge. Figure 1.6 shows networked SCs as shown in Figure 1.5 in
chronological order, and shows a dynamic structure. Moreover, although
each SC (SC-a to SC-f) is represented in simplified form in the figure,
realistically, each SC comprises multiple SCs that are stratified at the

business unit (or project unit) level. In the service development arena, actors from every specialization of public organizations participate in cross-functional teams (SCs that investigate subsystems) investigating each subsystem of the overall service architecture, and are organized in layers according to the service architecture (see Chapter 5 for a detailed discussion). Thus each SC comprises a modular structure service architecture (with a subsystem role) (Baldwin and Clark, 1997; Buckley, 1967). DoCoMo has achieved architectural innovation (Henderson and Clark, 1990) through networked SCs to create an i-mode service on a mobile service where previously there was none.

1.4 THE CONCEPT OF STRATEGIC COMMUNITIES AND NETWORKED STRATEGIC COMMUNITIES

One aspect of the Buckman Laboratories case is that in an issue-driven community, actors in differentiated specialist fields can address urgent problems within a dynamic and informal community. Features are urgency of context, varied specialties, dynamic human networks and collaboration. I believe that the issue-driven community has an informal organizational structure for knowledge integration possessing the features of an SC, or in other words, a feature separate from a community of practice (Brown and Duguid, 1991; Wenger, 2000).

In his publication, R.H. Buckman states the following concerning 'community of practice' (Buckman, 2004, p. 163):

> Given that definition, what I'm calling an Issue-Driven Community would be considered a Community of Practice. I prefer to differentiate between the two, however, because of the significant difference in the sense of urgency and the diverse population required to create the dynamic character I regard as the essential feature of an Issue-Driven Community. Generally speaking, Communities of Practice contain fewer members and do not have the same sense of urgency as Issue-Driven Communities usually do. They take a longer, slower look at developments in their field, which can also be valuable to an organization but on a different basis.

As a practitioner, I agree entirely with Buckman's views. The 'issue-driven community' Buckman Laboratory is precisely the sort of 'strategic community' that I have in mind, where a community that embodies various solutions to issues and strategic goals at organizational boundaries and knowledge boundaries is made up of actors with diverse knowledge.

In other words, I think of the issue-driven community as a place where members who share values and strategic aims combine to create new meaning aimed at learning and innovation. It is a learning community directed at incremental innovation and an innovation community creating new knowledge and radical innovation.

The different context of DoCoMo's i-mode development case shows similarities to the Buckman case in the areas of knowledge sharing and integration, but the DoCoMo case was structured more around NSCs crossing industry boundaries, while the Buckman case was structured around the networking of issue-driven communities. The hub-and-mode structure of DoCoMo's internal SC is networked to multiple external SCs (Barabasi, 2002; Watts, 2003; Kodama, 2005a, 2005b, 2005c). The networking of each SC created from different contexts and knowledge creates further new knowledge.

Next, regarding the features of SCs and NSCs, I would like to explain the difference between community of practice and project from the viewpoints of strategy, boundaries, network, personnel, capital provision and organization. A comparison between the SCs, NSCs and other organizational structures is given in Table 1.1.

Although SCs and NSCs share similarities with projects in real business scenarios, the organizational structure for each case is chosen according to an enterprise's particular management, and depends mainly on the strategy that the enterprise might take. For business developments that closely adhere to company-wide corporate strategies promoting ties between strategic enterprises and large-cale businesses, corporate projects for public organizations are formed on the basis of clearly established strategy plans and the assignments of top- and senior-level management. Clear milestones and goals are also detailed here. To execute these strategy plans fully, appropriate personnel are assigned to the project from within the company (and sometimes sourced from outside). The project follows a well-established management strategy (Ansoff, 1965; Hofer and Schendel, 1978; Mintzberg, 1978) that promotes business operations aimed at giving concrete expression to pre-defined detailed strategy plans within a fixed period, be it short- or long-term, and in so doing is also one of the especially effective organizational structures.

On the other hand, SCs and NSCs are applied in management environments characterized by difficult predictions, numerous uncertainties and a search for valid strategies. In the current business scene, a frequently adopted method is for specialists from each functional field relating to public organizations to gather and create in-house, closed, cross-functional teams and task teams, including this SC concept, in order to face challenges, solve new problems and create new business. The significance of the SC, however, is that the actors spontaneously and deliberately operate in a dynamic environment of SCs and NSCs (including remodeled communities) that cross industrial and corporate boundaries, and include clients.

In this context, the SCs and NSCs form and implement specific business concepts and ideas. Moreover, the actors use the SCs and NSCs to ascertain changes in the market by 'scanning the periphery' – searching for regional market changes (Day and Schoemaker, 2005) – and to create a new business model (mobile phone and automobile industries described in Section 1.1) by 'scanning inter- and intra-industry' borders for influential ideas.

Trial and error involving such methods as incubation is a necessary part of the process, and the SCs and NSCs take the position that a strategy will emerge from their actions. For the most part, middle management is at the center of the SCs and NSCs, forming virtual teams within and outside the company (including with clients), and generating emergent and entrepreneurial strategies (Burgelman, 1983a, b; Mintzberg, 1978). They then produce unprecedented demand and create new markets. The strategic community could be described as an engine of enactment (Weick, 1979).

The strategy-making process of the SCs and NSCs strengthens the emergent and entrepreneurial strategies side while also including the element of implementing deliberate strategies that confirm the strategic and market position aims of their own companies. Economic scope and range are pursued simultaneously by such means as strict testing of transaction costs within and outside the company, greater efficiency of strategic outsourcing, and enhanced strategic synergy with group companies.

Furthermore, SCs and NSCs are fundamentally different from projects in that project members are assigned mainly by the upper strata of enterprises, while in SCs and NSCs the community leader, who is a middle manager, forms virtual teams containing members from both within and outside the company through spontaneous and emergent thinking and action.

In the business area of new product and service development targeting architectural innovation (Henderson and Clark, 1990; Sanchez and Mahoney, 1996; Eisenhardt and Brown, 1998), actors have built modular SCs and are dynamically building the SCs' vertical and horizontal boundaries networks to embody new product and service architecture (whole system).

Points they have in common are that the activities of the SCs, NSCs and projects are authorized by upper strata inside the enterprise, and they are both able to obtain operating capital. However, a community of practice (Wenger, 2000) is informal and self-organized, its organization is formed virtually, and its organizational structure promotes improvements in the business process of daily operations, although in reality, it has difficulty obtaining personnel and capital support from within the enterprise.

Table 1.1 Comparison of organization structures

Organization Structure	Main Patterns of Strategy	Boundaries	Networks	Personnel	Capital Provision	Organization's Lifetime
Strategic Community & Networked Strategic Communities (SC & NSCs)	• Strategies under difficult-to-predict management environments • Strategic community forms business concepts and ideas as they emerge • Valid strategies must be sought through repeated trial and error (promotion of incubation) • Implementing deliberate strategies aimed at realizing strategic aims • Implementing strategic outsourcing and strategic group management	• Context sharing of abnormal 'ba' • Among actors: Creative abrasion Productive friction • Go beyond learning to pursue innovation • Pragmatism	• Building vertical boundaries network & horizontal boundaries network • Rebuilding flexible networked SCs • Modular structure networks	Community leader encourages all community members to resonate values based on clear visions and concepts, and to form a strategic community aimed at a uniform mission	Activities of the strategic community are authorized within the corporation (at top or senior management level), and securing capital required for daily operations is possible	As long as there is necessity of maintaining the strategic community
Project	• Strategies under management environments where analyses and forecasts are possible • Business strategies are formed at top or senior management level • Daily operations are pursued based on established strategy plans (clear milestones and goals)	• Transmitting correct information • Coordination • Information processing approach	• Network consisting mostly of project team members	Employees assigned by top management and senior management	Project activities are authorized with the corporation (at top or senior management level), and securing capital required for daily operations is possible	Until the project has been completed
Community of Practice	• Improvements in routine tasks at the workplace resulting from spontaneous behavior of employees are central • Improvements in the daily process of supplying products and services are promoted (improvements in TQM, customer service, etc.)	• Creating meaning and collaborating • Learning organization	• Specialist group network mostly comprises members from same line of work	Members who select themselves	Community activities are not disclosed within the corporation and many cases are not authorized. Securing capital required for activities is difficult. (Operated mostly on voluntary basis)	As long as there is interest in maintaining community

Adapted from Kodama (2002)

Furthermore, the SC members are organized to share '*ba*' (dynamic shared context in motion – Nonaka and Konno, 1998) transcending boundary, create new meaning in changing contexts, and to build trust among members (Vangen and Huxham, 2003) and resonance of value (Kodama, 2001). They accumulate dialogs and practices aimed at new issues and unknown challenges. The actors overcome friction and discord to pursue learning and further innovation.

The definitive difference between the SC and the community of practice is that although the community of practice is based mainly on the learning community (Lave and Wenger, 1990; Brown and Duguid, 1991; Orr, 1996) with the assembly of essentially the same types of specialist, the SC members have more diverse qualities. Of course, the SCs possess learning elements among different specialists, but beyond this is the element of innovation that transcends the learning routine and best practice. Friction, conflict and discord occur among SC actors (Carlile, 2002, 2004), but the dialectic and trade-off from the conflicting elements is transformed through creative abrasion (Leonard-Barton, 1992, 1995) and productive friction (Hagel and Brown, 2005) to promote collaboration among members.

In addition, an important focus of strategic management is the relationship between the strategy content and processes of the SC and NSC structures. The creation of new knowledge from these structures is strongly related to corporate strategy formulation and implementation. The positioning-based view (Porter, 1980, 1985) concerning the selection and development of new markets or the expansion of market share in existing markets, induces actors to implement SC and NSC structures in the strategy-making process. The result is an accumulation of new knowledge for individuals and the organization. The resource-based view (see, for example, Wernerfelt, 1984), on the other hand sees the embedded and accumulated resources (knowledge) in people and organizations (or throughout the whole company) as a result of the SC and NSC structures influencing the strategic structure by strengthening the existing position of the company and acquiring new market positions.

In order to construct a dynamic capability (Teece, Pisano and Shuen, 1997) to deal flexibly with changing corporate conditions, actors implement remodeled SCs and NSCs to refine existing knowledge and transform or acquire new knowledge. When positioning SC and NSC strategies, the first point is to gain a perspective of synthesizing the two strategic areas of positioning and resource. The second point is that as time changes, the SC and NSC structures should hold the perspective of micro-strategies (see, for example, Pettigrew, 1985; Johnson, 1987) by bridging strategic content, context and processes.

1.5 THE STRUCTURE OF THIS BOOK

This chapter has described the importance of knowledge creation in the ICT-driven, knowledge-based economy, and the concept of SC and NSC frameworks at its core. Chapter 2 discusses the relationship between SCs, NSCs and strategy, then presents a new theoretical framework (strategic activity cycle model) from a practice-based view of strategic management for actors both within and outside the company to formulate and implement strategies through the structure of SCs and NSCs.

Chapters 3 through to 8 discuss specific business scenarios regarding knowledge innovation from SC and NSC structures, including large corporations, joint ventures and customer-oriented solution businesses through detailed case studies. Chapter 3 uses chronologically ordered case studies to discuss details of new product development from the viewpoint of the strategic activity cycle model as it relates to new business creation among large corporations. Chapter 4 uses detailed case studies to discuss how micro and actors, networks organize as SCs and NSCs, and use dynamic processes that create new knowledge to cross intra- and inter-industry borders and generate regional activity through IT.

Chapter 5 describes SCs as modular structures, and how the layered SC networks can enable the development of new services by a process of architectural innovation.

Chapter 6 discusses the relationship between internal corporate ventures and SC structures. It looks at the business model of SC-structured support for large corporations as an important element of joint-venture success through detailed case studies of Japan–U.S. business ventures. Chapter 7 uses detailed case studies to discuss the knowledge creation process resulting from SCs where customers participate, and ICT businesses relating to education, medical treatment and welfare. It demonstrates the rigid SC structures that build trust and value resonance between the company and customers, and shows how a spiral learning process with the customer can lead to customer value creation.

Chapter 8 discusses the relationship between SC structures and ICT, presenting one perspective of the proper relationship between knowledge, people and ICT amid ICT progress and management change. It also looks at a case study involving corporate recipients of the Japan Quality Award to show how the knowledge people possess can simultaneously improve the efficiency of people's creativity and business processes and create new value for the customer through a spiral interaction with ICT.

In Chapter 9, I present new insights arising from detailed case studies compiled as a result of long-term fieldwork in real business. The insights regard a new model relating to the leadership behavior (called 'innovative leadership' in this book) of the actors in organizations implementing SCs and NSCs. One focal area is the sharing of new values by the actors (including clients) within and outside the organization, and the element of 'value-based leadership' that should lead to a general mobilization of knowledge based on practical wisdom both within and outside the organization. Another focal area is the element of 'dialectical leadership' that should synthesize the various paradoxes that actors inevitably face during strategy formulation and implementation.

Chapter 10 presents a number of implications concerning the thinking and behavior that corporate managers should display in order to realize knowledge innovation in the future.

2. Practice-based view of strategic management

2.1 THE BRIDGE BETWEEN THEORY AND PRACTICE

Chapter 1 outlined how strategic communities (SCs) and networked strategic communities (NSCs) provide the theoretical framework for the organizational behavior of actors who integrate distributed, differentiated knowledge. In this book, the greatest issue is to bridge strategic management theory and the daily practice of managers in the business field. An important focal point derives from the practical concept relating to invisible (or difficult to ascertain) actor activity from observation of the external divisions of companies or organizations where actors are daily involved in knowledge creating activities in their daily business lives.

Many scholars have reported on the importance of research into practitioners' practical activities, such as managerial work (Mintzberg, 1973; Kotter, 1982; Jarzabkowski and Searle, 2004), product innovation (Dougherty, 1992; Kodama, 2005b), learning and knowledge (Nonaka and Takeuchi, 1995; Orr, 1996; Wenger, 1998; Kodama, 1999; Brown and Duguid, 2001, Carlile, 2002, 2004; Orlikowski, 2002), strategymaking (Floyd and Lane, 2000; Dutton, Walton and Abrahamson, 1989; Huff, 1990), and technology and information management (Orlikowski, 2000). The creation of new knowledge at the business workplace arises from actors' daily practice (Orlikowski, 2002).

This research has opened the organizational 'black box', and has a micro-scale focus on strategizing and organizational behavior, such as the kind of strategies managers create and implement and the kind of interaction among practitioners that leads to the creation and sharing of new knowledge. Moreover, as collective cognition is embedded in organizational activities (Weick and Roberts, 1993), it is necessary to gain a better understanding of behavior among actors aimed at constructing a practical logic (Walsh, 1995) and to analyze further the relationship between cognition and strategy from a practice focus (Eden and Ackevmen, 1998). It is also necessary to conduct empirical studies and construct theories on the reality of the business workplace by integrating future strategy research into organizational theories (see, for example, Weick, 2004; Volberda and Elfring, 2001). 'Strategizing and organizing' research ascertaining process, change and power as strategy and organization transform over time is especially important (Pettigrew, 2003; Whittington, 2004).

In this book, I would like to present a new framework incorporating the concept of strategic and networked strategic communities from a focus on micro strategy, strategizing and organizing (see, for example, Whittingon, 1996, 2003; Johnson, Melin and Whittington, 2003). This will relate to practical logic for realizing strategies thought up by managers in realistic company situations on a daily basis involving what to think, why, and how.

First, I will explain why micro strategy, strategy and organizing are important for a large number of practitioners, including strategy researchers. Currently, a large number of practitioners emphasize not just strategic, analytical decisions but also daily activity and practice. These practitioners try their best to acquire the everyday, individual knowledge to respond swiftly, spontaneously, accurately and appropriately to unpredicted contexts and situations aimed at future business creation (strategic content such as responding quickly to urgent issues, developing and selling a new product six months down the line, or setting up a venture business). While individual capability and actions are important, group capability (such as teams, projects, and SCs and NSCs as dynamic structures) is more important still, and is the source of competitive edge for businesses. Weick (1987) says that 'execution is analysis and implementation is formulation'. In other words, he interprets implementation as 'what strategy is all about'. What is important for managers is not just that company strategists and consultants draw up excellent plans and proposals on paper (explicit knowledge), but how it will be implemented. The best consultants and managers recognize the importance of action and implementation, and it is all in the details and how they are performed (Teece, 1987).

Meanwhile, regarding the economic drivers for the strategy's micro approach, Johnson et al (2003) make the following points. The first is the resource-based view that a company's sustainable advantage lies in its micro assets, which are difficult to copy (Barney, 1986, 1991). The second is that recently, in a hypercompetitive environment (Brown and Eisenhardt, 1998; D'Aveni, 1994, 1995; Chakravarthy, 1997), the advantage has come to lie in the implementation (including trial and error) of an improvised and agile strategy-making process that goes beyond the execution of established routines to focus the managers', thinking and behavior more on the customer and the workplace (Brown and Eisenhardt, 1998; Kodama, 2003a). This has brought to an end the popularity of the traditionally static analytical strategy theory. Instead of a macro analysis that emphasized a market and company-oriented macro analysis there is now an emphasis on a micro focus that penetrates deep into the black box organization to carry out a detailed observation and analysis of individuals' thinking and behavior over time (see, for example, Pettigrew, 1985; Mintzberg, 1973; Johnson, 1987). This micro strategy perspective can deliver specific managerial implications for practitioners on a micro level, transforming the traditional reaction to the macro strategy theory of 'So what?' to 'I see! I get it!'

In his recent book, world-class practitioner Jack Welch said the following (Jack Welch with Suzy Welch, 2005):

> I know that strategy is a living, breathing, totally dynamic game ... In real life, strategy is actually very straightforward. You pick a general direction and implement like hell ... If you want to win, when it comes to strategy, ponder less and do more ... Obviously, everyone cares about strategy. You have to. But most managers I know see strategy as I do – an approximate course of action that you frequently revisit and redefine, according to shifting market conditions. It is an iterative process and not nearly as theoretical or life-and-death as some would have you believe.

Jack Welch sees practice as a key element of corporate strategy, and stresses the importance of innovation continually created from new knowledge through reacting to change, strong will on the part of managers, continual practice, and ascertaining best practice.

In this chapter, I would like first to outline established strategic theory, and then present a framework of how companies should create new knowledge and innovation amidst the great changes and uncertain elements of the twenty-first century from a practical viewpoint of strategy, organization, and SC and NSC structures.

2.2   BUILDING A PRACTICAL STRATEGY

Current corporate strategy is the practical, dynamic process of people thinking and formulating (many practitioners, including myself, recognize this). In the academic world, however, centered on the U.S., the removal of human subjectivity and values to make management studies increasingly scientific (see, for example, Simon, 1976) is gaining ground, and endeavors have come to focus on the growing elaboration of strategy analysis models and detailed, quantitative empirical studies. Of course, scientific management research is important on an academic level, but we cannot get away from the fact that the detailed frameworks of these analytical results are far removed from the practical thinking and behavior of many practitioners (Bennis and O'Toole, 2005; Gopinath and Hoffman, 1995).

The 'objective approach' of strategic theory separated from the values of people working in companies (such as their mental models of thought and belief) has ignored the practical aspect that strategy creation and implementation is carried out by subjective humans. It can be considered (Yu, 2003; Kodama, 2001) that future strategy theories will incorporate the thinking and activity of subjective human beings as functional reflective practitioners (Shone, 1983) rather than as passive machines, with the provision of new managerial implications for practitioners (and new micro-focus research implications for academics). Meanwhile, European scholars indicate that strategy theory analysis from a sociological viewpoint is more important than that from an economic viewpoint. The view of a company's strategic formulation and implementation as a social activity is also an important element of strategy theory (Jarzabkowski, 2004; Whittington, 2004; Chia, 2004).

2.2.1 Positioning-based and Resource-based Views

Traditional strategy research has generally pursued results on the basis of analytical, objective science. Porter's (1980, 1985) classic positioning-based view of macro-strategy, for example, introduced theories of the economic area of the industrial organization to company strategy. Porter's strategies, BCG (Boston Consulting Group) matrix, Project Portfolio Management (PPM), and SWOT (strengths, weaknesses, opportunities, threats) analysis had the merit of clearly presenting individual corporate strategy formulations, but did not indicate specific theories regarding strategy implementation. Moreover, although the 'habitat segregation theory' positioning functions adequately when industry order is maintained with stable, fixed players in a very slowly changing environment, it cannot adequately deal with changes to the detailed strategy-making process necessitated by business content change and the threat of unknown players in industries characterized by rapid market change and very competitive conditions. Moreover, an industry's competitive and transactional relationships are not inevitably determined by the bargaining power of either a buyer's or seller's market. Various factors, such as trust among companies, create a complex scenario.

A large body of opinion among practitioners holds that strategy formulation is accurate and reliable, but that implementation does not go well (I agree with this opinion). Since strategy formulation and strategy implementation are two sides of the same coin, it is impossible to tell clearly which is at fault if results are unfavorable. Whether strategy formulation lacks validity or whether the actors responsible for implementation lack business skills is a matter of debate in the business world. However, the two items of formulation and implementation should not be set up in opposition, but rather synthesized through dialectic. A key reason in many instances of failure is the separation within the company of the formulating and implementing processes.

The thinking of these traditional strategic theories as they concern practitioners is that while basic knowledge is important, the theories focus too much on strategy analysis and formulation, and the implementation aspect needs to be incorporated into the theory. Furthermore, a company being a group of individual actors, how does decision-making during interaction come about? And in this decision-making process, what kind of friction, conflicts and power structures exist within and outside the organization? It is essential to construct theories on a temporal axis about how actors formulate and implement strategy. To put it another way, as I mentioned at the start, it is important to have a practical dynamic strategic management theory for the company.

The resource-based view that pays attention to an organization's independent capability and competence (see, for example, Wernerfelt, 1984), has developed a micro-economics and organizational economics theory as a strategy framework. However, much of the debate about this resource-based view centers on macro-level empirical studies based on large volumes of statistical data, and a weak point is the lack of individual, specific answers to the question of enhancing competitiveness. Also, Priem and Butler (2001) complain that the definition of resources is typically all-inclusive and poor at discriminating between those resources that managers can practically handle and those beyond managerial control. Similarly, Porter's positioning-based view suffers from the weak point that the static nature of the theory cannot adapt to changing conditions. Furthermore, the organization that formulates and implements strategy is a 'black box', and the detailed process by which a resource of value is created and implemented as a strategy through human interaction is unclear.

As a development strategy from a resource-based view, Teece *et al.* (1997) suggested dynamic capability as the process of dynamically changing competences within and outside the company in response to changing environments. Eisenhardt and Martine (2000) suggested that dynamic capability was a strategic and organizational process of companies using internal and external resources (integration, reallocation, acquisition, resolution) in order to adapt to or conceive of changes in the market. In this way, the strategic theory's concern accomplishes evolution to more dynamic structures that reflect current corporate activity. There is currently no debate among management leaders regarding how companies can acquire this dynamic capability, however, and the clarification of these processes and mechanisms are issues for the future (Nonaka and Toyama, 2005).

Another current of thought is a resource-based view based on analysis of diversified, large corporations, developing into a theory that emphasizes the importance of competence acquisition through organizational learning at individual, group and organizational business unit and project levels. In recent years, this strategic theory has shifted away from the industrial economy model represented by the positioning-based view to a resource-based view including core competences, and a further development model of human and intellectual capital as the source of competitive edge (Bartlett and Ghoshal, 2002). Representative research includes 'core competences' (Prahalad and Hamel, 1990), 'knowledge-based view of the firm' (Grant, 1996a; Nonaka and Takeuchi, 1995), 'wellsprings of knowledge' (Leonard-Barton, 1995), and 'working knowledge' (Davenport and Prusak, 1998). The research series, including 'technology in practice' (Orlikowski, 2000), 'community of practice' (Brown and Duguid, 1991, 2001), 'knowing in practice' (Cook and Brown, 1999), 'strategic communities' (Kodama, 1999), and 'knowledge-based view: a new theory of strategy' (Eisenhardt and Santos, 2002), have been important in deepening the practical debate on how to share and activate the knowledge held by the individuals and groups in a company in order to create new knowledge. This is why the resource-based view is more relevant to a manager's daily activities, and enables the development of a more value-based approach to micro strategy, strategizing and organizing from observation and analysis of how strategies are formed and implemented.

2.2.2 Process Research

The positioning- and resource-based views above are theories relating to strategy content, and they have led to debate concerning the best strategies for adapting the environment and company. Strategy process research into means of formulating and implementing strategy, however, has led to debate centered around Ansoff (1965), Mintzberg (1973), Mintzberg *et al.* (1976), Mintzberg and Walters (1985), Johnson (1987) and Pettigrew (1977). Process research has been opening the organization's 'black box' and providing more detailed data and analysis concerning its internal strategic dynamics. As various elements are incorporated into the strategy-making process, the relationship between more detailed organizational dynamics and strategy formulation has become clearer. These elements include internal politics (Pettigrew, 1977; Galbraith and Nathanson, 1978; Narayanan and Fahey, 1982), organizations' internal and external power regarding decision-making (Guth, 1976; Mintzberg, Raisinghani and Theoret, 1976), organizational tension (Normann, 1977). The emphasis of process research on strategy formulation, however, has created a shortage of detail in the area of strategy implementation. Also lacking is micro-analysis of areas such as individual activity and power within an organization, conflict, and the decision-making and implementation processes. Johnson, Melin and Whittington (2003) have suggested the following six areas relating to this process research: deeper analysis of a manager's daily actions; a manager's detailed role and its activities and constraints; a manager's daily actions regarding strategizing activities; diversification or structure separation issues; strategy outcomes and links; and the scalability of general theories or issues. As with the resource-based view, more detailed process research could contribute to theories aimed at micro strategy, strategizing and organizing.

I have discussed above the pursuit of practical strategic management and the themes and development of existing strategy research issues. Next, I would like to propose a framework for a practice-based view of strategic management.

2.3 PRACTICE-BASED VIEW OF STRATEGIC MANAGEMENT

From the perspective of strategy and strategizing as practice, the key research question is in what context should an organization's personnel – top executives, middle managers and others – consider, formulate and implement strategy? Regarding a traditional, established strategy stream, Whittington (1996) indicates an emerging perspective on strategy as 'practice', and refers to the importance of practical theory for managers. Table 2.1 indicates the positioning of the practice-based view of strategic management as regards established strategy research. The horizontal axis indicates a large body of strategic thought with the focus on Who, Why, What, When, To whom and How a strategy should be formulated and implemented. One row shows the activities of a company or organization's macro units, and the other shows the micro units of the managers within an organization.

2.3.1 Practice-Based View: 'Who?'

'Who' represents analysis and consideration of organizational units such as industries, companies and inclusive business units in an industrial organization's macro strategy. In the practice-based view of micro-strategy, however, it is important to analyze the specifics of an organization's individual actors, and to pursue their thinking as regards strategy. In other words, strategy is created within the actor's mind, and the strategic viewpoint shifts from objectivity to subjectivity (Yu, 2003). Max Weber (1924/1947) suggested that action was a sign of an actor's subjective thinking. Strategists' thinking and acting processes arise directly from their own experience; those experiences create new knowledge, and strategic action is determined on this basis. Then knowledge is created from the next experience that follows the action (Mintzberg *et al.*, 1998), creating a subjective/objective duality. On a practical level, it is impossible to eliminate human subjectivity (values) completely from strategy formulation and implementation.

According to Giddens (1984), actors do not live in opposition to their environment, but practical consciousness (subjective) is created as they subconsciously absorb (objective) knowledge from their environment without sensing the contradictions. Through the accumulation of this practical knowledge, the actors have an impact on their environment once more. This is the synthesis of subjectivity and objectivity. Nonaka and Toyama (2005) suggested the importance of the interaction between objectivity (explicit knowledge) and subjectivity (tacit knowledge) as a knowledge-creating activity. Thus what should be regarded as important is not the opposition of objectivity and subjectivity, but their synthesis.

Weick (1979, 1995), on the other hand, held that organizations do not simply react to their environment, but react to an environment that is interpreted and enacted through a subjective framework created from experience. Weick (1995) also says that 'sense-making is the feedstock for institutionalization'. If institutionalization assumes shared sensemaking, we need to understand this as a recursive process of enactment to be explored in terms of how organizational actors influence and are influenced by organizational rules and norms (Johnson *et al.*, 2000, 2003; Barley and Tolbert, 1997). The pursuit of micro institutional theory is an important element of the 'practice-based view of strategic management'.

In this way, the positioning of the 'Who' in the practice-based view probes deep into the strategists' minds, focusing on the research target of specific actors within organizations promoting specific businesses. It is important, for example, to study change management from the viewpoint of 'Who', 'What kind of change has happened?' and 'In what way has it changed?'. Ohmae (2004) noted that a number of elements were necessary for companies and businesses to survive in the chaotic jungle of the twenty-first century, and that one of these was person-specific. Ohmae suggested the importance of specific individuals making and implementing decisions with specific timing. As in the case of NTT DoCoMo's i-mode, described in Chapter 1, innovation arising from new knowledge, especially in the business workplace, is created by forming SCs and NSCs implemented by specific actors (person-specific elements).

Table 2.1 Perspectives on strategy: practice-based view of strategic management

Issue / Level	Who	Why	What	When	To whom	How
Firm (Organization)	Industrial organization	Learning organization	-Policy -Planning -Positioning-based view -Resource-based view -Core competences	-Time pacing -Event pacing -Improvisation	-Alliance -M&A -Outsourcing	-Process -Product innovation
	Person-specific	Context-specific	Content-specific	Timing-specific	Connection & Network-specific	Practice-specific
Manager	-Who does it? -Who should we get to do it? -Who will become members?	-Why are we doing that? -Why is that happening?	-Establish specific strategic targets -Focus on target customers, target products and services.	-When will we do it? -Dynamics	-Human network -Tipping point -Connector -Changing specific networks	-How should we do it?

This doesn't mean that simply anyone will do. The roadmap for the future corporate vision and the future corporate grand design is drawn, and it involves specific actors who possess constantly self-improving 'people power' and 'concept power'. The specific actors are the leaders and managers at each management level within the organization, and comprise partner business leaders and managers as well as pioneering customers.

2.3.2 Practice-Based View: 'Why?'

'Why?' is the domain of context, with questions such as 'Why are we doing this business?' or 'What does it mean?' A classic example of traditional theory is 'organizational learning' (see, for example, Mintzberg, Ahlstrand and Lampel, 1998). This is the process of bringing out new meaning by aiming for reform in one's daily corporate routine. It is important to study best practice, total quality management (TQM), and other group or organizational activities. At Toyota Motors' workplace, for example, looking at quality improvement and daily problem solving, the actors at the workplace habitually use the device of asking 'Why?' five times for essential problems that cannot be solved at a glance. At the workplace, Toyota actors practise continuous reflection based on experience.

With a practice-based view, it becomes important to analyze more deeply from the viewpoint of individual actors' strategies within an organization. The excellent actor asks the question 'Why?' not as an onlooker, but as a realist. The actors make hypotheses about the ideal shape of the future, and what becomes important is strategic intent (Hamel and Prahalad, 1989), indicating the concepts of leveraging and stretching currently existing resources and capabilities in order to realize that shape. This does not involve considering strategy from a past and present viewpoint, but migrating to a viewpoint of 'creating the future'. When targeting future strategy, it is important to consider the present from a realistic viewpoint. The true strategy for a company does not derive from analysis of past events, but from actors creating a future vision from subjectivity, recognition, belief and thought. In order to do this, it is essential to perfect the construction, foresight, creativity and intuitive elements in the strategy planning process. In their search for future business creation, it is vital that actors jettison the hierarchy of path-dependent experience and function as a hierarchy of creativity (Hamel, 1996).

Toshifumi Suzuki, president and CEO of Seven and I Holdings, is pursuing managers' thinking from the future to today. In other words, from the era of analyzing the past and present to predict the future, we have entered the age of thinking about what the present should be like by considering what the future will hold. Without this process, companies would be unable to take up new challenges. When thinking from the future to the present from the customer's standpoint, realists come to see a quite different world. In this way, actors have an image of their company as forward-looking, and must think from the future to the present (Ackoff, 1981b).

The subjects and problems that actors face every day function as 'sensemaking' (Weick, 1995). They have to recognize and understand contexts that change over time, discover new meanings, and formulate and implement individual, specific strategies. When a formulated strategy does not work well, it should be changed swiftly and spontaneously, and implemented through trial and error repetition (Kodama 2005b, 2006).

2.3.3 Practice-Based View: 'What'

Concerning the content of macro-level strategies, until now companies have carried out policy research (see, for example, Rumelt, 1974; Markides, 1995) such as analyzing organizational pay-offs and diversification strategies, and investigating mergers and acquisitions (M&As) and joint ventures, in order to pursue the different strategic directions posed by the question of progressing 'Where?' A strategic planning approach of general tools and techniques including manager-oriented portfolio matrices, industry structure analysis and core competence analysis now permeates business (see, for example, Porter, 1980; Hamel and Prahalad, 1994).

The positioning of 'What' for the practice-based view of strategy necessitates analysis incorporating actors' individual, specific strategic content including individual products, services and business models. In reality, large companies especially have multiple business domains, with each domain comprising multiple products, services and business models. The accumulation of these individual businesses (including products and services) comes to be expressed as macro content. ICT business proceeds, for example, might derive from individual products and services. Different actors pursue these businesses with individual products and services, and these actors promote individual strategy content against individual context backgrounds. Actors pay careful attention to their own vision and strategic position (Markides, 1999), and implement specific strategies for the target customers, products and services in their domain.

Accordingly, the contents of the practice-based view of strategy must focus on and analyze individual actors' specific businesses, including products and services. The planning approach with manager-oriented tools and techniques, mentioned above, is a general theory. It is important for actors to embed these tools and techniques in strategy formulation and implementation for specific products and services.

2.3.4 Practice-Based View: 'When'

In traditional macro strategy incorporating positioning-based and resource-based views, the element of changing time is weak. In other words, in a situation defined by stable market conditions and fixed products, competitors, customers and markets where the movements are well understood, it is not necessary to incorporate the time variable. In the industrialized society of the last half of the twentieth century, centered on stable, predictable growth in the manufacturing industries, companies prospered as long as they invested the maximum possible resources, analyzed the market with sufficient capability, and determined strategy implementation timing in a systematic way.

In a situation of rapid environmental change with unpredictable market trends where competitors are also exposed to all kinds of investment risk, companies must consider the timing of strategy implementation more than they did in the past. With the practice-based view, actors must incorporate time-change variables into strategy, including the timing for implementing specific strategies and carrying out organizational reform to adapt to market changes. Insights can be gained from established research into industries subject to rapid change (see, for example, Brown and Eisenhardt, 1998), such as the timing to introduce a new product, and how and with what timing an organization should remodel. For such companies, it is important for change management to incorporate elements such as synergy, rhythm, pace and improvisation.

In present-day business, company leaders emphasize the elements of the above-mentioned Who-related timing ('When?' and 'To whom?') for specific businesses (strategic content) on a daily basis. Ohmae (2004) mentions the importance of the 'person-specific' and 'timing-specific' in business success. As an example, Ohmae emphasized the success of Cisco Systems. A man named John Chambers joined Cisco the second half of the 1990s, and then by acquiring appropriate resources and internal environments with good timing, created the success of the current Cisco Systems. To revisit the case of NTT DoCoMo's success outlined in Chapter 1, Mr Oboshi predicted the crisis in the mobile phone business, and chose the ideal time period for Mr Enoki to head development of next-generation services on the basis of a DoCoMo vision transforming volume to value. This element of timing was a major factor in the success of the new project.

With the practiced-based view of 'When?' actors pay attention to their own business areas, and monitor and analyze time processes to determine the timing for formulation and implementation of specific new products and services. They must then discover the causes and effects of their success or failure.

2.3.5 Practice-Based View: 'To whom'

The issue of 'To whom' relates to corporate efficiency and economics of scope based on the pursuit of competitive edge through the extension of existing resources, such as alliance theory and M&As in macro strategy, and transaction cost economics such as outsourcing (Williamson, 1975, 1981, 1985, 1991; Teece, 1982). The positioning of 'To whom?' in the strategy of the practice-based view, on the other hand, involves the human network that actors within an organization will form with other actors, both within and outside the organization. Numerous cases exist of individuals coming up with new knowledge and innovations, but as outlined in the case studies in Chapter 1, the business world throws up a great many cases of heterogeneous communication across the boundaries and connections between individuals. Specific connections and networks among actors create SCs and NSCs, and this creates new knowledge and innovation. The small-world theory of Watts and Strogatz (1998) and Watts (2003) suggests that a network of acquaintances could be created where no one is more than six stages away from anyone else in the world. Further, the creation of new knowledge and innovation speeds up as actors reach a tipping point (Schelling, 1978; Gladwell, 2000). Barabasi (2002) indicates the importance of human networks as hubs comprised of links and nodes. SCs can be either hubs or nodes. As shown in the case of i-mode in Chapter 1, new knowledge was created from the formation of networks centering on specific SCs.

On a related point, the blue ocean strategy of Kim and Mauborgne (2005) suggests the importance of a tipping point leadership through human networks of actors' specific connections. Actors drive reform through connections with 'kingpins' (respected figures with leadership qualities and a dynamic effect on their surroundings) holding power and influence in the organization. Actors' tipping point leadership is an important element enabling connections and networks aimed at driving business efficiently.

These connections and networks are not fixed, however, but change over time. Actors adapting to environments and conditions must effect planned remodeling. They must grasp the appropriate specific timing and always build changing connections and networks (SCs and NSCs) to acquire new knowledge and to create new knowledge through integration.

2.3.6 Practice-Based View: 'How'

In macro-strategy, the issue of 'How' is analyzed and considered at the business division or other organizational unit level. The classic example to date is a process research series (Chandler, 1962; Sloan, 1963; Johnson, 1987; Pettigrew, 1985; Freeland, 2000). The practice-based view of strategy places the pattern of action of individual actors within the organization as the source of the 'How?' positioning. In other words, it poses the question: 'How do actors strategize?' Strategy practice is not the same for everyone. Individual actors' thinking and action regarding strategy differs depending on the company, and strategy outcomes inevitably differ among companies in the same business domain and industry. Thus specific practice leads to the success or failure of strategic outcomes.

The issue of the 'How?' strategy in the practice-based view involves specific observation of actors' (including middle managers' and executives') actions; the question of how they formulate and make decisions on strategy; how they go about implementing the strategy; and finally, the kind of outcome. It is necessary to observe and analyze these points again and again (Floyd and Lane, 2000; Mezias *et al.*, 2001; Sama-Fredricks, 2003; Boyett and Currie, 2004; Kodama, 2005b). The process of actors accurately judging their own situation and discovering ideas and methods is especially important. Then they must further clarify the process by which they integrate the dispersed knowledge into the development of new products and services for the customer targets. The means of building SCs and NSCs as a way to create new knowledge is another important point of focus, in the same way as the question of how to build the 'To whom' connection and network mentioned above.

2.4   STRATEGIC ACTIVITY CYCLE MODEL

Next, I'd like to discuss how the chronological process of strategy formulation and implementation changes with a practice-based view of strategic management. When the framework for the change process is derived, one element that I have taken great care to consider is the process by which actors acquire new knowledge through the human network operating within and outside the company. As mentioned in Chapter 1, this is the analysis of the chronological process of SC and NSC formation. Another element is the cycle by which actors share knowledge and inspire each other to create new knowledge (including new products, services, and businesses. I undertook extensive fieldwork at organizations targeted for survey to take an inductive approach (Yin, 1994; Eisenhardt, 1989; Glaser and Strauss, 1967; Miles and Huberman, 1984) and analyzed in detail a chronological case study of implementation focusing on the above-mentioned six elements of the practice-based view: What kind of actors implement what strategy content, why, when (timing), to whom, and in what way?

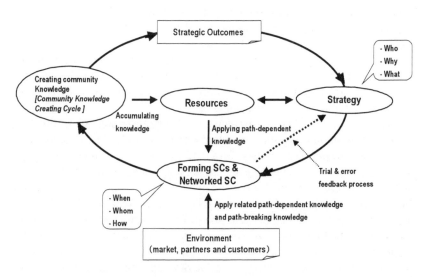

Figure 2.1   Strategic activity cycle

Next, I undertook multiple in-depth case studies from 48 new products, service developments and new business developments examples, and from comparative study of these cases I have derived a Strategic Activity Cycle framework relating to actors' strategic management practice (see Figure 2.1).

2.4.1   Strategy

The strategy part in Figure 2.1's Strategic Activity Cycle is the process by which actors formulate strategy. Strategy formulation in actual companies arises as a deliberate and systematic approach derived from the accurate distribution of internal resources, and from the existence of in-house emergent organizations (Mintzberg and Walters, 1985; Mintzberg, 1978), such as research laboratories and development and marketing divisions (Kodama, 2004) that create emergent and entrepreneurial strategies outside the realm of official planning. Deliberate strategies mainly promote reliable implementation of current mainstream business (such as research and development, sales, equipment investment, personnel and other forms of planning) in traditional organizations (Kodama, 2004). Entrepreneurial strategies, on the other hand, are cases where actors (many of whom are middle managers) pursue an independent vision, driven by independent strategies, based on a corporate vision and mission in areas that do not deviate greatly from overall strategy. This is relevant, for example, for joint businesses and ventures through new business development and strategic alliances with other companies. Meanwhile, emergent strategies have more creative features, and relate to proposals for new products and services at the workplace and urgent proposals from other companies.

In any case, these strategies go through an in-house decision-making process (the management level that makes the decision is determined by factors such as project scale, investment sum and level of importance) and are decided on after careful deliberation. This process varies according to company, but the more important the subject, the higher the management level (extending to boardroom) that the decision-making process is entrusted to. The complexity of the decision-making process also varies according to the scale and hierarchical structure of the organization. The decision-making process is especially strict for proposals with strong entrepreneurial and emergent strategy features, and the resource distribution process, also, is usually discussed in full. The larger the company, the more friction and discord arises from the process by which entrepreneurial and emergent strategy becomes part of a company's overall deliberate strategy (Kodama, 2003b). However, good leaders and managers are not afraid of disagreement. The actors will transform these conflicts into constructive and productive efforts through means of joint, extensive dialog focused on the strategy target.

2.4.2 The Structure of SCs and NSCs

The strategy that has passed through the formulation and decision-making process is then implemented by the actors. This process of implementation moving through the questions of 'When?' 'To whom?' and 'How?', is specifically important for real business. The traditional organization implements deliberate strategy by coordinating the transmission of accurate information and efficient business process implementation (Malone and Crowston, 1994) through the integration (Lawrence and Lorsch, 1967) of separate, differentiated work functions within the company. However, challenging goals (such as sales and customer acquisition targets) and urgent issues (such as responding to customers) facing mainstream business in traditional organizations may be addressed by cross-functional teams and task teams that cross work and function divisions. Flexible implementation of strategic outsourcing and collaboration aims to lower transaction costs and create synergy among company group members. Figure 2.1 shows how the SC and NSC structures do not only apply to in-house, path-dependent resources, but also positively take in external resources (Kodama, 2006).

Organizations that implement entrepreneurial and emergent strategies, on the other hand, do not just deepen and refine existing resources to create new business, but also acquire external resources (path-dependent resources assisting in-house resources, and the quite different path-breaking resources), including customers, through the construction of SCs and NSCs. Path-breaking resources, especially, are acquired through new knowledge from outside the borders of the company's own industry that accompanies strategic alliances and M&As. For future business, however, new product and service development is incubated as a prototype on a provisional, verifiable basis (Kodama, 2006). The result is feedback for the strategy formulation process in accordance with the situation (see the feedback arrows in Figure 2.1).

What is important in the SC and NSC structures is 'Who' – which actors, in which company, in which industry – to form an SC network with? If there are partners within the same industry possessing similar skills and technology, there should be few problems choosing an appropriate partner, but for an SC formation crossing industry borders, the overall actor composition must be considered, including relationships with competitors, power issues across industries, and consistency of corporate culture. The i-mode case from Chapter 1 demonstrated how the basic strategy goal of trust building and construction of shared values created a win-win partnership. Instead of a partner dominating through a vertical integration, it is important to have boundary management that creates a positive impact among the various industries through collaboration and reciprocal support.

Moreover, as mentioned above, the element of timing is important in strategically implemented decision-making. The result changes greatly depending on when and with what timing actors implement strategy. The timing of chronological axes for SC and NSC structures has a great impact on new product and service development decisions and market introductions. These SC and NSC structures must be remodeled according to the situation. The above-mentioned SC and NSC connections and networks are specific networks subject to change.

In a rapidly changing market environment, it is necessary to look beyond the development of existing resources to acquire new knowledge and establish new positioning from integration of existing resources or acquisition of path-breaking differentiated knowledge. This entails scanning within the same industry, including domains on the periphery of the actor's own company, for products and services, and scanning neighboring industry boundaries as well as completely unrelated industries, for diverse business trends. Through this scanning, actors establish new cognitive frames by interpreting fresh meaning through new sensemaking (Weick, 1995; Daft and Weick, 1984). These new cognitive frames propel actors to formulate and implement new strategies aimed at new challenges (Bogner and Bar, 2000; Walsh, 1995). The DoCoMo case in Chapter 1 evolved dynamically through trial and error as a result of the development of path-dependent resources for the i-mode technical platform. The acquisition of path-breaking resources led to the development of a new business model built on a win-win model with other industries.

2.4.3 Sharing, Inspiration, Creation and Accumulation of Community Knowledge

I will here refer to SCs and NSCs as 'communities'; new knowledge (specifically, new products, services and business models) is referred to as 'community knowledge'. New knowledge from the SCs and NSCs communities is created by actors and applied in the workplace. Competence, skills, and expertise become embedded and accumulate in the actors and organizations. In this section, I would like to describe the concept of the Community Knowledge Creating Cycle. This is comprised of the four processes of sharing, inspiration, creation and accumulation (see Figure 2.2).

The sharing process consists of extensive dialog resulting in the concerned parties understanding the vision and objectives pursued by the different organizations regarding the sharing of knowledge. The inspiration process involves contact, and entails inspiring and extending various aspects of community knowledge within the organization in support of identifying problems, challenges and solutions, so that the vision and concept can be realized on the basis of community knowledge shared by the different organizations concerned. The process of creation involves creating new community knowledge on the basis of the community knowledge inspired and extended within the circle of organizations concerned. The process of accumulation involves methodically accumulating within the community, as valuable expertise, the various aspects of community knowledge garnered through the processes of sharing, inspiring, and creating.

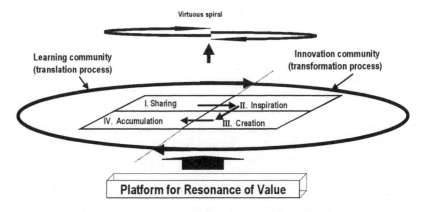

Notes:
I.   Sharing – Understanding and sharing existing knowledge held in the community
II. Inspiration – Propagating knowledge through inspiration related to existing knowledge
III. Creation – Creating new knowledge
IV. Accumulation – Storing diverse new knowledge born in the process of inspiration, propagation
     and creation

Figure 2.2   Community knowledge creating cycle

I will explain these processes specifically in the following ways. Among SCs and NSCs comprised of actors from diverse specialties and backgrounds, tension, conflict and friction are monitored (see, for example, Kodama 2001, 2005b). Within the community, the actors dynamically share individual context, information and knowledge (tacit and explicit) through dialog while sharing one strategic goal in the community. This is the sharing stage illustrated in Figure 2.2. Further new meaning is created from dynamically shared context, information and knowledge within the community. Then the actors work to create an action plan embodying the strategic goals incorporating the various points and issues learned from each other. Some learning communities promote the translation process (a feature of semantic boundaries) to derive new meaning among actors as they consider the knowledge boundary features at the sharing stage (Carlile, 2002, 2004).

Within the community, however, individual actors robustly state their opinions concerning specific issues, formed from their own values and areas of expertise, so that opinions clash and passions often flare. The higher the strategy target hurdle (product development difficulty or business model complexity are examples), the newer the subject matter, or more uncertain the market, the greater the collision, friction and conflict among actors (Carlile, 2002, 2004). Among individual actors there are cases of battles where opinions clash and neither side is prepared to compromise. Especially among heterogeneous members, such battles at the business workplace are likely to lead to high-quality knowledge creation or innovation (Johansson, 2004). The Buckman Laboratories and i-mode cases described in Chapter 1, which always created new community knowledge, comprised heterogeneous communities of actors. In these cases, however, capable actors engaged in constructive debate, and the community members were able to narrow down the problem to a solution through mutual understanding. The community has to advance by integrating opposing propositions through dialectic dialog (Kodama, 2005b). This is the inspiration stage illustrated in Figure 2.2. Meanwhile, considering the feature of the knowledge boundary between the actors at the inspiration stage, some innovation communities also promote the transformation process (a feature of the pragmatic boundary) for jointly-held existing knowledge (Carlile, 2002, 2004).

At the inspiration stage, dialectical dialog is promoted and conflict links to collaboration. At the creation stage illustrated in Figure 2.2, the actors solve specific issues through collaboration, target knowledge creation for strategic goals, integrate knowledge dispersed in the community (NSCs), and create new community knowledge.

Product development, for example, follows a process whereby the basic and detailed designs of the entire system architecture and subsystem are completed, then specific prototypes are completed and integrated, and then each job and function division (including research, development design and manufacturing) is linked to the completion of a commercial product. Further, the new products and services are introduced to actual markets through strong links with advertising, publicity, sales, distribution and service divisions. In this creation stage, the current products and businesses are included and the target strategy implemented, and then the innovation community is formed as a transformation process delivering change to the market and customer.

In the accumulation stage illustrated in Figure 2.2, the community knowledge accumulates as individual actor and organizational resources. This knowledge comprises the actors' competences, skills and expertise gained at the creation stage, and that acquired through business application of markets and fields, such as introduction of new products and services to the market. At this accumulation stage, actors form a learning community as a translation process, and discover reflection (Shone, 1983) and sense-making of new meaning through interaction with the market (customers) as a result of strategy implementation. Then the actors form new cognitive frames and look for the next strategic challenge.

Through these strategy implementation cycle series of community knowledge, strategy outcome can be acquired (see Figure 2.1). However, this strategic activity cycle is not over in a single cycle. The community knowledge creating cycle and the strategic activity cycle simultaneously link and spiral upward (see Figure 2.2). At the accumulation stage, the actors once more face the challenge of forming SCs and NSCs to realize new strategic formulations through the new sense-making learning process.

2.4.4 Managing the Strategic Activity Cycle

Realistically, multiple strategic activity cycles exist within the company. Actors concerned with different individual services and business (mainly corporate middle management, including project leaders, team leaders and managers) are following these strategic activity cycles individually. The senior executives with rights and responsibilities for many of these projects (products and services), moreover, must manage many of these strategic activity cycles simultaneously.

There are a number of themes that can be creatively and efficiently driven by the strategic activity cycle. One is integration of the strategic activity cycle by reacting to the individual strategy-making processes (deliberate strategy, emergent strategy and entrepreneur strategy) mentioned previously. In order to maintain continuous growth capability, it is necessary to promote current mainstream business (exploitation activity) and future-oriented business (exploration activity) together (Tushman and O'Reilly, 1997; Kodama, 2003b). In other words, it is necessary to promote strategies for integration with exploration businesses through emergent and entrepreneur strategies, mainly supervised by emergent organizations; also, integration with exploitation businesses must be a deliberate mainstream strategy mainly supervised by traditional organizations (Kodama, 2004). Organizations that possess the features of these three strategy-making processes may have minor differences in structure and operation, but generally the managers can be said to recognize the meaning of and need for integrative strategies on a day-to-day basis. The implementation, however, is difficult, and becomes more complex still when relationships with external partners and customers are factored in. This is because the larger the business, the greater the conflict between mainstream and new business, and the greater the friction arising within the organization (Burgelman and Välikangas, 2004; Thusman and O'Reilly, 1997; Kodama, 2003b). By overcoming these issues and integrating multiple strategic activity cycles, however, strategic corporate output can be maximized.

Another theme is that of demand – specifically, how to achieve a community knowledge cycle through the formation of SCs and NSCs in a strategic activity cycle. One of the important areas of thought and action for prospective actors is the Resonance of Value (Kodama, 2001) model within the community (see Figure 2.1). This model is similar to the idea of share value (O'Reilly and Pfeffer, 2000) for companies and organizations, but from a practice-based view, it is important to clarify the detailed process whereby actors can create resonance of value or share value.

There are numerous issues (including the one above) concerning how to construct and manage a strategic activity cycle. In Chapters 3 to 8 I will discuss these points through in-depth case studies drawn from real business scenarios.

3. Knowledge innovation through strategic activity cycles

3.1 THE STRATEGIC ACTIVITY CYCLE OF LARGE COMPANIES

In this chapter, I will use in-depth case studies to discuss how the concept model of the strategic activity cycle described in Chapter 2 is managed by actors in the large-company business arena. From a practice-based view, the actors' thinking and behavior are characterized by the following three features.

3.1.1 Synthesis of Timing

The first is the 'synthesis of timing'. This refers to the thought processes behind the timing-specific elements that should feature in decision-making when actors are formulating and implementing strategy. Specifically, these are the timing strategies for thinking of the present from the future and thinking of the future from the present. Considering the strategic activity cycle in Figure 2.1 from the viewpoint of implementing timing strategies, the two kinds of strategic activity cycle in Figure 3.1 exist in the companies' strategic processes.

In Figure 3.1, exploration activities to search for future business (Cycle A) are cycles where actors in emergent organizations targeting potential markets (individual, specific products and services) formulate and implement strategies through trial and error. Exploitation activities that promote current mainstream business (Cycle B), on the other hand, are cycles where actors in traditional organizations systematically formulate and implement strategies. The timing strategy of thinking of the present from the future means that a link exists from Cycle A to Cycle B's strategic processes. In other words, it implements future business embedded company-wide in the mainstream business core. Because of this, it becomes possible to implement market-oriented future business as realistic mainstream business, and to create new markets.

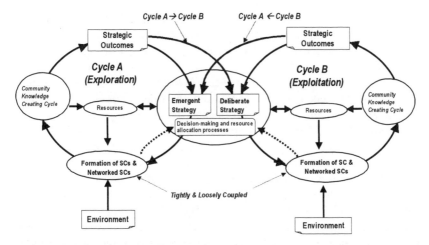

Figure 3.1   Integrated strategic activity cycles

Conversely, timing strategies thinking of the future from the present link Cycle B to Cycle A's strategic processes. In other words, they link the strategy-making process from an actor's process of knowledge sharing and inspiration to the formulation and implementation of strategy targeting the search for new business opportunities (Cycle A as exploration activity) within the current mainstream business implementation (Cycle B as exploitation activity).

In reality, it is essential for actors in large companies to formulate and implement timing strategy through these two thought processes. Actors must implement this timing strategy consciously and deliberately, and actors in the top and middle management levels must interact while realizing the strategy. This is an element of a strategy's timing synthesis.

Of course companies continue to pursue incremental innovation through Cycle B as an exploitation activity, but such companies operate in industries where environmental and technological change has been relatively slow. Moreover, some companies exist that pursue radical or discontinuous innovation and reap profits through Cycle A as an exploration activity. These include research and development ventures and companies in fields such as ICT, biotechnology, and medical supplies with a management foundation in patents and licensing.

3.1.2   Synthesis of Strategic Space

The second feature is the synthesis of strategic space. This is an issue related to the construction of networked SCs, and requires integrated management of tightly and loosely coupled NSCs. An understanding of actors' new generation of meaning and interaction promotes interactive conversion of tacit and explicit knowledge, and creates an SC as a learning community (Nonaka and Takeuchi, 1995). Furthermore, actors pragmatically solve specific problem points and issues and create SCs as innovation communities (Kodama, 2005c). In addition, in order to integrate knowledge among SCs distributed within and outside the company, actors use strong networked ties to embed the deeply connected and diverse knowledge of individual SCs to networked SCs (see, for example, the i-mode case study in Chapter 1). However, actors must remodel the networked SCs constructed as strong ties from rigid value chains (Porter, 1985) and value networks (Christensen, 1997) in response to changing environmental and market conditions. NSCs with strong ties can change to become loosely coupled network SCs, or the SC could disappear altogether, as companies face issues such as path-dependency (Rosenberg, 1982; Hargadon and Sutton, 1997), competency traps (Levitt and March, 1988; Martines and Kambil, 1999) and core rigidities (Leonard-Barton, 1992, 1995).

With loosely coupled networked SCs, on the other hand, actors form multiple SCs within and outside the company, and undertake peripheral region and boundary scanning among industries. This applies, for example, to consortiums with potential outside partners and customers, incubation, and joint experiments. By combining internal SCs (SCs whose influence affects decision-making within the company) and weak network ties, however, the linked, weak SCs search for and monitor future business opportunities. Then the actors accurately ascertain the timing of business opportunities, and convert weak and strong ties to realize knowledge integration in one go.

3.1.3 Management of the Strategy-making Process

The third feature is the combined management of the strategy-making process. This is closely related to the combined management of two strategic activity cycles from the first feature of timing strategy – it is the integration of emergent or entrepreneurial strategy centered on Cycle A and deliberate strategy centered on Cycle B. The linkage of future strategies (emergent or entrepreneurial) to deliberate strategy as current mainstream business has prioritized in-house creation of clear decision-making processes and resource allocation processes (Christensen and Raynor, 2003). The decision-making process requires that strategic outcomes from several emergent or entrepreneurial strategies developing in-house are fully examined, and appropriate resource allocation decisions for individual strategies (including new products, services and businesses) implemented after thorough dialog and discussions among top and middle management teams. During such times, management's 'disciplined imagination' (Weick, 1989) becomes important, and the clarification of strategy and technology priorities and decision-making processes must be open to managers within the company.

The above three elements for the implementation of strategic activity cycles influence strategy formulation and implementation in large companies. In the following section, I will describe a specific business case linking the implementation and results of Cycle A with Cycle B as corporate mainstream business for the purpose of exploration activity. (I will also discuss business cases linking Cycle B with Cycle A in Chapter 4).

3.2 NTT'S MULTIMEDIA BUSINESS (A CASE STUDY)

3.2.1 Expansion of the Video Conferencing Market in Japan

During the 1994 New Year holidays, the then-president of Nippon Telegraph and Telephone Corporation (NTT), Japan's largest telecommunications company, announced that NTT was going to transform itself from a phone company into a multimedia company. It was a time of great change, and NTT, with its 48-year history in the telephone-based network business, faced a future of forging new, multimedia-based businesses. Against this background, a small-scale multimedia promotion organization was inaugurated within the structure of the NTT main office staff.

At the time, NTT's basic policy for promoting multimedia was to exploit existing, functional network technology to offer multimedia services to its customers. NTT named its policy 'Multimedia for Today (Now-ISDN)'. It utilized an ISDN multimedia network-compatible communications scheme as a platform, and offered customers various application services based on this platform.

NTT promoted ISDN-based videoconferencing systems and videophones (video communication terminals) as its hallmark applications. Since video applications were virtually unknown in the Japanese market, the founding of a new business became a big issue at NTT.

At first, three employees, including a senior and assistant manager, set to work drafting a plan to establish a market for ISDN-based video communication. Their vision was to construct a new, video-communication based culture out of Japan's telephone-based communication. They were presented with innumerable business problems. Here are a just a few of them:

- How to develop a low-cost, high-quality desktop video conferencing system for the business market.
- How to develop a business structure to facilitate sales, maintenance and after-sales service while promoting the NTT-developed video terminals.
- How to enhance the sales and technical skills of the employees to facilitate marketing, sales, installation, maintenance and after-sales service for these video terminals that were breaking new ground.
- How to promote the video terminals NTT would produce.

At the time, the task force of just a few employees found it nearly impossible to make progress with these products. But the motive force behind the video-based businesses turned out to be community management, based on the creation of strategic communities within and outside the company that related to individual business processes, including development, marketing, sales, maintenance and after-sales service.

In one such instance, a community leader at NTT headquarters' Multimedia Promotion Department demonstrated innovative leadership in exploiting the relationships of empathy and resonance he had built with other leaders, both within and outside the company, to create various business communities. He managed these community groups simultaneously (thus creating networked SCs), and worked to promote video multimedia through the creation of new businesses, as shown in Figure 3.2.

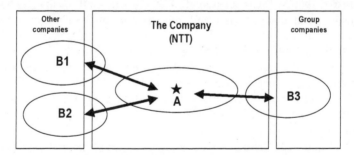

Notes:

★: Community leader manages a group of strategic communities comprehensively and network-enables each SC

A: Strategic communities contained within the company (Build a sales system across branches and stores within the company and establish a service front system)

B1:   Strategic communities outside the company (Form strategic partnerships with PictureTel – joint development)

B2:   Strategic communities outside the company (Establish sales channels outside company)

B3:   Strategic communities outside the company (Strategic outsourcing to group companies)

Figure 3.2 Strategic community creation at NTT

3.2.2 Systematically Creating Strategic Communities

Various organizational methods have been the focus of attention for enabling large companies to achieve significant strategic innovations (Markides, 1998). Their common essence is the idea of a strategically-minded innovator in a large company constructing an organization distinct from the main company. This organization can be contained within, but separate from, the main organization (Figure 3.3, Pattern 1), or can be a separate subsidiary (Figure 3.3, Pattern 2). However, while these organizational patterns are extremely effective for strategic innovation, problems always occur due to issues of harmony between the cultures of the old and new organizations. Overcoming these problems requires vigorous leadership from top management, and a revolution in corporate culture.

To promote the kind of strategic business innovation that leads to the long-term development of such phenomena as continuous organizational invigoration and creation of new business, the vital issue is not how to engage in strategic business practices and operations using only the company's internal resources (knowledge and talent). The key issue is how to create strategic communities based on collaboration (including virtual collaboration through ICT-based networks) or various external (human) resources, including customers, so as to develop innovative businesses such as the one described in the NTT case study (Kodama, 1999a).

In this section, I will outline three points that comprise the important elements of strategic community management shown in Figure 3.2. They differ from the processes of strategic innovation-based management shown in Figure 3.3, Patterns 1 and 2.

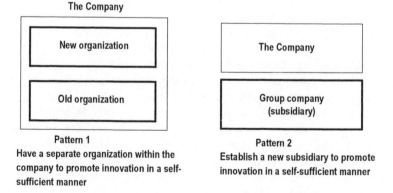

Figure 3.3   Forms of strategic innovation in large companies

Point 1 is to have an exceptional, ambitious community leader use an in-house network of personal relationships to create a new strategic community within the company, and in so doing lay the foundation for moving forward with new, strategic businesses within the existing organization (Pattern 1), rather than investing new resources in various separate organizations that will promote strategic businesses in a self-sufficient manner (Patterns 2). This latter approach enables the strategic community of the new business, with its new corporate culture, to bring about a new strategic mindset in the many employees of the company's other organization who retain the old corporate culture. In other words, it allows the new strategic community to play the role of a catalyst that joins and harmonizes the new and old corporate cultures. (See Figure 3.2, strategic community A.)

Point 2 is for the community leader to obtain, through strategic outside partnerships and outsourcing, the resources (knowledge and talent) needed to promote strategic business creation externally, and for him or her to make use of the relationships of empathy and resonance developed with leaders in other businesses to create an external strategic community. Another important activity is the creation of business communities through strategic partnerships with businesses in other industries, with the goal of discovering new markets and expanding markets for products and services generated during the strategic creation of new businesses. The community leader must search out key people in other industries and work with them to cultivate and expand new markets. Strategic joint development, sales partnerships and outsourcing formed with businesses in other industries are ways of doing this (see Figure 3.2, strategic communities B1, B2, B3).

Point 3 is for the community leader to use innovative leadership to manage simultaneously several groups of strategic communities, of the two types described earlier, in a comprehensive manner. The community leader and other actors build NSCs in order to combine each SC's knowledge and construct a new video communications business model incorporating product development, sales and maintenance services. As described in Chapter 2, actors, including the community leader, must also work to facilitate the continuous sharing, inspiring, creation and accumulation of community knowledge within each of these business communities.

Accordingly, ambitious community leaders, who play an important role through their primary concern of promoting the creation of strategic businesses, have to rely on their own ability to create strategic communities continually and systematically, using the relationships of empathy and resonance they have developed with leaders within and outside the corporate structure, including relationships with leaders in other industries, while comprehensively managing these multiple strategic community groups. The community leader perceives the confederation of these diverse, sometimes customer-inclusive, strategic communities located both within and outside the corporate organization as a virtual corporation, and strategically promotes its businesses.

3.2.3 The Creation of a Strategic Community with PictureTel Corporation of America

The PictureTel corporation is an example of strategic community B1 in Figure 3.2.

Developing a core engine for multimedia services – Phoenix Multimedia Conferencing System
In February 1995, NTT agreed to form a strategic partnership with PictureTel Corporation, based in Boston, Massachusetts (subsequently acquired by the US company Polycom, currently the world's biggest player in the videoconferencing market), which had a track record of achievement in the core multimedia field of video communications. The partnership's purpose was the joint development of a next-generation desktop videoconferencing system to be called Phoenix (Nihon Keizai Shimbun, 1995). Many manufacturers in Japan and abroad were already selling ISDN-based videoconferencing systems, but even for the time, product prices were high, amounting to around one million yen for a desktop model and several million yen for a room-type videoconferencing system. These prices, as well as the unfamiliarity with operating methods for videoconferencing, were among the reasons it had yet to take off.

For NTT, the objective of the strategic partnership with PictureTel was to ignite the Japanese video terminal market in a single stroke, and at the same time launch the new videoconferencing system as a driver for Now-ISDN. NTT's target unit sales price was set at under 200 000 yen. This pricing brought major changes in the desktop videoconferencing system market (see 'Phoenix' in Figure 3.4).

The key factor behind the success of this strategic alliance was the empathy and resonance of the values held by the leaders of NTT and PictureTel. The corporate philosophy of PictureTel is 'Redefine the way the world meets.'

NTT introduced the multimedia communications infrastructure referred to as ISDN, which is readily available today for a wide range of customers and large number of uses. The infrastructure was intended for use in the fields of education, medicine and welfare as well as the business sector. In the telecommunications sector, the world's carriers urgently needed to migrate from a diminishing returns business model centered on conventional analog voice traffic to a stepped-up return model of non-voice traffic centered on digital video and data. In the area of cyber businesses supported by multimedia that merges networks, content and a variety of applications, there was a strong possibility of creating new businesses spurred by diverse alliances among companies and organizations in different lines of business.

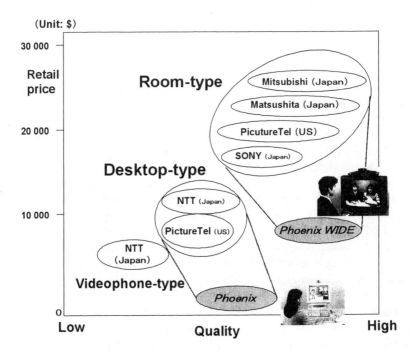

Figure 3.4   Global market for videoconferencing systems

Alliances in the multimedia arena adopt a style wherein organizational actors from unfamiliar corporate cultures form a community in which people liaise and create solidarity with each other in order to achieve their business goals. The leaders involved in this project are required to be constantly innovative and to have strategic vision and energy.

This was the case with the three actors in the Multimedia Promotion Department (an organization with the features of an emergent organization) who drove the promotion of the joint development strategy with PictureTel. The president at the top outlined the vision while middle managers advanced emergent strategies through trial and error implementation of individual, specific strategies and technologies. First, the three actors mobilized a strategic activity cycle (Cycle A) as an exploration activity, and then implemented a community knowledge creating cycle (Figure 3.5) formed by creating SCs with PictureTel. Actors from both companies determined the technical specifications (hardware and software) for this strategic community (B1), implemented a trial prototype, and finally achieved the world's first 'Phoenix'. Many difficult questions were raised through the new developments. At this point, collaboration with technicians from Microsoft, NEC and other companies became vital.

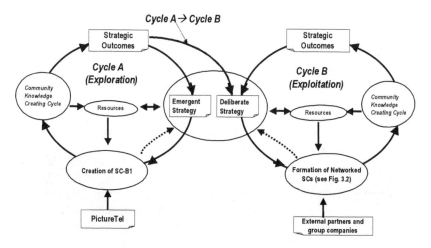

Figure 3.5   Integrated strategic activity cycles

Then issues that the Multimedia Promotion Department actors had to develop simultaneously had to be authorized in the decision-making process as a whole-company sales strategy regarding the development schedules of new products. Because they belonged to a large company, the actors came to recognize the barriers between the divisions. It became necessary to form strategic communities to gain the understanding of both parties and create new meaning for NTT's vision and future strategies. These SCs would be formed through tough negotiations with organizations connected with management, sales, technical services and other areas in NTT branch offices and branches throughout Japan.

Then the middle management level at each organization and the employees at the lower levels engaged in debate until a consensus was reached. After that, the actors in top management engaged in productive (and at times adversarial) debased focused on decision-making meetings. The company's highest decision-making body then gave its authorization, and the emergent strategy, promoted mainly by the emergent organization's actors, was advanced as the entire company's deliberate strategy, embracing the traditional organizations of the management and technical services departments.

3.2.4 The Creation of Strategic Communities within NTT: Establishing an Organization for Business Promotion

This case study correspond, to strategic community A in Figure 3.2.

Establishing an in-house sales organization
The task confronting the community leader of the Multimedia Promotion Department, which at that time had no sales organization, was to create a business community, including the sales departments of NTT branch offices and branches throughout Japan, for the purpose of outsourcing the marketing of the Phoenix. It was necessary to foster a deep knowledge of and identification with the Phoenix in the many NTT employees who had never before handled video terminals.

A group of community members, mostly made up of community leaders, transformed employees' feelings toward the promotion of multimedia terminals by means of product explanation meetings, training meetings and other educational activities throughout the approximately six months leading up to release. By the time the Phoenix went to market, NTT had trained approximately 1000 employees in Phoenix sales and technology.

Using straightforward instruction, a group of community members (chiefly community leaders) cultivated personnel who would act as key people in offices throughout Japan. And so a virtual business community was formed between the Multimedia Promotion Department at NTT headquarters, NTT's branch offices and NTT branches, through activities to motivate employees to promote the sales of these new products. The new corporate culture of this new business community gave rise to an innovative mindset in other employees who had previously been immersed in the old corporate culture. As a result, this virtual business community expanded greatly, and the Phoenix is now positioned as NTT's mainstay video multimedia product.

Establishing a customer service system
In response to various inquiries arising from Phoenix users with regard to technical issues and network faults, one of the major issues the community leader at the Multimedia Promotion Department had to deal with was how to establish a sales system while creating a stronger complaints department backed by a nationwide network of customer service desks.

At the time, the ISDN service center, or 113 Service Center (which had 40 front desks across the country), was answering technical enquiries about

ISDN terminals and lines and accepting troubleshooting requests. The community leader at NTT headquarters Support Department and the Multimedia Promotion Department, which exercised overall control over those nationwide ISDN service centers, formed an in-house business alliance and began accepting Phoenix customer service requests at ISDN services centers across the country.

At first, employees felt insecure about the new technology and products. To counter this, community leaders worked hard on improving employee skills through on-the-job technical training or nationwide briefings intended for each ISDN service center. The actions of these community leaders also contributed to the creation of important in-house strategic communities in line with the establishment of the sales network.

In this way, NTT used the in-house strategic community A (Figure 3.2) to form its deliberate strategy on sales plans and technology services for the entire company. It did this through intense dialog and collaboration with the emergent organization of the Multimedia Promotion Department, the traditional organizations of the headquarters' management and technology services divisions, and NTT branch offices and branches throughout Japan. The actors' tactics for implementing this deliberate strategy included the pursuit of efficiency through activating the resources of external sales channels and the pursuit of synergy through technology links with NTT group companies. The tactics took the shape of strategic community B2 and B3, and are described below.

3.2.5 The Creation of Strategic Communities Outside the Company

Enlarging extra-corporate sales channels and establishing a maintenance organization

To boost sales through channels other than those funnelled from NTT sales departments in branches and stores, NTT entered into sales tie-ups with Otsuka Shokai, a major System Integrator (SI) vendor, and LAOX, a PC and home appliance volume retailer. Outside agency agreements with about 100 companies were successfully concluded before initiating sales of Phoenix. NTT entered into partnerships with companies in its group (NTT-TE) to outsource maintenance and after-sales service strategically. This was an example of strategic outsourcing within the NTT group for the purpose of sharing and accumulating knowledge and expertise related to the Phoenix. NTT utilized this outsourcing arrangement to offer its video terminal customers a high-quality service package that included maintenance and after-sales service.

NTT's endeavors to form business communities through strategic partnerships and outsourcing related to extra-corporate sales, maintenance, and after-sales service, built a sound foundation for Phoenix.

Support for internal and external communities over the new video information networks

To support the strategic community groups both within and outside NTT that were associated with sales, maintenance and after-sales services, the community leader at the Multimedia Promotion Department in NTT headquarters introduced desktop videoconferencing systems and groupware which would connect each community internally and to others using ISDN and the Internet in the form of a new video information system (referred to as the Phoenix Customer Service Network: See Figure 3.6).

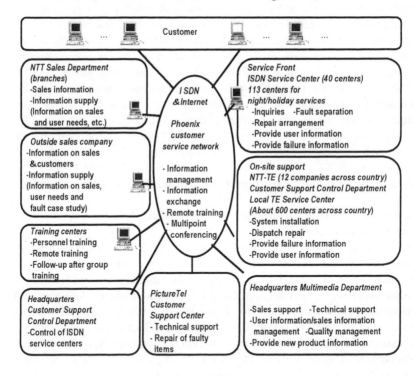

Figure 3.6   Construction and role of Phoenix Customer Service Network

The goal was to provide high-quality customer services through a virtual community created using the Phoenix Customer Service Network. This network was applied in three modes. The first mode was to accumulate and share sales and maintenance information, such as sharing of customer or fault case information, within and among communities. Customer needs as well as product and system improvement requests would be promptly collected, stored in a database and shared. The second mode was to operate a sales and maintenance information exchange and conduct virtual conferences nationwide. For example, information would be distributed between sales branches or to community members at multipoint videoconferences linking ISDN service centers, and information exchanges would be actively calculated so as to enhance the value of the information. The third mode was to be follow-up personnel training conducted after product briefings through remote training via the videoconferencing system, or as part of mass training.

The introduction of the system allowed community competencies such as information, knowledge and expertise within and among the communities to be accumulated and shared efficiently, and at the same time provided leadership support tools comprising multimedia sales, maintenance and after-sales services, which enabled the business cycle to progress smoothly in the form of leadership support tools for the community leaders.

Prompt decision-making by community leaders at the Multimedia Promotion Department and innovative leadership redoubled the will to introduce these large video information network systems.

In this way, actors soundly implemented deliberate strategies through forming NSCs from each SC in Figure 3.2 (A, B1, B2 and B3). The actors from traditional and emergent organizations fully mobilized Cycle B's strategic activity cycle (Figure 3.5), and the actors in the emergent organization of the Multimedia Promotion Department further formulated and executed emergent strategy by repetition of trial and error aimed at new product development. Next, they activated Cycle A, appropriately grasping the timing of product creation, and linked it to the deliberate strategy of Cycle B as the subsequent overall strategy. In this case, actors responded to technology (narrow band to broadband, ISDN to IP, the increasingly high performance of semiconductor chips) and the market (corporate user to mass user, customizing and solution proposals for private users) and on that occasion formed SCs and NSCs with optimum partners, undertaking further remodeling in response to the situation.

3.2.6 Japan Launches Sales of World's First Multimedia Conferencing System

In March 1996, NTT began selling Phoenix, the world's first desktop-type multimedia conferencing system to be compatible with Windows 95 and the

PCI local bus in the hope that it would be the killer application to make 'Multimedia for Today (Now-ISDN)' a reality (Nihon Keizai Shimbun, 1996). Phoenix was truly a world first and a first in Japan among multimedia products, in terms of both its cost and functionality. Its amazingly low cost of 198 000 yen redefined multimedia and established a videoconferencing market in Japan at a single stroke.

On the launch date, NTT's vice-president (later to become president), Junichiro Miyazu, presided over a Phoenix sales kick-off ceremony at LAOX's 'The Computer' Shop in Akihabara, home to Japan's largest computer electronics shopping town (Nikkei Sangyo Shimbun, 1996). The impetus to mobilize this senior figure from big business stemmed from innovative leadership centered around the community leader at the Multimedia Promotion Department in an endeavor extending from the formation of tie-ups with PictureTel to the launch of sales. This took just about one year. The community leader created a group of strategic communities within and outside the main organization in order to energize each organization within NTT and reform mindsets with the aim of encouraging community members to promote multimedia businesses. The Phoenix's sales for 1997 amounted to a 70 percent share of the Japanese market for desktop videoconferencing systems.

Phoenix is currently positioned as a video multimedia product representing NTT. Phoenix quickly evolved in a succession of upgrades from the initial NEC-PC98 model to a DOS/V model (Nihon Kogyo Shimbun, 1996) and NEC-PC98/DOS integration models (Nikkei Sangyo Shimbun, 1997c). The success of Phoenix, which was formed as part of a strategic alliance with PictureTel, was achieved through the introduction of a new product on to the market. Commercialization and sales of room-type videoconferencing systems referred to as Phoenix WIDE (Nikkei Sangyo Shimbun, 1997a) triggered radical price-cutting sales that swept the room-type videoconferencing system market, having much the same impact as the original Phoenix. Phoenix WIDE has now come to command an impressive 50 percent share of the room-type videoconferencing system market.

3.2.7   Results Achieved by Strategic Communities (Strategic Outcomes)

Figure 3.7 shows activities by each SC (A, B1, B2 and B3) in chronological order.

Achievements by SC–B1
SC–B1 achievements divide into two main areas. First, in order to create a new video culture in Japan called video communications, it developed a new high-quality, low-priced Phoenix videoconferencing system accepted by

many customers. As NTT and PictureTel were working out the details of the contract, the community successfully determined the technical specifications of the new product and made decisions on the procurement contract terms within about five months. In the joint development process after the contract was signed, NTT's community members stayed in the U.S. for a long period to execute a development project by cooperating on various issues. Activities included technical discussions for the creation of a prototype, quality checks on software having complex and various functions, localization into Japanese, and creation of technical and user manuals. Needless to say, information sharing and dispatches were actively performed via the latest communication tools available at that time, including the Internet and TV conferencing. As a result, the Phoenix desktop multimedia conference system was born in Japan as a global first. The second achievement was commercialization of an updated version of Phoenix (DOS/V model and PC98/DOS integration models) and a new line-up of products (Phoenix WIDE).

Achievements by SC-A
SC-A achievements progressed through the following five stages. First, it established a sales structure for NTT Sales Department (branches) at about 200 locations nationwide, and core community members at each branch promoted Phoenix sales in each area. Second, it established a customer service counter structure at the customer service center at about 50 locations nationwide. The center in each area provided centralized customer services to handle inquiries and troubleshooting. Third, it provided training for new technologies, sales expertise and skills to about 1000 sales staff and customer service staff (in the six months before NTT began selling Phoenix). For this training, a special facility was constructed in three months and the staff were given training to provide meticulous knowledge, expertise and skills. Fourth, it established a database of sales information, customer needs and technical information through the Phoenix customer service network that connects Tokyo and the customer service centers forming the sales base in each area, and promoted sharing of information, knowledge and expertise among communities using both Phoenix and the Internet. Fifth, as a noteworthy achievement, the sales team successfully expanded sales applications for Phoenix. That is, it developed new usage for videoconferencing by selling the videoconferencing system for the distance learning, telemedicine and welfare markets as well as for the usual corporate meeting purposes. I will discuss details of this later.

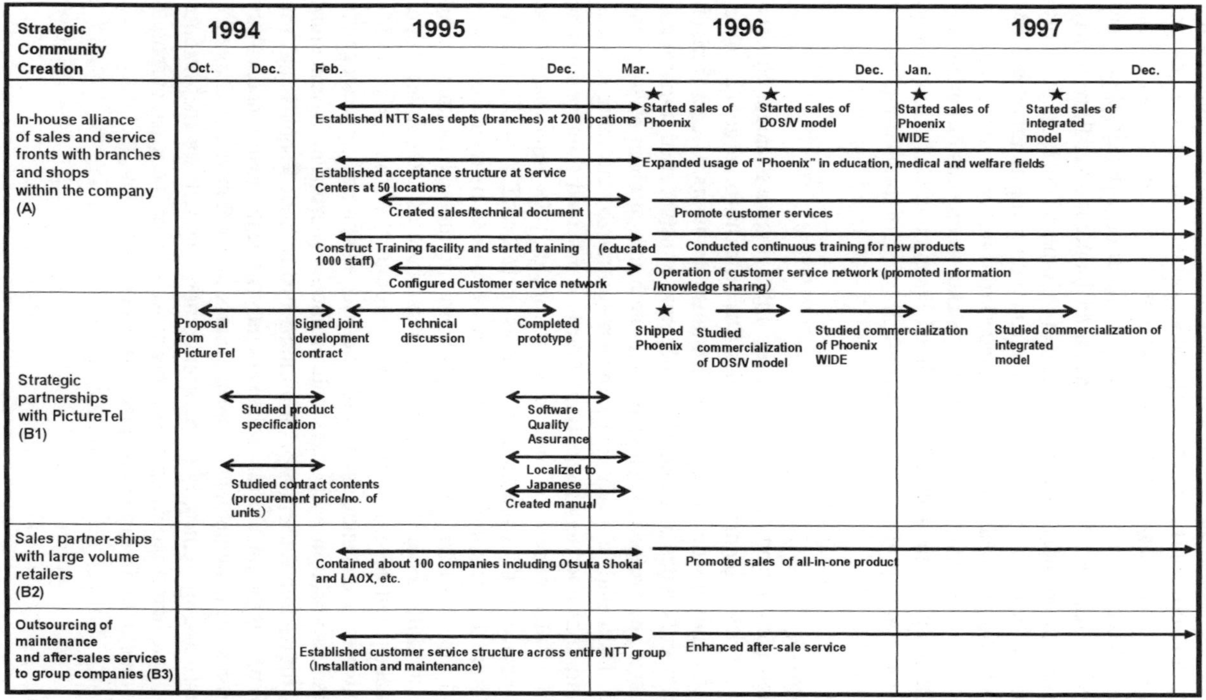

Strategic Community Creation	1994		1995		1996		1997	
	Oct.	Dec.	Feb.	Dec.	Mar.	Dec.	Jan.	Dec.

Figure 3.7 content (timeline):

In-house alliance of sales and service fronts with branches and shops within the company (A)
- Established NTT Sales depts (branches) at 200 locations
- ★ Started sales of Phoenix (Mar.)
- ★ Started sales of DOS/V model
- ★ Started sales of Phoenix WIDE (Jan.)
- ★ Started sales of integrated model
- Established acceptance structure at Service Centers at 50 locations
- Created sales/technical document
- Expanded usage of "Phoenix" in education, medical and welfare fields
- Promote customer services
- Construct Training facility and started training 1000 staff) (educated
- Conducted continuous training for new products
- Configured Customer service network
- Operation of customer service network (promoted information /knowledge sharing)

Strategic partnerships with PictureTel (B1)
- Proposal from PictureTel
- Signed joint development contract
- Technical discussion
- Completed prototype
- Studied product specification
- Software Quality Assurance
- Studied contract contents (procurement price/no. of units)
- Localized to Japanese
- Created manual
- ★ Shipped Phoenix
- Studied commercialization of DOS/V model
- Studied commercialization of Phoenix WIDE
- Studied commercialization of integrated model

Sales partner-ships with large volume retailers (B2)
- Contained about 100 companies including Otsuka Shokai and LAOX, etc.
- Promoted sales of all-in-one product

Outsourcing of maintenance and after-sales services to group companies (B3)
- Established customer service structure across entire NTT group (Installation and maintenance)
- Enhanced after-sale service

Figure 3.7 Activities of strategic communities

Achievements by SC–B2 and B3

NTT entered into a sales agent contract with about 100 outside sales companies, including large mass merchandisers and large sales companies, and NTT and sales agent communities set up a product package called Phoenix + PC + ISDN to promote sales to ordinary households using a discount method. This all-in-one product came preinstalled with the Phoenix board and software and bundled with ISDN line connection devices. This type of product held great advantages for users because anybody could easily perform TV conferencing, without special knowledge and skills, by simply switching on the system and connecting it to an ISDN line. With the Phoenix system installed in an all-in-one package integrated with an ISDN line and strategic outsourcing to NTT group companies, technical expertise and skills were handed down in order to promote the customer services (installation and maintenance) provided by all group companies.

3.2.8 Formation of a Value-Harmonized Platform in a Strategic Business Community

If innovation is to be achieved based on the creation of a strategic business community, it will become important to form an intra-community, value-harmonized platform involving all of the community members. What is meant here by 'value' corresponds to the idea, thought and spirit of the entire community respecting the vision and concept upheld by the community leader with a view to business achievement by the community.

What we have observed through this case study of the value harmonization process may be summarized as follows: In order to have the value outlooks of all the community members resonate, a shift becomes necessary from the existing set of values (or old values) to a new set of values. A value-harmonized platform is created through the four-tiered process of 'sharing, contact-triggered inspiration, creation and resonance' of value outlooks (Figure 3.8).

The first step – the sharing of value outlooks – provides the stage for studying and understanding the new value outlook (idea, thought and spirit respecting the vision and concept introduced by the community leader) in the light of which the community members have indicated the direction they feel the community should take. In the case of strategic alliance with or strategic outsourcing to an outside party, this first step will also provide the opportunity for the two partners to understand and study each other's corporate value outlook and management vision. Community members study the difference between the existing and the new value outlook through constructive conversations with community leaders so as to arrive at an understanding of the essentials of the new value outlook.

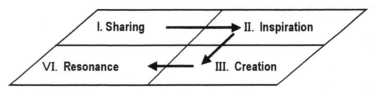

I.   Sharing Step
       Study and understanding of new sense of value advocated by community leaders and study and understanding of different corporate value and management visions.

II.   Inspiration Step
       Inducement of new sense of value in the communities through destroying the old sense of value held by community members or the fusion of a different sense of corporate value or management visions.

III.   Creation Step
       Creation of new sense of value in communities.

IV.   Resonance Step
       Resonance of ideals, will and spirit of all community members for new value in communities.

Figure 3.8   Resonance process of value in community

For example, for a community member in community A (in-house community) in Figure 3.2, who has for many years been handling the old and sedate market for analog telephone business that no longer promises profitability for the future, the new multimedia business dealing in digital applications, PCs and video-networking is a major challenge. This member is deeply entrenched in a fixed value system in which he or she is a mere cog in a giant corporate machine called NTT, and is content to attend uneventfully to the daily routine in exchange for fixed pay (or couldn't care less what went on in the workplace as long as he or she is paid). This value system is significantly hampering the member from acquiring a new sales style or new technical skills. But following repeated, constructive conversations with the community leader, who speaks to him or her enthusiastically, the community member is beginning to show signs of opening up to the idea of studying and understanding the new value system.

The second step – contact-triggered inspiration of a value outlook – provides the stage for discarding old values in favor of new ones advocated by the community leader that will spread within the community. Furthermore, in cases of strategic tie-ups or strategic outsourcing, there is a stage at which the sense of value on both sides is absorbed and then spread, fusing the corporate values and management visions of the two sides. One of the triggers that is an important process in this dissemination is to induce risk awareness. At in-house community A, the community leader persuaded members of the need to establish new multimedia business in order to survive in the ICT and multimedia world of the future. The important thing is that the innovative leadership of the community leader gradually eliminates the old values by encouraging risk awareness.

The third step – the creation of a value outlook – provides the stage for the creation of new value outlooks within a community, rooted in new value outlooks introduced by community leaders. At in-house community A, this would be an intra-community setting for new value creation where community members individually engage in self-improvement as they strive for the new objectives of a new multimedia business. It would also be at this stage that challenging objectives are set, such as an organized acquisition of new sales and technical skills.

The last step – the resonance of value outlooks – is where the mental vectors of idea, thought, and spirit of community members in their entirety resonate to the values newly created within the community to cultivate a sense of unity. A value-harmonized platform will form itself within the community, and at this stage in-house community A members would individually acquire new knowledge, skills and expertise, improve competence, and come to recognize their own 'unflagging courage' and their true selves with respect to the new multimedia business.

The value harmonization process in the communities illustrated in Figure 3.2 is expanded in Figure 3.9. For the community members, value harmonization within in-house community A is, in fact, no less than a fight against habit. With extra-company communities (B1, B2, B3), however, it becomes important for the community leaders to locate and identify partners most likely to benefit both parties, create new values to be shared with the extra-company leaders through reciprocated influence and fusion of the two corporate value systems and management visions, and assure in an organized manner that resonance occurs between the two systems. In either or any of the communities, a value-harmonized platform will be created under the innovative leadership of community leaders upholding new visions and concepts, enabling its eventual development into the innovation process (sharing – inspiration – creation – accumulation) of the community knowledge creating cycle.

Thus value harmonization within A provides a platform for resonance of value (Chapter 2, Figure 2.2) and an important element to enable the creation of new knowledge from SCs and NSCs.

Strategic Community Creation	Sharing	Inspiration →	Creation →	Resonance
In-house alliance of sales and service fronts with branches and shops within the company (A)	For the vision of how to expand in the new business area called multimedia, promote study and understanding of new sense of value through constructive conversation within communities	Shake the old sense of value by inducing awareness of inherent dangers (destroying old sense of value)	Establish vision and concept through creation of new sense of value that systematically form new sales and technology style	Establish idea, will and spirit so that all of community members have common new sense of value and individuals obtain knowledge and skills
Strategic partnerships with PictureTel (B1)	The two sides study and promote understanding of corporate sense of value of the other and management vision for development of multimedia business	Induce new sense of value by fusing corporate sense of value and management vision of both sides and establishing strategic partnership	Establish new vision and concept of both sides toward the development of multimedia business, and create new sense of value to aim at dissemination of new video image culture in Japan	Establish idea, will and spirit to generate new core competence so that the joint development personnel on both sides have a new, common sense of value and share and fuse the core competence of both sides
Sales partnerships with large volume retailers such as Otsuka Shokai, LAOX (B2)				Establish idea, will and spirit to generate new sales style such that the sales personnel on both sides have a new, common senses of value and fuse the sales skill on both sides
Outsourcing of maintenance and after-sales services to group companies (B3)	Study to understand corporate value and management vision on both sides and reconstruct a sense of value from the viewpoint of group management	Induce new sense of value that is aware of management vision called optimum group management	Create new sense of value to aim at promotion of new group corporate strategy called development of multimedia business	Establish ideals, will and spirit so that all employees of group companies work within the new sense of value.

Creation of resonance platform of new sense of value

Figure 3.9 Resonance process of creating sense of value in strategic communities

3.2.9 Strategic Management as Practice in the MPD Case

Taking on board the president's vision of moving from phone booth to multimedia room, the initial action was undertaken by the Multimedia Promotion Department's middle managers. One of their roles was to digest the vision from the top and instill it as specific strategy. In the MPD case, the middle managers recognized and understood the contexts of the ideal shape of NTT's future and the multimedia revolution vision, and they embarked on product development that was quite different from that for existing emergent products. Having followed a traditionally independent development strategy over many years, NTT came to grips with new acquisitions, cooperation and creativity in collaboration with the best partners in the world as a means of realizing target products as strategic content.

With the focus on the strategic activity cycle, actors from emergent organizations, driven by exploration activity and aiming to realize future-oriented strategies, shared new context and meaning with actors from traditional organizations. Fixing on the release of Microsoft's Windows 95 as the timing for the launch of new products, it became crucial for actors to push joint development with PictureTel. Moreover, actors had to form strong SCs in-house while promoting a highly volatile emergent strategy of new product development in order to link developed products' to the company-wide deliberate strategy. The implementation of this deliberate strategy required the construction of internal and external NSCs as specific connections and networks, and close collaboration with partner companies (including group members) became urgent.

Superficial utterances about 'vision' and 'mission' from top management are not enough to bring about change in the corporate culture of the traditional large company. In order to permeate through to the employee at the distant end of the workplace, it is important to display prototypes and boundary objects (Carlile, 2002; Cramton, 2001; Star, 1989), including specific products and businesses, as in this case. The actors had strong feelings about this. One of the mantras for this new product was to 'transform NTT's corporate culture'. Changing the values of working people is no small matter. Community leaders, however, exhibited 'value-based leadership' to mobilize knowledge within and outside the organization based on sharing new values with numerous actors in connected companies, and to build resonance of value and practical wisdom. I will explore the community leaders' 'value-based leadership' in more detail in Chapter 9.

4. Dynamic creation of networked strategic communities

4.1 LINKING DELIBERATE AND EMERGENT STRATEGIES

Chapter 3 looked at in-depth case studies of large companies' strategic activity cycles to illustrate the linkage from emergent strategy (Cycle A's strategy-making process) to deliberate strategy (Cycle B's strategy-making process) as an important element of new business expansion. In this chapter, I would like to look at another in-depth case study to illustrate the converse process – that of the formulation and implementation of new, emergent strategies from the contents of deliberate strategy (Cycle B) fixed as mainstream business, and how new knowledge is created in the form of new business content (Cycle A).

This chapter focuses on two issues, and describes the development process of an ambitious project in Japan that occurred over five years. The first issue involves important elements in the process by which a large company's informal project teams build a new business model from an emergent strategy through trial and error, targeting the expansion of existing business regions. The second involves a new knowledge creation process of integrative competences (Kodama, 2004) through dialectical leadership in the networked SCs. An example of establishing networked SCs will be a business case involving the promotion of a regionally-based electronic network in Japan that makes use of information and multimedia technologies. The case study will examine how the network of SCs – involving the central government, the regional government, public agencies, the private sector, Non-Profit Organization (NPOs) and other parties – promoted electronic networking in a regional setting in Japan to create the world's first multimedia village project. It will also consider the impact on such areas as education, medical care, social welfare and regional administration from the standpoint of a new knowledge creation process through the synthesis of diverse knowledge within the networked SCs.

In this in-depth case study, my analysis of knowledge creation focuses on the degree to which, and process by which, the SC networks have created new knowledge based on new technologies, social and customer needs, and diverse content diffused beyond the boundaries of the SCs. I then analyze the case from two angles. The first examines the characteristics of SC networks that triggered the synthesis of knowledge diffused from the three individual SC boundaries of involvement in collaboration (DiMaggio and Powell, 1983), embeddedness in collaboration (Granovetter, 1985; Dacin et al, 1999), and resonance of values (Kodama, 2001) by which the SCs were formed. The second examines the integrative competences used by strategic communities, comprising community leaders within networked SCs, to integrate dialectically the diverse SC knowledge that is distributed in the new knowledge creation process into a big project.

4.2 PROMOTION OF ICT DIFFUSION IN REGIONS OF JAPAN: THE WORLD'S FIRST MULTIMEDIA VILLAGE PROJECT AIMS TO REVIVE DEPOPULATED AREAS

4.2.1 The Importance of Promoting Diffusion of Regional Information Technology

Regional governments throughout the world, seeking to realize a regional society characterized by material wealth and a high quality of life, are actively taking steps, listening to requests and complaints brought to them daily by residents, and developing measures in order to solve regional problems in fields such as education, medical care, social welfare, the environment, industry, tourism, city planning and disaster prevention. Recently, finding transverse solutions – solutions that reach across different fields – has become a matter of some urgency, particularly as regards individual problems in areas such as education, medical care and social welfare.

Over the past few years, newspapers, television and other mass media outlets have made frequent use of the expressions 'diffusion of information technology', 'multimedia', and 'the advent of the advanced info-com society'. But there has been little discussion of the basic issues concerning the kind of influence and constructive effects that ICT diffusion would exert on the lives of ordinary people, and especially on regional residents, outside of business fields. The essence of IT lies in overcoming distance and time in various human endeavors, from daily life to business, and broadening the range and possibilities of human activity. Affordable, increasingly user-friendly info-com technology has many fields of application (the Internet is the most prominent example) and holds great potential for addressing the needs of residents and solving regional problems in order to achieve regional societies characterized by greater material wealth and a higher quality of life.

4.2.2 Background and Aims of Measures

Multimedia-based enrichment of regional communities is becoming an important topic in the 21st century. As the population declines due to a falling birth rate and society continues to age, progress is being made in the social structure with regard to internationalization and the decentralization of authority to the local level. For village residents in various regions to lead secure, healthy and enjoyable lives, we must work to enrich local, intra-village communities, encourage inter-village communication, and improve the environment for lifelong learning, beginning our efforts with enriching fields such as health insurance, social welfare, medical care and education, and improving regional government services. The Multimedia Village Project is a measure of how far the government and the private sector – the Ministry of Posts and Telecommunications, regional governments, and Japan's largest telecommunications carriers (NTT and others) – are collaborating and coordinating their efforts. The project is based upon a special scheme concerned with working to overcome the depopulation problem, improve the living environment in mountain villages and revitalize them, while investigating the question, 'What kind of multimedia would village residents be glad to use?'

4.2.3 Formation of Networked Strategic Communities

4.2.3.1 Mission and challenges
In September 1997, Nippon Telegraph and Telephone Corporation (NTT), Japan's largest telecommunications company, launched a new-generation videophone named 'Phoenix mini' throughout Japan. Though the initial target market was business and virtual classroom communications, it began to catch on for household use, helped by features that allowed the enjoyment of high-quality, two-way video communication at the world's lowest price of 198 000 yen a pair.

At that time, as ISDN and the Internet continued to spread, NTT's traditional organizations, comprising operational headquarters, nationwide branches and business offices, focused their promotions on sales of this videophone. As a result of the formation of NSCs (see Figure 3.2), the strategic activity cycle (Cycle B in Figure 3.5) was driven forward by actors in the Multimedia Promotion Department (MPD). Around 50 actors in the

MPD, including managers, and around 1000 in traditional organizations were involved in sales promotion of the video communication business.

The collection of customer needs and technical queries arising from the daily sales activities of the actors gave rise to debate around such questions as 'Why is Information and Communication Technology (ICT) necessary?' and 'What needs are there, except for business?' Marketing and development executives came to embrace the starting point of 'ICT is a tool designed to help a wide range of people in society', from the focus of one of the tenets of NTT's corporate philosophy – that of contributing to society. Then the actors searched for new business domains focusing on specific questions posed by the developed system, such as 'How can we contribute to the aging society, depopulation, medical treatment, welfare and other issues?' After that, a new project targeting these issues was developed within the emergent organization of the Multimedia Promotion Department (actors participated in new task teams while carrying out their original work, and created cross-functional teams). These newly-constructed projects focused on support for promoting information in depopulated areas all over Japan and support for medical treatment in remote areas (mentioned later), and actors took on the challenge of this new business, crossing the boundaries of industries that NTT had had no experience of up to that point.

The organizational behaviour of actors such as these functioned as a link to the strategy-making process of strategic activity Cycle A, driving exploration activity from strategic activity Cycle B, which comprised the exploitation activity of daily sales promotion (Figure 4.1). Then the NSCs newly constructed for strategic activity Cycle A (Figure 4.2) accelerated the formulation and implementation of emergent strategy and gave birth to new knowledge of new services – virtual knowledge-based services such as the Medicine Pack Service (mentioned later).

The vision and concept under which the NTT project leader pursued the popularization of the videophone called for lending a hand in the areas of medical care, insurance, social welfare and education for aged populations, including the bed-ridden, in remote regions. This vision and concept was also intended to have an impact on society through selecting one remote village in Japan and connecting all its households by videophone to the rest of the country. A larger frame of the project concept, called the Multimedia Village Project, envisioned the creation and provision of new values to large numbers of elderly people through multiple applications in the areas of medical care, health insurance, social welfare and education. The project leader's vision and concept was to realize such a multimedia village in Japan and to create a new template for a model project – the first of its kind in the world.

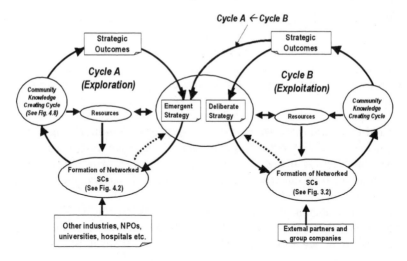

Figure 4.1   Integrated strategic activity cycles

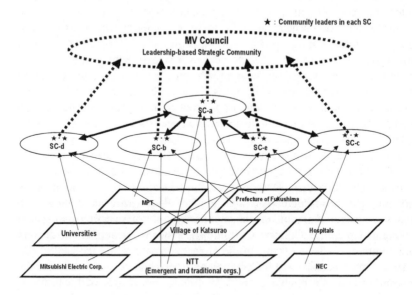

Note: MV = Multimedia Village

Figure 4.2   Formation of strategic communities and networked SCs

Several obstacles stood in the way of the project's launch, however:

- Difficulties with financing the installation of equipment to support the videophone and associated systems, and securing subsidies from the Ministry of Posts and Telecommunications and other government sources.
- The problem of selecting one village from among many, and then building consensus among the villagers for the introduction of the videophone to each village household.
- The problem of distributing extensive videophone applications to the areas of medical care, insurance, social welfare and education.
- The videophone, when it was developed, made its debut flashing the catch phrase, 'So easy to use, anyone can use it'. It was not certain, however, whether elderly people unfamiliar with such equipment would be able to master it. A host of other problems also needed to be addressed.

4.2.3.2 Decision-making based on past accomplishments

For the project leader, selecting a village posed a major challenge. The next challenge was to secure consensus and cooperation at the level of the local prefectural government under whose jurisdiction the village would be hosting such a large-scale project. NTT did have a track record of working with Fukushima Prefecture to institute a multimedia-supported, virtual-format, lifelong learning program. Koriyama Women's University, for example, which celebrated the 50th anniversary of its foundation as an educational corporation in 1996, launched a 'Multimedia Telecommunications-Based Lifelong Continuing Education Service' as one of its commemorative projects (Fukushima Minpo Shimbun, 1997).

This program put in place a PC-based teleconferencing system, a multi-room teleconferencing system that enabled participation with a regular TV set or simple monitor hookup, and an interactive, lifelong continuing education course accessible to subscribers through teleconference hook-up with multiple points of access. Specifically, multimedia-based, interactive classes were inaugurated in the framework of a network linking the 'Lifelong Learning Center' to multiple citizens' centers in farming communities.

Under the slogan of 'Attend college courses near your home', the program promoted lifelong learning while making a significant contribution to reversing the dwindling number of educational opportunities. A course linking the Center to three citizens' centers in the prefecture in real time offered a total of five lectures around the general theme of respecting regional needs and focusing on such subjects as 'Real problems in everyday life', 'Themes that make our lives worth living', and 'Events of topical social interest'. The participants were enthusiastic, and lively debates unfolded as village participants and lecturers engaged in a stimulating exchange of knowledge. In August 1997, NTT also coordinated a link-up between Fukushima Prefecture and faraway Brazil, providing an opportunity for, among other things, an exchange of opinions between the Fukushima Governor and Fukushima-born residents of Brazil.

Against this background, the first thought on the project leader's mind was to target a village in Fukushima:

> I believed Fukushima Prefecture possessed a sufficiently deep-rooted culture receptive to the teleconferencing system and the videophone. The telecommunications-based, lifelong, continuing education course had won acclaim from housewives and the elderly, and we had successfully made the Fukushima Governor, the highest-ranking official of the prefecture, cognizant of the value of video communications. We therefore decided to choose a village in Fukushima as the primary candidate. Of the several villages in the prefecture, we chose Katsurao-mura, where Katsurao Middle School, known for its emphasis on Internet use in its curricular program, was located. Katsurao-mura became the site of the Multimedia Village Project. We believed that the leadership of the Governor would be key to the launch of this large-scale project. Our first and most important task, then, was to make a presentation of the project's vision and concept before the Governor and secure his consent.

4.2.3.3 Forming strategic communities and networked strategic communities

In January 1998, the NTT project leader in the Multimedia Promotion Department, together with the traditional NTT organization comprising the branch manager of NTT Fukushima and like-minded colleagues, gave a presentation of the project's vision and concept before a panel of executive-level core leaders including the Fukushima prefectural governor and Katsurao-mura village mayor. Following an exhaustive discussion, the empathy and positive response of the core leaders was obtained in support of the project, and an SC (SC-a) was formed (Figure 4.2). Keeping pace with the formation of the SC-a, the NTT project leader then gave a presentation of the project's vision and concept to the executive director and senior officials of the Ministry of Posts and Telecommunications (MPT), and tried to gain financial support for the project. Then a strategic community (SC-b) between NTT and the MPT was formed, and several problems and issues regarding the allotment of funding and the effect of the project on social welfare were discussed within the SC-b (Figure 4.3, Phase 1).

In the process of pursuing political and financial issues in greater detail and solving a number of problems in Katsurao-mura households, NTT collected data on the village's need for the videophone and other related multimedia systems, and discussed the issue with the MPT, including the Fukushima prefectural governor and representatives of Katsurao-mura, with a view to realizing the aims of the project. Through this process, SC networks linking SC-a and SC-b were formed during this phase (Figure 4.3, Phase 2).

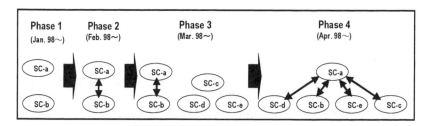

Phase 1: Creating SC-a with Prefecture of Fukushima, Village of Katsurao and NTT
           Creating SC-b with MPT, Village of Katsurao and NTT
Phase 2: Networking Strategic Communities with SC-a and SC-b
Phase 3: Creating SC-c with Prefecture of Fukushima, Village of Katsurao and Universities
           Creating SC-d with Prefecture of Fukushima, Village of Katsurao and Hospitals
           Creating SC-e with Mitsubishi Electric Corp., NEC and NTT
Phase 4: Networking Strategic Communities with Village of Katsurao, Prefecture of Fukushima,
           MPT, Universities, Hospitals and NTT

Figure 4.3   Networking strategic communities at the big project

As a result of the negotiations and the consensus with MPT, the Fukushima prefectural governor and Katsurao-mura village officials moved to finalize the proposal in which the experiments in e-learning, remote health care and telemedicine were planned through extensive collaboration with universities and hospitals. They then made further project presentations to several universities and hospitals. In this process, they formed new SCs with the universities (Koriyama Women's University and Fukushima University) (SC-c) and hospitals outside the village (SC-d) for collaboration on the project (Figure 4.2). The NTT project team, on the other hand, formed an SC with system vendors (Mitsubishi Electric Corporation and NEC) (SC-e) to realize the concept of the multimedia village from the standpoint of technology using ICT and multimedia. A variety of technical issues concerning video communications and transmission of educational and medical content were thoroughly discussed (Figure 4.3, Phase 3).

Accordingly, an umbrella networked project centered on Katsurao-mura in SC-a was formed, linking SCs b–e to SC-a, and through it, to each other. The aim of this network was to coordinate the interactive functions of different entities to bring the Multimedia Village Project to fruition, and a decision was made to work out the details (Figure 4.3, Phase 4). A proposal based on a vision and concept developed by an NTT project leader initiated the realization of a community as an executive-created project, which in turn provided a vehicle for the mutual sharing of values held by the core leaders.

In April 1998, the Katsurao-mura Multimedia Village Promotion Council (the MV Council) was formed to work across various organizations, including hospitals and schools, the Ministry of Posts and Telecommunications, the Ministry of Education, Fukushima Prefecture, Katsurao-mura, Fukushima University, Koriyama Women's University, medical associations, villagers' livelihood cooperatives and NTT (Figure 4.2). The purpose was to take further steps toward the accomplishment of the project. The MV Council was established by the core leaders in each of the various organizations, and took on the name of the Leadership-based Strategic Community (LSC). The LSC sought to promote and verify the experiment of introducing the videophone-based multimedia system to remote village communities across the nation. From this initiative it was hoped that the Multimedia Village Project idea would be accepted throughout the country. The core leaders of the various organizations (government agencies, Fukushima Prefecture, Katsurao-mura, universities, hospitals, medical associations, NPOs and others) will hereafter be referred to as 'community leaders'.

As part of the specifics of the experiment's implementation, two subcommittees were formed, one for health maintenance and well-being and one for education. The Health Maintenance and Well-Being Subcommittee was to provide care, medical consultation, health counseling and other services for the aged while using the experience to confirm the possibility of realizing a diverse, videophone-based, remote medical care and consultation service in the future. It was also decided that the Education Subcommittee would organize videophone-aided remote classrooms, seminars and inter-school student exchanges, and provide support for lifelong learning in farming communities so as to create an educational environment that would eliminate regional disparities.

In this way, a community was created through the systematic institution of the MV Council as it moved from a core leadership-centered to a strategically organized approach. With a view to bringing the Multimedia Village Project ever closer to inauguration, the MV Council studied every minute detail relating to the conceptual foundation of the Project, such as the design of the system structure, matters pertaining to medical care, insurance, social welfare and education, consensus-building presentations to the villagers, and the test run schedule. Thanks to the swift action of the community, the village residents (the customers of the project), were able to deepen their understanding. Equipment installation was completed by June

1998, and a test run of the videophone-aided Multimedia Village Project was implemented under a three-year plan ending in March 2001. Figure 4.4 shows a conceptual drawing of the Video-Net established in Katsurao-mura (Nihon Keizai Shimbun, 1998a, b; Nihon Kogyo Shimbun, 1998a, b; Wudunn, 1999).[2]

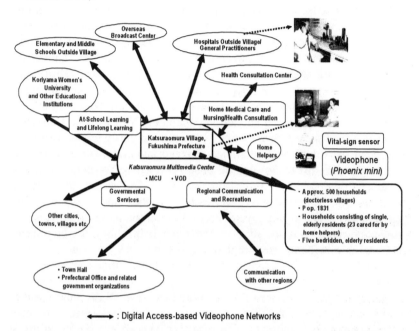

◄────► : Digital Access-based Videophone Networks

Note: MCU = Multipoint Connection Unit; VOD = Video-on-Demand.

Figure 4.4   Video-net in Katsurao-mura Village, Fukushima Prefecture

By laying digital access lines in all 473 of the households in Katsurao-mura as well as in the schools, the town hall and other public facilities, organizers prepared an environment where videophones could be used freely under a Multimedia Village System (MV System) that would be put in place. The equipment installed consisted of a Multipoint Connection Unit (MCU) (Kodama, 1999b), which permitted a maximum of 94 locations to be simultaneously connected to the multimedia center in the town hall to make arrangements and hold meetings, and a Video-On-Demand (VOD) based video server (Kodama, 1999b), from which diverse graphical information could be searched for and retrieved using a videophone. Residents took the initiative in expressing opinions, such as 'I'd like them to put a lot of information relevant to my everyday life on the video server', 'Aren't there any applications that let children play and have a good time?' and, 'I want to use my videophone to talk to family and friends outside the village'.

In the experiment, as a measure to promote the spread of information technology and revitalize mountain village regions, cheap, user-friendly multimedia was put to practical use, and methods were examined for applying multimedia in various fields, starting with medical care, social welfare, education and government services, with the ultimate objective of promoting the spread of information technology. Specifically, the experiment verified how bi-directional communication can be put to practical use with user-friendly, videophone-based graphical information, with the aim of reversing population decline, improving the living environment of mountain villages and revitalizing the villages.

Amid a rapidly shrinking and aging population, Video-Net was installed in public facilities and each home in Katsurao-mura to provide services meeting the individual needs of village residents and demonstrate the impact of these services, with the aim of molding a village community where everyone, from children to the elderly, could feel secure and lead a worthwhile life. The Video-Net successfully enabled individual residents from all walks of life to gain greater access to information and knowledge. A multimedia center was installed in the town hall, public facilities were networked to each home using digital access lines, and health preservation, social welfare, education services and government information were made available.

Thus, with the vision and concept proposed by an NTT project leader serving to trigger a sympathetic resonance of the value systems of core leaders, organized community creation on a grand scale was harvested out of a group-level, community-creating effort, resulting in the provision of services to the customers – the village population.

4.2.3.4 Innovation in new knowledge creation
The biggest challenge for the MV Council (LSC), was how to provide truly worthwhile content and applications for the village residents (the customers), using a completed MV system as the platform. This major challenge addressed the human side of the proposal that was to look at breathing life (software) into the vessel we called the MV system (hardware).

The challenges faced by the LSC at the time of start-up were the consolidation of the Multimedia Village Project, the conceptualization of the MV system, and the design and building of the system. In the stages following start-up, the content and applications relating to services in the fields of medical care, insurance, social welfare and education (all services already realized) were made available to villagers as virtual knowledge-based services (Kodama, 1999) offered on the MV system platform, the new task being to work out a way to make the system accepted throughout the community.

4.3   DYNAMICS OF NETWORKED SCs

In this section, I will use important concepts derived from the in-depth case study to consider the sort of impact that the SC networks and integrative competences, established through dialectical leadership of the community leaders, had on new knowledge creation (the output of the MV Council). First, I will analyze the characteristics of SC networks that created the trigger for the synthesis of knowledge diffused from the boundaries of individual SCs, distributed from the three dimensions of their involvement in collaboration, embeddedness in collaboration and resonance of the values on which they were formed. Second, I will discuss the integrative competences that the strategic community, comprising community leaders within networked SCs, used to synthesize dialectically the diverse knowledge of the SCs distributed in the project's new knowledge creation process.

4.3.1   Characteristics of Networked SCs

Information and knowledge within communities is both sticky and leaky. It is important, however, that the networked SCs make the leaky aspect work in a positive manner and that community leaders of all SCs promote the sharing and inspiration of knowledge beyond the SCs' boundaries. The act of transcending boundaries stimulates deep, meaningful learning, which in turn opens possibilities for the generation of new knowledge and creativity. Radical new insights and developments, such as the project discussed here, often arise at the boundaries between SCs (Grant and Baden-Fuller, 1995; Grant, 1996b). Organizations face the dilemma of having to reconcile the conflicting needs of rapid access and synthesis of relevant new knowledge with the long time frames needed for knowledge creation and synthesis. Networked SCs based on extensive inter-organizational collaboration offer a possible solution. The need for businesses and society to transcend the boundaries of SCs has grown in recent years as industry markets become more uncertain and both technology and customer needs change more rapidly. It is not possible to rely on one practical experience and the knowledge of a single organization to solve the complex problem of synthesizing technology and social needs shown in this case. The community leaders of organizations need to build SCs actively inside and outside the organization, including with customers, then to transcend the boundaries of the SCs and network rapidly.

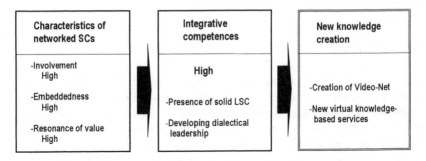

Figure 4.5   Evaluations of new knowledge creation in the case

The first important element in the formation of networked SCs is collaboration. Strong interaction among community members, strategic partnerships among organizations that form networked SCs, and interactive information sharing within networked SCs are not the only conditions required for extensive collaboration as defined by DiMaggio and Powell (1983). High levels of involvement in the collaborative process, developing a strong mutual awareness that SC members are involved in a common enterprise, are also essential. Figure 4.5 shows the results when I evaluated the networked SCs of the MV Council, with weight given to the factor of high involvement.

The second important element in the formation of networked SCs is embeddedness, which describes the degree to which collaboration between SCs is enmeshed in inter-organizational relationships. This element highlights the connection between collaboration and the broader inter-organizational network. Highly embedded collaborations between SCs were observed as an expanded network of SCs centered on Katsurao-mura came into being.

The third important element in the formation of networked SCs is the resonance process of values in the community. This is the process whereby all community members, in their effort to fulfill the networked SC's mission and goals, share and resonate values aimed at realizing the business. This idea of the resonance of values is also the same as the hidden value, espoused by O'Reilley and Pfeffer, that enables the shared values within the formal organization or community to produce new knowledge or competences (O'Reilly III and Pfeffer, 2000). The resonance of values in networked SCs with partners inside and outside the organization (Kodama, 2001) leads to dialectical ideas and strength to act among community leaders, and turns into a capability for generating new knowledge that forms the new core for the networked SCs. High levels of resonance value were observed in the networked SCs of the MV Council, which had succeeded in the project (Figure 4.5).

Next follows a supplementary explanation of the three factors relating to the networked SCs obtained from the field study mentioned above. High involvement, the first element of networked SCs, refers to the condition in which specialized engineers and professionals in the networked SCs thoroughly understand and share each other's knowledge of the various core technologies and content created in each SC through member dialog and collaboration. The specific knowledge of core technologies and content that was created in each SC is as follows (Figure 4.6).

SC-a, comprising Katsurao-mura, Fukushima Prefecture and NTT, created knowledge that formed concepts aimed at realizing the future Multimedia Village Project that resulted from merging the social and technological contexts. SC-b, comprising NTT and the MPT (the overseeing body), created a road map for bringing outlying regions into the information age in order to realize SC-a's new concepts from the standpoint of national policies and financial resources. In SC-c, Katsurao-mura, Fukushima Prefecture and local universities collaborated to develop a new e-learning system. In SC-d, Katsurao-mura, Fukushima Prefecture, and local hospitals collaborated to develop a new e-healthcare system. And in SC-e, NTT, Mitsubishi Electric and NEC collaborated to develop a total system that could realize the Multimedia Village concept from a technological standpoint.

The development results (core technologies and content) created by these SCs grew into knowledge that was deeply shared through close dialog and collaboration within the networked SCs. Much of the data from interviews and other sources confirm that the condition of high involvement had been attained. One NTT manager commented as follows:

> To make this project a success, we not only needed to tackle tangible issues such as developing technology and finding finances, we also needed to address intangible issues such as developing support for residents' education, medical care and welfare services and to integrate these with the tangible resources. If we could not achieve a deep and thorough understanding of specialized knowledge among the various organizations involved, it would have been impossible to produce a system that residents would truly enjoy using. Our first mission was, therefore, to ensure that members of all these organizations were able to share this knowledge at a deep level.

High embeddedness, the second element, refers to the condition in which knowledge created in each SC transcends SCs' boundaries and is deeply shared among them, and is then generated as new knowledge by integrating the various bodies of knowledge from the networked SCs. The main feature in the NSCs of each case is that the element of high embeddedness facilitates the integration of the core technologies and contents of each SC and creates concrete new knowledge as development results (Figure 4.5).

High resonance of value, the third element, refers to the condition in which NSC members share deeply and empathize with a vision for development that the members of NSCs aim to achieve through close dialog and collaboration. This observation was obtained by myself from discussions with many community members. An NTT director, for example, commented:

> It was important for us to develop a system that appealed to the human heart and sensitivities, so we had to devote considerable thought to devising a system that residents found user-friendly and enjoyable at the same time. We therefore had many debates on what sort of IT would be meaningful to the lives of village residents. The extensive dialog among members of all organizations that enabled us to empathize and share uniform values was extremely important.

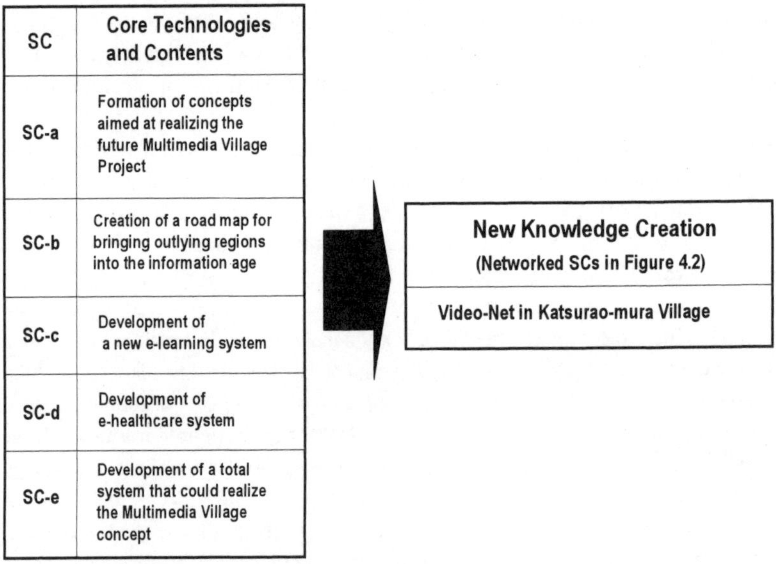

SC	Core Technologies and Contents
SC-a	Formation of concepts aimed at realizing the future Multimedia Village Project
SC-b	Creation of a road map for bringing outlying regions into the information age
SC-c	Development of a new e-learning system
SC-d	Development of e-healthcare system
SC-e	Development of a total system that could realize the Multimedia Village concept

New Knowledge Creation
(Networked SCs in Figure 4.2)

Video-Net in Katsurao-mura Village

Figure 4.6   Core technologies and contents of SCs and new knowledge creation of networked SCs

To carry out these dialogs, community leaders and other members needed to build a platform for resonating values and creating relationships of mutual trust (Vangen and Huxham, 2003) while engaging in ongoing mutual exchanges, deep collaboration, high involvement and high embeddness at the boundaries of multiple, diverse SCs. An evaluation of networked SCs can be found in the project's characteristic pattern of rapid networking among SCs, realizing high involvement, high embeddness and high resonance value. These effects can establish the leadership-based strategic community and produce the integrative competences based on their dialectical leadership (Figure 4.5).

4.4 INTEGRATIVE COMPETENCES THROUGH DIALECTICAL LEADERSHIP OF COMMUNITY LEADERS

Discord and conflict are common occurrences among networked SCs. These elements are harmful factors in the effort to synthesize the knowledge possessed by the SCs. The leadership-based strategic community (LSC) thus endeavors to promote synthesis over discord.

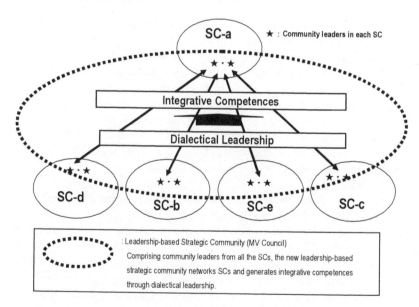

Figure 4.7 Integrative competences through dialectical leadership of community leaders

The role of the LSC is: 1) to synthesize the knowledge of all SCs in the networks formed by community leaders and comprising personnel from various levels of participating organizations, including top management and middle management (Figure 4.2); and 2) to generate integrative competences for the combined network power of all SCs through dialectical leadership (Figure 4.7). The ability of community leaders in the SCs to unite comes from a solid LSC possessing the elements of high involvement, high embeddedness, high resonance of value and trust building. In order to create knowledge, which is the ultimate aim of the networked SCs, community leaders need to understand and share thoroughly each other's knowledge through the SCs that they have formed. This engagement among community leaders is the element of high involvement. The solid LSC then integrates all the diverse knowledge that was shared among the SCs and creates new knowledge as networked SCs. This comes as a result of the element of high embeddedness. In order to produce the elements of high involvement and high embeddedness within the LSC, I have been able to confirm, through dialogs with community leaders, that it is particularly important for community leaders to build high resonance of value and trust among each other (Vangen and Huxham, 2003). A Katsurao-mura village leader commented as follows:

> To bring a project of this scale to a successful conclusion, it was important for leaders in the various organizations to build relationships of trust. This project required a diverse range of specialized knowledge. Experienced leaders in such fields as government policy, finance, education, medical care, welfare, technology development and politics needed to build relationships of trust and to exercise their own expertise to the greatest extent of their ability. To achieve this trust, it was vital that they shared and empathized the visions and values that would bring the project to fruition. This trust enabled them to share specialized knowledge in various fields and then to integrate this knowledge to give substance to the new concepts that represented the ultimate aim of the project.

The above four elements of the solid LSC thus produce the integrative competences that lead to knowledge creation.

The LSC also needs to balance the various paradoxical elements and issues within SCs in the network in order to realize these integrative competences. The LSC needs to enable community leaders to conduct dialectical management based consciously on dialectical leadership and engage in dialectical dialog to solve the various differences and issues that result from learning among the community leaders. When this is achieved, the LSC actively analyzes problems and resolves issues, forms an arena for the resonance of new values, and creates a higher level of knowledge.

Dialectical management is based on the Hegelian approach, which is a practical method of resolving conflict within an organization (Benson, 1977; Peng and Nisbett, 1999; Seo and Creed, 2002).

The balancing of paradoxical elements and issues involves the synthesis of divergent views among organization members coming from different corporate cultures on the one hand, and the synthesis of divergent business and social issues, such as the different management, technology or customer needs procedures, on the other. In the case of the MV Council, synthesis was required in three areas: 1) the values of many employees possessing a broad diversity of viewpoints and knowledge shaped by the different organizational cultures to which they belong; 2) balancing customers' needs and high technology presented by firms; and 3) balancing political aspects and social needs. The LSC plays a central role in synthesizing the paradoxical elements and issues in the specific areas of human resources, elements among seeds and needs, and political issues. The dialectical leadership, with the new ideas and approaches of the community leaders who have adopted the methods of dialectical management in their efforts to synthesize paradoxical elements and issues, make new knowledge creation and innovation possible.

The LSC promotes dialectical dialog and discussion among community leaders in order to cultivate a thorough understanding of problems and issues. By communicating and collaborating with each other, community leaders become aware of the roles and values of each other's work. As a result, they are able to transform the various conflicts that have arisen among them into 'constructive conflicts' (Robbins, 1974). This process requires community leaders to follow a pattern of dialectical thought and action in which they ask themselves what sorts of actions they themselves would take, what sorts of strategies or tactics they would adopt, and what they could contribute toward achieving the project and the innovation of new knowledge creation. In achieving new knowledge creation and innovation, the LSC promotes the empathy and resonance of the community leaders' values, and the combined synergy and dialectical leadership among the community leaders has resulted in the high levels of integrative competences that have enabled the MV Council to realize this big project and form new, virtual knowledge-based services in the medical and educational fields. In another sense, it can be seen that the MV Council has used the resonance of values among community leaders in their SCs and their leadership synergy based on dialectical leadership to form the LSC and develop high levels of integrative competences, which in turn have generated a solid network of SCs (Figure 4.5).

4.5 COMMUNITY KNOWLEDGE CREATING CYCLE

Actors integrated distributed knowledge and created new knowledge from the formation of NSCs in Cycle A (see Figure 4.1), which are networks of diverse organizations comprising, for example, the different industry types, non-profit organizations, hospitals and universities indicated in Figure 4.2. Then the knowledge created through the community knowledge creating cycle of Figure 4.1 is described on a temporal axis, as follows.

The biggest challenge for the MV Council community was how to provide truly worthwhile content and applications for the village residents (the customers) using a completed MV system as the platform. This was a major challenge that addressed the human side of the proposition that was looking at breathing life (the software) into the vessel we called the MV system (the hardware).

One of the basic requirements for the continued development of a created community consists of innovation of community knowledge in terms of information, knowledge, skills, know-how, experience and other factors that follow the steps of sharing, inspiration through contact, creation and accumulation described in Chapter 2.

The challenges faced by the community at the time of start-up were the consolidation of the Multimedia Village Project, conceptualization of the MV system, and designing and building of the system. To build the best MV system possible for the residents of Katsurao-mura, who could then share the information and knowledge held by organizations comprising a variety of businesses, knowledge-exchange sessions were organized within the community in the form of constructive dialog between community leaders, among whom figured a number of strategic community members. Ever mindful to exploit content and applications that would breathe life into the village and build new values, the leaders encouraged the creation and accumulation of community knowledge in terms of both 'hard' and 'soft' aspects, namely by consolidating the Multimedia Village Project, conceiving, designing and constructing the MV concept, and refining the method for providing virtual knowledge-based services in the areas of medical care, insurance, social welfare and education (see the Start-Up Phase in Figure 4.8).

In the post-start-up stages, the completed content and applications in the fields of medical care, insurance, social welfare and education were made available to villagers as virtual knowledge-based services offered on the MV system platform, with the subsequent task of making the system accepted throughout the community.

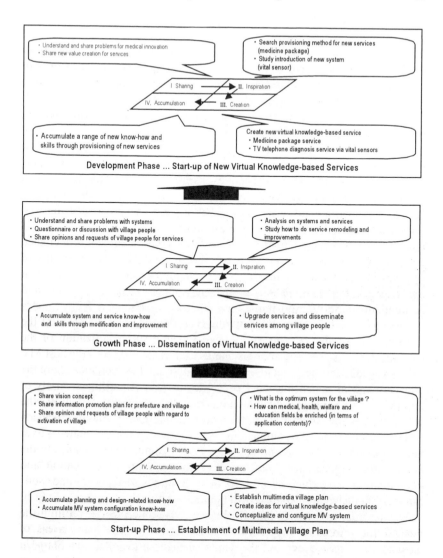

Figure 4.8 Community knowledge creating cycle (Katsurao-mura Project)

As an example of medical care services, it became possible to provide remote videophone health consultations, thus lightening the physical burden of commuting to a hospital for patients and their families and improving the efficacy of house calls for doctors. As an aspect of a comprehensive social welfare and medical care support initiative for the elderly, it became possible for a home helper to check the appearance of his or her elderly charges via videophone screen at any time, permitting early detection of emergencies and detailed care. It also became possible to receive at-home calisthenics instruction from the social welfare center. Furthermore, a mechanism was established whereby hearing impaired residents could use VOD to retrieve videophone-based sign language assistance and graphical information related to insurance and social welfare on demand.

Services in the area of education included a range of lifelong learning programs provided via videophone by Koriyama Women's University and other institutions so that village residents could avail themselves of various educational opportunities from home. Participation in nationwide seminars, cooperative learning and inter-school exchanges via videophone and in real time were also made available to offer children in depopulated areas an educational environment in which regional differences were irrelevant. Uses for school-centered videophone were expanded, among them joint research announcements with elementary and middle schools outside the village, debates and student exchanges with other schools, videophone-based inspection of classes by parents and guardians, and remote English conversation classes taught by non-Japanese English teachers.

Applications for administrative and other services in new fields outside medical care, insurance, social welfare and education were given pioneering test runs. Experiment organizers, for example, produced informational video content, including a government guide and data relating to shopping, recreation and various services, and stored it on the VOD server. This allowed users to search for and retrieve this diverse graphical information, and to use and enjoy readily everything from governmental information to window shopping and karaoke. Moreover, a multipoint video connection service was used to allow numerous individuals to engage simultaneously and interactively in such activities as making appointments and participating in seminars. In this way, village residents were easily able to participate in videoconferences held in their own village, or anywhere in Japan, from the comfort of their own homes.

Further improvements to the virtual knowledge-based services were made through the process of flagging problems with the system and services by means of opinion surveys and interviews carried out to reflect the opinions and wishes of the villagers. To achieve this, a spiraling innovation process of sharing, inspiring, creating and accumulating community knowledge through repeated service offerings was developed. This phase coincided with the community's growth period (Growth Phase in Figure 4.8). Virtual knowledge-based services were thus established on firm ground through organizational learning based on the spiral process of community knowledge.

The development phase of community knowledge also provided the launch stage for yet newer virtual knowledge-based services (the Development Phase in Figure 4.8). As the search continued for applications in various fields that contribute to new medical care innovations, such as remote medical care using vital-sign sensors and home delivery of medicine to chronic patients based on videophone medical examinations, a new era of resident-centered multimedia got its start in this village of Katsurao-mura (Nikkei Sangyo Shimbun, 1999, Asahi Shimbun, 1999).

The following illustrates how this has happened. The provisions of the existing Japanese Medical Act require a face-to-face meeting between the diagnosing physician and the patient for drug prescriptions to be dispensed. But this law makes it necessary for residents of geographically remote, doctor-deprived villages such as Katsurao-mura afflicted with chronic ailments (patients with relatively stable conditions such as diabetes or hypertension) to undertake trips of several hours expressly to visit doctors for drug prescriptions. This is an onerous burden for the elderly. To remedy this situation, the community producer engaged in aggressive negotiations with the Ministry of Public Health and Welfare, the governmental organ regulating medical care. The result was a legalization of medicinal home delivery on the basis of videophone-aided remote diagnoses (Medicine Pack Service). The creation of the Medicine Pack Service was a major boon for elderly sufferers of chronic disorders. Thus, the innovative creation of new services based on virtual knowledge arose from a sharing and inspiring of new and unprecedented knowledge and an accumulation of skills and expertise.

The whole community of Katsurao-mura strove for self-improvement under the slogan of providing quality services to its customers (the villagers), and innovating new knowledge. It was this innovation that created abiding new values for the community's customers.

4.6 STRATEGIC MANAGEMENT AS PRACTICE IN THE KATSURAO-MURA CASE

Actors in the sales workplaces of traditional organizations are driven by the daily, routine business of new product sales and solutions – the exploitative activity of best practice comprising horizontal development of daily business reform and improvement activities, as well as examples of sales success). They aimed to share customer information constantly with actors from the emergent organizations of new product development divisions through the formation of NSCs (Figures 3.2 and 3.5). The middle managers of both organizations, especially, collaborated closely and worked positively at developing experiments and incubation with new usage methods, potential customers and lead users relating to videoconferencing systems and videophones. Amidst informal meetings and exchanges of opinion, the trend to establish big business related to multimedia solutions exploiting the Internet and videophone gradually grew, driven by middle managers.

How can this kind of dialog enable ICT to help regions affected by progressive depopulation and ageing? Despite having no direct relation to NTT's and others' corporate profit, actors came to have deep discussions about how to exploit the ICT revolution to advance regional activity as a social contribution from Japan's leading companies. The content of this dialog and discussion became an important context for middle managers looking for the next challenge. They undertook the significant duty of formulating individual, specific strategic content on the nebulous issue of 'The development of regional ICT'. It was important to create a new business strategy framework rather than rely on established business activities. Common points are shared with every country, but to mobilize senior citizens in Japan, it was essential to create a large, consensus-based framework for strategic aims incorporating the authorities (governments and administrators). As a result, the strategic community thought of receiving ICT investment as funding aid from government, local authorities, private enterprise and others. Comprehensive debate among relevant organizations put the 'multimedia village structure' at the core of formulated strategic content. To implement the questions of 'Who', 'Why', 'What', 'When', 'To whom', and 'How', as specific strategies (as mentioned in the above case), the requisite timing was ascertained to encourage the strong intentions and regional activities of Katsurao-mura in Fukushima Prefecture, and NSC construction was improvised (systematically and through trial-and-error, cautiously and audaciously) under the leadership of private companies such as NTT, with partners enabled by new and potential knowledge. Then new, virtual knowledge-based services were created in the region by achieving a 'multimedia village structure' through trial and error. Amid a constantly changing context, community leaders from each SC (Figure 4.2) displayed a dialectical leadership that dynamically synthesized diverse knowledge and created new knowledge.

From the viewpoint of the 'strategic activity cycle', the development of the future vision of regional ICT from actors' daily exploitative activities inspired the actors, and the actors then became able to link strategies to explorative activity cycles as new emergent strategies. Moreover, the strategic outcomes of Katsurao-mura precipitated the next strategic activity cycle (Cycle A in Figure 4.1). So Cycle A led to further formulation and implementation of emergent strategies.

No example of an experiment comparable in size or as technologically advanced as Katsurao-mura's Multimedia Village Project can be found anywhere in the world. Amid the digitization (conversion to ISDN) of public circuits, Video-Nets allow homes, schools and regions to be linked through advanced multimedia services on the basis of videophones whose user interfaces are simple to master. In today's climate, where the formation of a truly free communication society is anticipated, much is expected from this project as a means of building a model of an ideal society and sounding out new, ideal forms of regional communication and culture.

The community leader's next strategic step was to deploy the Katsurao-mura test case, which provided a multimedia village project template, to other Japanese villages and towns. His project team contacted regional governments throughout the country to sell them the project idea and concentrated on forging community ties with the key people, namely the core leaders. The upshot was that a second multimedia village project was launched in Nosegawa, Nara Prefecture, in April 1999 with a project budget in the order of 65 million yen. The project installed an MV system under a similar scheme to the Katsurao-mura project in which a government subsidy was put to use (Asahi Shimbun, 1998). At the same time, the formation of a community with the participation of local entities including hospitals, a medical association and universities enabled work on the content and applications relating to the areas of medical care, insurance, social welfare and education.

Furthermore, the project size was scaled up from village to town when it was decided, in November 1999, to launch Japan's first multimedia town project based on a similar scheme and with the support of a Government subsidy in Yajimamachi, Akita Prefecture, with a project budget of the order of 120 million yen (Akita Sakigake Shimbun, 1999).

Thus, success with one community (the case of Katsurao-mura with a project budget of approximately 75 million yen) led to success with other communities (the cases of Yasakugawa and Yajimamachi) in a spiraling chain of strategic community creation, providing an example of an important management process for this case study.

NOTES

1. Government (Ministry of Posts and Telecommunications) subsidies, made available under the heading of regional electronic networking promotion (Networking Facilities Upgrade Project Grants-in-Aid), include a facilities-building costs component, one-third of which is shouldered by the Government and the remaining two-thirds by regional governments (prefectures, cities, towns, villages). In the case of the Katsurao-mura project, the total construction cost came to 75 million yen, an amount covered in equal parts by the Ministry of Posts and Telecommunications, Fukushima Prefecture and Katsurao-mura. This total construction cost

was incurred by the VOD (Video on Demand), MCU (Multipoint Connection Unit), networking equipment and other multimedia center-related construction components. NTT agreed to undertake the building of the entire multimedia center, proceeding to lease videophones free of charge to all 500 households in the village and putting the Video-Nets system in place. For the Video-Nets concept and virtual knowledge-based services applications, see Kodama, 1999b.

2.   Many television stations, newspapers and other media produced stories on the world's first videophone-aided multimedia village project realized in Katsurao-mura. Prominent among them were TV Tokyo (*World Business Satellite*, aired 18 May 1998), TBS (*Wide Show*, aired 11 May 1998), and NHK (news).

3.   A patient receives a diagnosis via videophone, then the doctor writes a prescription if needed, faxes it to a pharmacy outside the hospital, and mails it to the patient. The pharmacy prepares the medicine according to the prescription facsimile, and an employee then takes it directly to the patient's home and compares the original prescription with the facsimile. If they match, the employee exchanges the medicine for the original prescription and payment (including a delivery fee). Patients eligible for home delivery include those with chronic illnesses, such as high blood pressure and rheumatism, who are in a stable condition. (Home delivery of medicine on the basis of videophone diagnosis was approved by the Ministry of Health and Welfare in April 1999.) The 'Medicine Pack Service' was the first of its kind in Japan in the area of medical care, and the event was reported by Japan Broadcasting Corporation (NHK) in nationally broadcast television programs, such as *Ohayo Nippon* (*Good Morning Japan*) (9 December 1999) and *News at Nine* (1 December 1999).

5. Architectural innovation in cross-functional multi-projects

In this chapter, I present a basic framework in which the integration of various organizational boundaries between heterogeneous organizations both inside and outside a corporation creates new knowledge. The chapter presents a detailed case study involving joint new product and service development of a mobile multimedia system by NTT DoCoMo (a mobile communications carrier in Japan), Fujitsu, NEC and large telecommunication manufacturers including high-tech companies based in the U.S. This case study illustrates the dynamism in which new knowledge is created by simultaneously promoting the formation of a horizontally integrated network among strategic communities between the three corporations (including customers) and a vertically integrated network among strategic communities within the corporation. The dynamic capability through the networked strategic communities enabled NTT DoCoMo, Fujitsu and NEC to build new business models aimed at customers and achieve successful architectural innovation (new product and service development).

5.1 A CASE STUDY OF NEW PRODUCT AND SERVICE DEVELOPMENT

Until now, the main functions of second-generation (2G) mobile phones have been voice communication and accessing of text-based web information on the mobile Internet (through, for example, i-mode), which have been enjoying explosive growth in Japan as well as Europe (*Business Week*, 2000). Now, however, technological breakthroughs in areas such as semiconductors, low power consumption, networking and video compression have enabled promising video applications with mobile videophones that are completely new and different from the videoconferencing systems and conventional videophones that exploited fixed communications networks such as ISDN or the Internet (Kodama, 1999b).

93

In Japan, third-generation (3G) mobile communications services, launched in October 2001,[1] enabled communications via mobile phones provided by DoCoMo. Once a video delivery system to mobile phones becomes operational, video communications will be possible anywhere at any time. This technology therefore holds the potential to revolutionize the lives of individuals.

DoCoMo promoted the popularization of the mobile phone, 3G's most popular application. At that time, one of DoCoMo's big issues was the establishment of new business in a video streaming distribution platform and its video-based applications. These were almost unheard of in the Japanese market, and presented a new challenge for the world's first new product and service development.

At first, seven employees, including a team leader, set to work drafting a plan to establish a market for 3G-based video streaming applications. Their vision was to create a new culture in Japan, based on video transmission, out of the country's telephone and text-based mobile communications of the past. They were presented with the business challenge of developing the following:

- A live video distribution platform capable of simultaneously delivering live video to multiple mobile phones, such as mobile phone terminals and PDAs (Personal Digital Assistants), as a 3G mobile communications service.
- The kind of video content (live and on-demand video information) that would be required for customers in DoCoMo's efforts to promote its video streaming service.
- A business formation that would facilitate sales, maintenance and after-sales service in DoCoMo's efforts to promote the mobile video streaming service.

The ten team members were passionate about realizing a video streaming platform that used mobile videophone so that users could access video content anywhere, at any time (see Figure 5.1). These members had experience with fixed-line video streaming systems in such areas as marketing, product development and sales. Though the new field was unknown to them, they firmly believed that a mobile multimedia culture using video streaming would evolve at some time in the future and that this was a theme in which they should become engaged, especially while the market remained undeveloped.

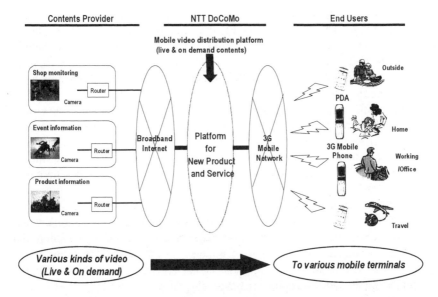

Figure 5.1 Video streaming platform for mobile phones

At the time, moving forward with these issues was a practically impossible task for just ten employees. However, the motivating force behind these video-based businesses turned out to be network-based community thinking and action based on the creation of communities outside the company, including customers (Wenger, 2000), that related to each individual business process: new product and service development, marketing, customer services, maintenance, after-sales service and so on.

There were many negative opinions within DoCoMo about the development of this platform. 'Is there really a need for several people to engage in video streaming on their mobile phones' tiny LCD screens when there is no 3G-mobile phone market yet?' and 'Should we risk development capital for this sort of service?' were two of the questions. There were problems outside DoCoMo as well, such as the uncertainty that any manufacturers would be willing to share the considerable risk involved in developing this technology.[2]

To bring their vision to fruition, however, the ten members – including a team leader – made persuasive presentations at related divisions within DoCoMo to reach a consensus. They also visited several corporate customers who were already using video streaming services over a fixed broadband network to see if they could collect any information on potential needs for video streaming. In addition, they held several unofficial meetings with manufacturers in Japan and overseas, exchanging views on joint R&D and the possibility that their vision could be achieved. As a result, the ten members were able to obtain a consistent understanding and empathy, along with a resonance for the vision and value of 'Realizing future mobile multimedia', among groups within DoCoMo, Fujitsu and NEC (the large telecommunications manufacturers) and among corporate customers.

Through ample dialog, the ten team members aimed to form strategic communities for the purpose of sharing business context and knowledge among groups within DoCoMo, Fujitsu and NEC, and among customers. The first strategic community was SC-a, comprising the service planning team and the development division within DoCoMo; the second was SC-b, comprising DoCoMo's and Fujitsu's network development division; the third was SC-c, comprising DoCoMo's and NEC's software development division; and the fourth was SC-d, comprising specific corporate customers. The actors in the four strategic communities engaged in close dialog, created shared knowledge for the purpose of realizing mobile multimedia, and at the same time agreed on the need to understand new knowledge concerning platform development for a new video service. These four strategic communities had the characteristics of the semantic boundary described by Carlile (2004), as they formed networked strategic communities among specific customers – DoCoMo, Fujitsu and NEC – and promoted the sharing of business context and knowledge (see Figure 5.2).

DoCoMo's service planning team, however, needed to leap over a number of hurdles in the way of realizing the new platform. As illustrated in Figure 5.2, SC-a brought in additional related groups which uncovered practical problems and issues. Thus novelty arose in SC-a, and the boundary characteristics as shared meaning changed from a semantic to a pragmatic boundary (Carlile, 2004). Behind this rise of novelty was a major issue concerning the need to acquire development resources (development expenses) within DoCoMo and build an internal structure aimed at new product and service development. To this end, the service planning team needed to reach a consensus among related divisions at DoCoMo (corporate sales, consumer sales, development, equipment, maintenance, procurement, planning and other divisions) and clear a multitude of decision-making processes (internal procedures) within DoCoMo. The service planning team was able to obtain a final green light after resolving various conflicts within the company and making numerous adjustments through political negotiations.

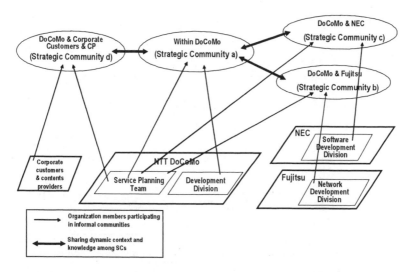

Figure 5.2   Formation of four strategic communities (Dec 2000 – May 2001): strategic communities as semantic boundaries

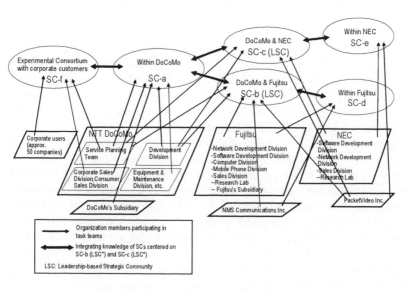

Figure 5.3   Horizontally integrated NSCs (customers, DoCoMo, Fujitsu, NEC): external integration capability of knowledge through integration of pragmatic boundaries (SCs)

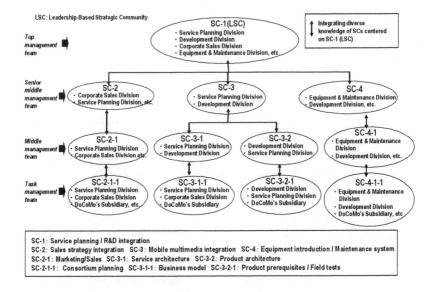

*Figure 5.4   Vertically integrated NSCs (DoCoMo): internal integration
            capability of knowledge through integration of pragmatic
            boundaries (SCs)*

SC-a, as in Figure 5.2, changed to a pragmatic boundary (see Figure 5.3)
that involved a larger number of related groups (including DoCoMo
subsidiaries such as DoCoMo Systems Inc. and DoCoMo Service Inc.). A
structured model comprising numerous cross-functional task teams shown in
Figure 5.4 was formed within DoCoMo in order to pursue detailed studies
regarding the specifics of the new product and service development, the type
of business model to be built, and the means of construction. Figure 5.4
represents a development of the detailed functions (required tasks) and
structure (management level) of the SC-a in Figure 5.3. Pragmatic boundary
SCs were formed at each of the various levels of management (top, senior
middle, middle, task and others). At the same time, these SCs were
vertically integrated between the levels of management to form NSCs. The
process represented the integration of various pragmatic boundaries within
DoCoMo.

I will now describe the characteristic SCs of Figure 5.4. SC-1 is an SC
comprising a team of leaders (top management) who are in charge of related
divisions at DoCoMo. They have complete authority to formulate and
execute this new product and service development. SC-2 comprises a team
of senior middle management that pursues studies towards realizing the
development from the customer side. SC-3 comprises a senior middle

management team studying the service and product architecture that is to form the platform for the business model at the core of the development. SC-4 consists of a senior middle management team that studies the efficient equipment investment, construction method, equipment operation and customer services required to give physical shape to the development. Numerous SCs are thus formed within DoCoMo and its subsidiaries, and the network of vertically integrated SCs consolidates new knowledge produced from individual SCs, creating an internal integration capability. Though people in charge of each SC support this internal integration capability, the most important role is played by the team of leaders in SC-1 (the leadership-based SC, or LSC) who need to address simultaneously issues in diverse business areas such as marketing, sales, technology development, equipment and maintenance in order to hand down final decisions.

Having arrived internally at the decision to proceed with this new product and service development, in May 2001 DoCoMo agreed to form strategic partnerships to develop jointly mobile streaming video systems. It formed a partnership with Fujitsu to develop an experimental and trial system and with NEC to develop a commercial system. For DoCoMo, the objective of the SCs was to cover the Japanese mobile video streaming market in a single stroke while launching the new wireless video streaming service to promote the 3G mobile market. Strategic Communities B and C between DoCoMo, Fujitsu and NEC in Figure 5.2 migrated to SC-b and SC-c in Figure 5.3 respectively; as a pragmatic boundary, this promoted joint development aimed at realizing more concrete new products and services.

Participants in the SC-b comprised members of Fujitsu's network development division, middle managers and staff members from the research laboratory, the software development division, the computer division, the mobile phone division, the sales division, Fujitsu's subsidiary companies, PacketVideo Inc. and NMS Communications Inc. in the U.S., all of whom repeatedly discussed experimental and trial product specifications required by the product architecture, business models and services. SC-c participants comprised members of NEC's software development division, middle managers and staff members from the research laboratory, the network development division, sales division and PacketVideo Inc., all of whom repeatedly discussed commercial product specifications required by the product architecture, business model and services.

The jointly developed SC-b and SC-c in Figure 5.3 are part of the horizontally integrated NSCs of DoCoMo, Fujitsu and NEC. SC-b and SC-c are equivalent to the pragmatic boundaries that produce new knowledge after obtaining external integration capability through partnership and collaboration in the strategic alliance between communications carriers and vendors.

At Fujitsu and NEC, on the other hand, company-wide development structures were established as a result of the strategic alliances with DoCoMo. SC-d and SC-e (Figure 5.3) began to form as pragmatic boundaries involving various related divisions within Fujitsu and NEC. SC-d and SC-e developed into layered structures. In the case of Fujitsu in SC-d, the merging and integration of different technologies in specialized fields – video, mobile communications, semiconductor, hardware, software, computer and human interface – were required for large-scale new product development. Therefore, experts from various locations – the research laboratory, the software development division, the mobile phone division, the computer division as it relates to software technology, Fujitsu's subsidiary companies, PacketVideo Inc. and NMS Communications Inc. – gathered to form an internally structured model of the kind of cross-functional task team shown in Figure 5.5. This figure represents the SC-d of Figure 5.3, which has developed with detailed functions (the knowledge and tasks of various experts) and structures (components that configure the product when the overall system has developed into subsystems). SCs that formed pragmatic boundaries were created at each of the various levels of management (top, senior middle, middle, task management), and at the same time these SCs were vertically integrated between the levels of management, forming NSCs. In other words, the process represented the integration of various pragmatic boundaries within Fujitsu.

In the case of NEC in SC-e, experts from various locations, including the research laboratory, the network development division and PacketVideo Inc., gathered as joint development partners to form an internally structured cross-functional task team.

Next, I will describe the features of the SCs in Figure 5.5. SC-1 is an SC comprising a team of leaders (top management) who are in charge of related divisions at Fujitsu and have complete authority to formulate and execute this new product and service development. SC-2 comprises a senior middle management team that pursues studies in system architecture. SC-3 comprises a senior middle management team that examines the connectivity between new product and mobile phones. SC-2-1 and SC-2-2 comprise middle management teams that study software and hardware architecture forming the core of each new product development. SC-2-3 comprises middle management teams that study system integration and the application development of new products. SC-2-1-1, SC-2-1-2, SC-2-2-1, and SC-2-2-2 comprise task management teams including the many staff of Fujitsu's subsidiary companies, PacketVideo Inc. and NMS Communications Inc., who study detailed architecture and sub-systems of hardware and software components forming the core of each new product development.

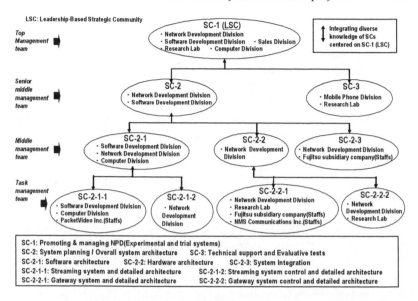

Figure 5.5   *Vertically integrated NSCs (Fujitsu): internal integration capability of knowledge through integration of pragmatic boundaries (SCs)*

In reality, Figure 5.5's SC structures are even more complex. This is because product architecture is dependent on product functions or structures, (integral or module, or any type of component that is a combination of these) and the overall system breaks up into the many subsystems that make up its layered structure (see, for example, Simon, 1996; Clark, 1985; Baldwin and Clark, 2000). Accordingly, in the process of developing individual subsystems, individual SCs were formed as cross-functional teams of technical experts in the fields of hardware, software, systems, video processing, sound processing, semiconductor design, semiconductor communication interfaces, human interfaces and others. As the overall system develops into a multi-layered structure of subsystems, as shown in Figure 5.5, the form of the SC is also structured into a hierarchy.

Many SCs were thus formed within Fujitsu and NEC, and the network of vertically integrated SCs consolidated new knowledge produced from each of the SCs and created an internal integration capability at Fujitsu and NEC. Though the people in charge of each SC support this internal integration capability, the most important role is played by the team of leaders in SC-1 (in Figure 5.5) (hereafter, LSCs) who need to simultaneously address issues in various business areas, such as the integration of different technical fields, production management and total development management, in order to hand down final decisions.

Next, as the first step toward a prototype commercial service, DoCoMo's Service Planning Team further expanded the number of corporate customer members (including content providers) in SC-d (see Figure 5.2) to execute new product and service development that responds to the potential needs of corporate customers. The team also planned to form an experimental consortium utilizing a prototype of the new product.

The main aims of the consortium were to verify the experimental platform for video streaming, use empirical tests to evaluate marketability, and work toward the development of applications that support the services. Building cooperative relationships with customers by having corporate customers (including content providers) use DoCoMo's trial services in actual business situations and provide feedback reflecting their positive impressions, complaints, requests and various other views through questionnaires, was an important process for DoCoMo. As a result of advance negotiations with corporate customers, which involved asking them to buy mobile videophones and pay for the communications charges, sign non-disclosure agreements concerning the details of the trial, and participate in surveys and interviews, DoCoMo formed the Experimental Consortium with about 50 of these corporate customers. The implementing of experiments that DoCoMo had never conducted before involving the use of prototypes and customers (the element of uncertainty was an example of novelty) transformed SC-d in Figure 5.2 to the pragmatic SC-f in Figure 5.3. The involvement of the internal corporate sales division and the service planning team in charge of close mediation with customers (receiving direct requests and complaints) and the close collaboration with the development division were also required for SC-f. SC-f merged with SC-a within DoCoMo, forming NSCs that were horizontally integrated between corporate customers and DoCoMo. Meanwhile SC-b in Figure 5.3, which engaged in joint development between DoCoMo and Fujitsu, bridged SC-a within DoCoMo and SC-d within Fujitsu and was oriented towards NSCs that were horizontally integrated among corporate customers, DoCoMo and Fujitsu, as shown in Figure 5.3. In other words, the pragmatic boundaries between the corporate customers, DoCoMo and Fujitsu – all of them different companies – became integrated. These horizontally integrated NSCs contributed to the creation of new knowledge in the form of service concepts linked to customer needs and views from the market, giving rise to an external integration capability at DoCoMo and Fujitsu.

DoCoMo balanced the external integration capability produced by the horizontally integrated NSCs in Figure 5.3 and the internal integration capability produced by the vertically integrated NSCs at DoCoMo and

Fujitsu in Figures 5.4 and 5.5, and promoted the Experimental Consortium. DoCoMo conducted experiments through the consortium to study and verify the applications by each company based on actual usage.[3] As part of the experiments, DoCoMo conducted interviews and surveys concerning additional functions aimed at improving convenience and practical usage time.

After establishing the experimental consortium, DoCoMo created horizontally integrated NSCs (SC-a, SC-b and SC-d in Figure 5.3) to launch a video streaming trial service called 'V-Live' beginning in April 2002.[4] 'V-Live' provides a video streaming platform that enables numerous people to see video contents via 3G video-enabled phones.

By the time the trial service started, the Experimental Consortium had completed its work, SC-f in Figure 5.3 had disappeared, and DoCoMo had promoted the development of the service to general corporate users and consumers. DoCoMo's service planning team, however, formed links with the corporate sales division and consumer sales division in order to collect requests and complaints from existing users and pursue sales activities aimed at obtaining new customers. The service planning team and development division in SC-a of Figure 5.3 carefully examined the requests from customers for additional improvements in services, and SC-b and SC-c, representing strategic alliances for joint development with Fujitsu and NEC for the subsequent commercial service, engaged in specific technical studies.

Following the start of the trial service, as a third step, DoCoMo, through the creation of horizontal NSCs (SC-a, SC- and SC-e in Figure 5.3), finally launched 'M-Stage V-Live' as a commercial service for 3G mobile phones beginning 1 May 2003.[5] The commercial system was jointly developed and integrated through NSCs with DoCoMo and NEC. 'M-Stage V-Live' is a one-to-many video streaming service that enables users to download or stream a variety of live and archived content. Following the successful launch of the 'V-Live' trial service, DoCoMo offered the commercial service to 3G mobile phone users in Japan. 'M-Stage V-Live' provided by DoCoMo is expected to become a key application service for 3G mobile phone handsets, contributing to the widespread expansion of video streaming content.

Thus the new technology for the above products developed not only through experiments, trials and commercial services, but also through the continuation of both the external integration capability produced by the horizontally integrated NSCs concerned with new product and service development and the internal integration capability produced by the vertically integrated NSCs at DoCoMo, Fujitsu and NEC.

5.2 FRAMEWORK RESULTING FROM THE QUALITATIVE STUDY

The distinctive organizational behavior obtained from the field investigations of this study created a network of SCs that represented a variety of pragmatic boundaries promoting new product and service development both inside and outside the organization. The NSCs that were formed have two characteristics.

The first characteristic is that the NSCs were horizontally integrated among corporations that include customers. This horizontally integrated SC network promotes the external integration of knowledge at the pragmatic boundaries among corporations (including customers) so that the corporation can provide products and services that match market needs. This networking is referred to as external integration capability. The second characteristic is that the NSCs were vertically integrated among the layers of management within the corporation. This vertically integrated network of SCs consolidates required core knowledge spread out within the corporation so that it can be used to realize new business models and develop new technology. In other words, it promotes the internal integration of knowledge at the pragmatic boundaries between the various layers of management inside the corporation. This networking is referred to as internal integration capability. The balancing of these external and internal integration capabilities creates the integrative competences (Kodama, 2004) that become the driving force for corporations as they create new markets in response to dynamic environmental changes. By simultaneously building these two different types of SC networks, NTT DoCoMo, Fujitsu and NEC in this case study were able to acquire new product and service development capabilities.

Furthermore, from the analysis of this case study that comes in a later section, I will identify five vital factors in the formation of SCs and NSCs. The first factor is involvement (DiMaggio and Powell, 1983). Involvement refers to the level of understanding and sharing of existing knowledge, and the degree of understanding and sharing required for generating new knowledge, through interaction and collaboration among organization members who are members of SCs and NSCs. The second factor is embeddedness (Granovetter, 1985; Dacin *et al.*, 1999). Embeddedness describes the degree to which collaboration between organizations (SCs and NSCs) is enmeshed in inter-organizational relationships. Deep embeddedness is an important factor that embeds the tacit and explicit knowledge of actors at organizational boundaries deeply into the SCs and NSCs in order to create new knowledge. The third factor is resonance of value (Kodama, 2001). Resonance of value refers to unifying the views and desires of organization members through a deep understanding of, and sympathy, for the vision and mission arising from the diverse values that members possess. The fourth factor is networked SC formation speed. This describes the speed at which SCs are networked. The fifth factor is leadership-based SC, referring to SCs formed by leaders within NSCs.

The above five concepts promote the building of NSCs and the integration of core knowledge in pragmatic boundaries inside and outside the corporation, and are important elements in the generation of a corporation's internal and external integration capabilities as integrative competences. Details of these factors will be provided below.

At the corporate level, integrative competences (Kodama, 2004) can be thought of as a collection of competency combinations that can be used to share and assess knowledge across the various types of boundaries. From the standpoint of strategies, rather than describing a company as an integration of resources (Barney, 1991), it can be more completely described as an integration of different types of boundaries (SCs) where knowledge must be shared, assessed and consolidated (Carlile, 2004). Thus, in a rapidly changing and highly uncertain business environment, it is most important for corporations to form SCs dynamically (or rebuild SCs as needed) and, by way of their integrated, networked links, to stimulate the desired new knowledge through the process of integration and transformation.

5.3 CHARACTERISTICS OF NSCs

In this section I will describe four factors leading to the building of NSCs extracted from the case analysis. First, I will analyze the characteristics of SC networks that triggered the synthesis of knowledge from the boundaries of individual SCs according to their involvement in collaboration, embeddedness in collaboration, resonance of values, and the speed at which the NSCs were formed (Table 5.1).

Information and knowledge within strategic communities is both sticky and leaky. It is important, however, that NSCs make the leaky aspect of knowledge in strategic communities work in a positive manner and that leaders of all SCs promote the sharing and inspiration of knowledge beyond the SCs' boundaries. The act of transcending boundaries stimulates deep, meaningful learning, which in turn opens possibilities for the generation of new knowledge and creativity. Radically new insights and developments, such as the big project in this case, often arise at the boundaries between SCs (Grant and Baden-Fuller, 1995; Grant, 1996a). In particular, organizations often face the dilemma of having to reconcile rapid access and synthesis of relevant new knowledge with the long timeframes needed for knowledge creation and synthesis. NSCs based on deep inter-organizational collaboration can offer a possible solution.

Table 5.1 Evaluations of networked strategic communities

Characteristics of networked strategic communities (SCs)	Concepts
1. Knowledge sharing through deep collaboration among SCs	High involvement (DiMaggio and Powell, 1983)
2. Sharing and integrating tacit and explicit knowledge among SCs	High embeddedness (Granovetter, 1985; Dacin *et al.*, 1999)
3. Understanding, empathizing, and resonating common missions among SCs	Resonance of value (Kodama, 2001)
4. Forming networked SCs at high speed	Improvisation (Brown and Eisenhardt, 1998)

The need for businesses and society to transcend the boundaries of SCs has been increasing in recent years as industry markets become more uncertain and technology as well as customer needs change more rapidly. A single practical experience and knowledge of a single organization is not the only way to solve the complex problem of synthesizing technology and social needs that is shown in this case. The leaders of organizations need to build SCs actively inside and outside the organization, including with customers, and then to transcend the boundaries of the SCs and network them in a speedy manner.

One important element in the formation of NSCs is deep collaboration. Close interaction among SC members, a strategic partnership among organizations that form NSCs, and interactive information sharing within NSCs are not the only conditions required for deep collaboration as defined by DiMaggio and Powell (1983). High levels of involvement in the collaborative process (the development of a strong mutual awareness that SC members are involved in a common enterprise) are also essential.

Close involvement is the situation in which the knowledge comprising various core technologies and the expertise that members of NSCs have accumulated through extensive dialog and collaboration are thoroughly understood and closely shared among technical experts and customers within the NSCs. The specific core technologies and expertise gained in each SC are described next.

In SC-a in Figure 5.3, for instance, this knowledge is of the human resources structure, and includes manuals, training and technical skills, the business model and the service architecture for the operation and support systems concerning new services within DoCoMo. In SC-b in Figure 5.3, knowledge of the service architecture and enabling product specifications based on the business model devised and closely examined by DoCoMo, plus knowledge of product architecture, functions and other aspects devised and closely examined by Fujitsu, were merged and integrated to produce new knowledge. In SC-d in Figure 5.3, this knowledge represents the core technology that resulted from the merging and integration of video, mobile communications, semiconductor, software and other computer technologies within Fujitsu. SC-f in Figure 5.3 collated specific customer needs through the Experimental Consortium with progressive corporate users (approximately 50 companies) utilizing DoCoMo and mobile solutions. These needs included improvements in function and ease of use in the prototype systems. This is equivalent to the accumulation of knowledge known as 'customer competence' (Prahalad and Ramaswamy, 2000, 2004).

The development results and expertise created by the various SCs are deeply shared through extensive dialog and collaboration within the NSCs, and the condition of high involvement has been confirmed from numerous interviews and other sources. A DoCoMo manager, for example, stated:

> While product development that ultimately results from technological expertise is important, it is not enough to satisfy customer needs. We therefore need to receive different types of feedback on trial services through experiments with progressive customers before we offer the services commercially, and to incorporate this feedback into the development of the products and services we eventually offer. To achieve this, we need to engage in deep sharing and collaboration of knowledge with partners, including customers.

Low involvement, on the other hand, goes no further than the simple sharing of information among customers and partners; it does not assume any deep sharing or collaboration of knowledge.

The second important element in the formation of NSCs – embeddedness – describes the degree to which collaboration between SCs is enmeshed in inter-organizational relationships. This element highlights the connection between the collaboration and the broader inter-organizational network. Highly embedded collaborations between SCs were observed as an expanded network of SCs centered on the reason for DoCoMo's existence. High embeddedness refers to the situation in which knowledge (tacit and explicit) created by the SCs transcends individual SCs and is closely shared among all the SCs, and the NSCs integrate this knowledge to generate new knowledge. It is characteristic of NSCs that they integrate the core technologies and expertise of each SC and create specific knowledge as a result of new development. (Low embeddedness, on the other hand, goes no further than the simple sharing of information among customers and partners; it does not assume any integration of knowledge.)

The third important element in the formation of NSCs is the resonance process of values in the community. This is the process whereby all SC members, in their effort to fulfill the NSCs' missions and goals, share and resonate values aimed at achieving the business. High resonance of value refers to the situation in which SC members of NSCs engage in extensive dialog and collaboration in order to share and empathize closely the visions for their development goals. This concept of high resonance of value was obtained from a considerable volume of data in the form of many interviews between myself and SC members. A DoCoMo SC leader, for instance, stated: 'It is important for us to understand core technologies and customer needs deeply, and to share and empathize uniform values closely, such as how to develop the system and achieve the goal, with partner members, including customers'. (Low resonance of value, on the other hand, assumes a situation where approaches to product development among customers and partners and user viewpoints do not sufficiently converge.)

This idea of the resonance of values is also the same as the hidden value, espoused by O'Reilley and Pfeffer, that enables the shared values within the formal organization or community to produce new knowledge or competencies (O'Reilly III and Pfeffer, 2000). The resonance of values in NSCs with partners inside and outside the organization leads to dialectical ideas and strength to act among SC leaders and becomes a capability for generating new knowledge that forms the new core for the NSCs. High levels of resonance value were observed in the NSCs which had succeeded in the large project.

The fourth important element in the formation of NSCs is speed. This element of speed in the formation of networks was not discussed in any depth during research into inter-organizational networks. It must be considered, however, by businesses in industries undergoing rapid change or whose technologies are rapidly advancing. In this case, a major feature of success at DoCoMo, Fujitsu, NEC and other companies is the fact that they formed their NSCs very quickly, in around 15 days, among customers and partners. A DoCoMo manager states that the formation of NSCs is similar to the following value of improvisation: 'We need to brainstorm together with partners and customers in order to develop our product or service faster than anyone else in the world. Speed is the essence of survival for us.' And a senior manager at Fujitsu remarked: 'When an urgent issue or problem occurs, it is important for team members to get together and immediately make a decision about what to do'. (If NSCs are formed slowly, on the other hand, the ultimate goal of development will, of course, fall far behind schedule.)

The decisive factor behind this rapid formation of NSCs is improvisation, which is an especially important concept when developing innovative products and services in an environment where market needs are uncertain due to ongoing rapid changes, and where technology is also changing (Brown and Eisenhardt, 1998). Speed and flexibility are particularly essential when making organizational decisions in tie-ups with external strategic partners. From the viewpoint of strategic logic, companies need to jump into the confusion, keep moving, and seize opportunities quickly as they pursue them in unpredictable, rapidly changing, ambiguous markets (very characteristic of the 3G mobile phone market in this case study) (Eisenhardt and Sull, 2001). DoCoMo, Fujitsu and NEC needed to go along with this flow (the speedy pattern of forming NSCs).

The above four concepts contribute to the building of solid, vertically and horizontally integrated NSCs, and each at the same time produces internal and external integration capability as it creates new knowledge.

5.4 THE BUILDING OF INTEGRATIVE COMPETENCES FROM INTERNAL AND EXTERNAL INTEGRATION CAPABILITIES

This detailed case study showed that a balance of internal and external integration capability at DoCoMo, Fujitsu and NEC became the source of integrative competences for enabling new product and service development. While integrative competences are enabling the corporation to give birth to new markets as it responds to changes in the market environment, it is important, from the practical viewpoint of maintaining ongoing competitiveness, that the corporation uses its integrative competences to integrate knowledge flexibly, representing resources inside the corporation and knowledge from outside the corporation. By building SCs and NSCs through promptly enacted activities inside and outside the corporation, it stimulates the building of business model concepts and the implementation of trials, making it possible to achieve the ultimate goal of new product and service development.

As shown in Figure 5.6, internal integration capability refers to the ability to integrate the core knowledge of individual SCs within DoCoMo, Fujitsu and NEC, encompassing such areas as service architecture, product architecture and component technology. Internal integration capability can be produced from vertically integrated NSCs. In the new product and service development of this case study, it was necessary to engage in a major review of the technical architecture of the product as a universal existing framework in addressing the issues of new business models and complex technical integration that utilize mobile phones. As Henderson and Clark (1990) pointed out, when basic technology is transferred (as in cases where product architecture is changed), the response of the corporation can be protected by the internal structure of the development organization, as it reflects the technological architecture that created this structure. Though the cases of DoCoMo, Fujitsu and NEC had significant restrictions in their existing organizational structures as they struggled to reach their goals, by flexibly forming organic NSCs within the corporation, they were able to respond to new product and service development as an architectural innovation. On the other hand, external integration capability refers to the ability of SC-b at DoCoMo and Fujitsu and SC-c at DoCoMo and NEC to integrate customer competencies and core knowledge, such as business models and service/product architectures consistent with customer needs, at DoCoMo, Fujitsu and NEC. This capability emerges from horizontally integrated NSCs.

An important insight here concerns how NSCs should be structured in order to integrate the core knowledge of each SC. The insight obtained from field studies into vertically integrated NSCs was the presence of teams that played central roles in SCs comprising the NSCs, and from the viewpoint of social network theory, this SC was positioned like a hub or node that had centrality (Barabasi, 2002; Watts, 2003; Kodama, 2005b). This was the LSC in Figures 5.4 and 5.5 that comprised the top management team with the ability to manage diverse tasks, such as various technology and business processes and cross-cultural issues, and the authority to make final decisions. It was possible to confirm the existence of an LSC within DoCoMo, Fujitsu and NEC. Leaders within the LSC had the role of integrating the core knowledge of multiple SCs within the company.

The viewpoint obtained from field studies into horizontally integrated NSCs, on the other hand, represents the presence of SC-b that bridges SC-a in DoCoMo and SC-d in Fujitsu, and of SC-c that bridges SC-a in DoCoMo and SC-e in NEC (Figure 5.3) and promotes joint development tasks. This SC-b and SC-c mainly comprise leaders such as middle and task managers at DoCoMo, Fujitsu and NEC (including top managers and senior middle managers as needed depending on the details of important issues or decisions to be made). These leaders have a uniform authority with respect to all tasks. In other words, SC-b and SC-c are equivalent to an LSC in that the members share dynamic business contexts and core knowledge in their respective corporations. As a pragmatic boundary, it is also possible for the

LSC to create any new knowledge required for new product and service development.

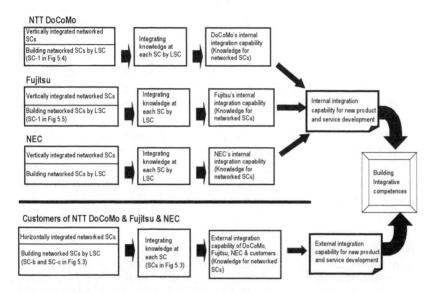

Figure 5.6   Integrative competences through internal and external integration capabilities

5.5   RESEARCH FOR THE FUTURE

This chapter has identified concepts and frameworks required for knowledge creation from the case study of NSCs in the field of creating unknown markets in a rapidly changing environment. The important point in the new information obtained from the case study concerns how the knowledge from outside and inside the company, including customers, is mobilized to create unknown markets and produce new products and business models. To this end, it is necessary to form strategic communities that are not tied to existing organizational structures or cultures and to reform paradigms of new organizations that have promoted the formation of networks.

Though the concept of the networks of strategic communities has been gained from a previous case study, the research described in this chapter was not able to establish whether the concept could be applied to all cases of new product development or business model development. As a future theme, I need to verify this concept in a large number of cases in diverse industries, scenarios, market structures and competitive environments, across national differences, and among multinational corporations and domestic corporations. Another issue for the future concerns investigating the impact that the cultural and leadership context (such as Western and Japanese management styles) might have on the formation of NSCs and knowledge creation. This element involves trust and power and is an important factor in the formation of NSCs comprising players in a variety of fields.

On the other hand, when we consider the increasing sophistication and specialization of technology in recent years and the growing complexity of business models utilizing ICT, it is becoming increasingly difficult to create completely new knowledge and generate innovation from the knowledge and core competencies possessed by a single company (this is an issue directly confronting many innovators at leading-edge companies). While the networked strategic community is considered to be a valid management method for creating undefined future markets in a turbulent, dynamic environment, from now on we need to research this concept more thoroughly from both the theoretical and practical points of view.

NOTES

1. FOMA (Freedom Of Mobile Multimedia Access) is the service brand name for DoCoMo's third-generation mobile communications system (IMT-2000). The FOMA market experienced rapid growth from December 2002, reaching 10 million subscribers as of February 2005.
2. DoCoMo has been focusing internal resources on R&D and service development tasks, mainly for forming business model proposals and developing product and service architecture. Accordingly, the development and manufacturing of the hardware and software that enable DoCoMo's planned business model or product and service architecture are executed through joint development by DoCoMo and internal and external manufacturers.
3. PacketVideo and NTT DoCoMo team up to deliver world's first one-to-many live video streaming via 3G network. Technical details are discussed in Ohira *et al.* (2003a, b).
4. NTT DoCoMo V-Live is to begin its user-paid service in cooperation with PacketVideo. Fujitsu and NMS Communications Jointly Develop Wireless Video Gateway System for 'V-Live' Trial Service of Mobile Handsets by NTT DoCoMo.
5. NTT DoCoMo started video streaming service for 3G FOMA phones. See website (www.3g.co.uk/PR/April2003/5281.htm).

6. Business innovation through joint ventures supported by major businesses

6.1 INTRODUCTION

Corporate venturing, including joint ventures, has become an important management method as a crucial strategy for new business development (Von Hippel, 1977; Burgelman, 1983a; Block, 1982; Block and MacMillan, 1993; Gompers and Lerner, 1999; Albrinck et al., 2001). Corporate venturing can be applied strategically and effectively to encourage corporate innovation and create new capability as a corporate growth driver. Recent high-tech organizations are frequently using corporate ventures collaborated with both inside and outside the corporations as a way of dealing with today's complex business model. In particular, in ICT, multimedia and broadband business, the close collaboration between various actors from different backgrounds and industries is a crucial factor to create new knowledge and business models. The new business ideas can be produced through the formation of NSCs, including external partners and customers (Kodama, 1999a).

Diverse emerging businesses in the multimedia arena have capitalized on the Internet, while other information networks have developed alongside ICT and multimedia technologies. These trends stem from the acceleration of business development, especially for large companies, through strategic alliances among heterogeneous ventures in the multimedia sector, and the development of new business promoted by venture companies that combine their core competencies.

The videoconferencing market has experienced explosive growth over the past six years. With the advent of desktop videoconferencing that runs on PCs, videoconferencing systems are no longer the preserve of large enterprises but are finding their way into small and medium-sized enterprises and other fields of business. Recently, videoconferencing systems have grown into a new and prospective telecommunications medium, evolving such high-tech implementations as data conferences and videoconferencing in the local area network (LAN) environment or via the Internet.

Unlike conventional point-to-point conferencing systems, currently available MCUs (Multipoint Connection Units[1]) allow videoconferencing to be conducted by linking three or more locations at a time. However, due to the expense of MCUs and the complexity of system operation, with the exception of some leading-edge companies, multipoint videoconferencing systems have not enjoyed popular support. Under such circumstances, international telecommunications carriers and system vendors are endeavoring to launch 'multipoint connection service' businesses as a means for the user to implement multipoint videoconferencing without the need to purchase or otherwise acquire MCUs.

This chapter deals with a case study in the multimedia sector and focuses on multipoint connection venture businesses for the world's largest videoconferencing system, which was created by joint venture businesses funded through investment from heterogeneous U.S.–Japan businesses. The chapter indicates the importance of enterprise strategy implemented by a large business-support type venture model based on strategic alliances with, and assistance from, the original investing companies as key factors in the creation of a new market in the multimedia sector, and in ultimate success.

6.2 STATUS OF MULTIPOINT CONNECTION SERVICES AROUND THE WORLD

In the U.S., the total number of videoconferencing systems of all sizes is expected to top the 20 million mark by the year 2007. The number of videoconferencing systems in Japan, meanwhile, is expected to grow to an impressive two million. The growth of multipoint connection services and proprietary ownership of MCUs will also accelerate. AT&T began providing multipoint connection services in 1994, followed by a number of other companies, including MCI and Sprint. Worldwide service is also available outside the U.S. market. In Europe, telecommunications carriers are focusing their services on domestic markets. MCU connection fees per hour average $50 to $60 per terminal.

In Japan, prior to 1995 and the subsequent establishment of NTT Phoenix Network Communication Inc., which is the subject of this study, the market for videoconferencing systems was immature. KDDI Communications Inc., a subsidiary of KDDI, had only one access point (MCU connection point) in Tokyo, with a charge of $50 per terminal. In the eyes of users, this technology was saddled with costly access communication fees.

At the beginning of 1996, NTT began to implement a new multimedia strategy from the perspective that the anticipated proliferation of multipoint connection services provided by videoconferencing systems would lead to major growth in application in the fields of business, education, medical care and welfare. The key point of the strategy was to study adaptable business mechanisms to use multipoint connection services at low cost.

6.3   BEGINNING OF INCUBATION AT NTT

In March 1996, an incubation project team was inaugurated under the control of the Multimedia Promotion Department at NTT Headquarters, with the aim of implementing a multipoint connection service business for the marketing of videoconferencing systems.

In order to review the business feasibility of the connection service, NTT had been studying MCU function checks, operability and serviceability by capitalizing on this service during national meeting events and seminars intended for NTT branches and stores. NTT had also been soliciting a wide range of customers who purchased NTT's desktop videoconferencing system for a trial run of this service and collecting the customer's opinions and requests.

Figure 6.1 depicts the multipoint connection service videoconferencing system trial deployed by NTT. About 1200 multipoint meetings were conducted over a period of nine months, and about 10 000 terminals were connected online with the videoconferencing system to discuss up-to-date issues on business, education and events. Because this service was expected to be compatible with a wide range of applications, including business, education, welfare and entertainment, NTT decided to launch specific business planning.

6.4   CHALLENGE FOR FEASIBLE BUSINESS PLANNING

Specific issues with relation to feasible business planning included determining low-price MCU charges (MCU connection fees) for subscribers and ease of access to MCU at low communication fees (communication fees for connection to access points equipped with MCUs). The business set-up enabled a large number of users to share the benefits of MCU, and required the installation of a large amount of MCU equipment to allow for a large number of access points nationwide, with MCU fees reduced to a minimum. The project team, therefore, foresaw that user facilities would improve significantly and many users would come to use the multipoint connection service.

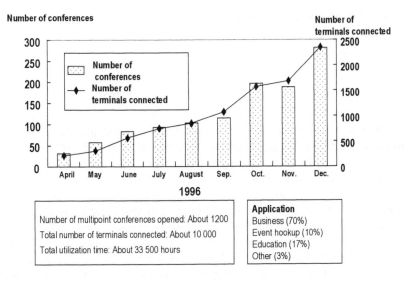

Figure 6.1   Trial run of multipoint connection services (April – December 1996)

Table 6.1   Outline of NTT Phoenix Network Communication Inc.

Location	Tokyo
Founded	July 1997
Capital	490 000 000 yen
Description of business	Multipoint connection serviceConstruction of multimedia network
	Outsourcing operation
Employees	13
Controlling share	NTT (44.3%),
	PictureTel (19.9%),
	Otsuka Shokai (11%)
	Canon Sales Inc. (5%)
	NOVA (19%)
	NTT-TE (10%)
	NTT-PC (1%)

6.5   INCORPORATION AND BUSINESS PROCESS OF THE JOINT VENTURE BUSINESS

To enable videoconferencing system users to use the multipoint connection service at reasonably low charges, NTT's project team studied the business planning for the multipoint connection service in Japan to be implemented by the strategic alliance of heterogeneous companies set up between the U.S. company PictureTel (now Polycom), professional videoconferencing system maker Otsuka Shokai, major telecommunications system integrator (SI) and sales company Canon Sales, major language school, NOVA, and NTT group companies NTT-TE and NTT-PC. After mutual discussions about the specific business plan, a joint-venture videoconferencing multipoint connection service company (NTT Phoenix Network Communication Inc., hereafter NTT Phoenix) was founded in July 1997 (Nihon Keizai Shimbun, 1997a) (see Table 6.1).

6.6   WHY THE JOINT VENTURE-TYPE MODEL WAS CHOSEN AS THE BUSINESS PLAN

NTT did not provide a multipoint connection service due to a number of factors arising out of both internal and external sources, as follows:

- In Japan, charges for telecommunications services provided by NTT required the approval of the MPT (approval of telecommunications charges took an average of six months or longer).
- Distribution of multipoint connection service required competencies such as MCU video-related technology, marketing of the video service, and sales efforts that were lacking at NTT in the past.
- Because NTT is a large organization, organizing the system (personnel and resource developments) to carry out the project took a considerable amount of time.

The project team at NTT considered the foregoing factors on an overall basis and determined to work out a venture business plan in alliance with companies blessed with competencies at the core of the business, such as expertise in technology and services.

6.7 INNOVATIVE PROJECT LEADERSHIP

The challenge assigned to the NTT project leaders was to find candidate businesses with which a strategic alliance could be formed in order to implement the venture business. In particular, the alliance with U.S. PictureTel, which boasts an impressive 50 percent of world market share, provided NTT with an important partner in its efforts to develop the video network business in Japan.

At the time, NTT formed a partnership with PictureTel to work on the development of a next-generation desktop videoconferencing system (Nihon Keizai Shimbun, 1996) and released an NTT-branded product dubbed 'Phoenix' (Nihon Keizai Shimbun, 1996). The leaders of both organizations formed a common consensus over the challenges of overcoming the new hurdles in an attempt to evolve from the development of a videoconferencing system to the development of new video network business. A natural outgrowth of this move in October 1996 led to the formation of a strategic alliance to study the feasibility of the multipoint connection service business in Japan.

The success factor in the strategic alliance with PictureTel was the empathy and resonance for the sense of value envisaged by the leaders of both the NTT and PictureTel teams. The corporate belief of PictureTel is to 'Redefine the way the world meets'. Leaders at PictureTel added:

> Our corporate belief is to esteem humanism rather than technology. Unfortunately, however, it is not possible for us to meet whomever we really want to see whenever we want. You can talk to your mother living in a remote home town over a phone, but it is difficult for you to find out about her health or whether she is lonely from her voice alone. But if you can see her face and hear her voice, both you and your mother will no longer be lonely.
>
> This is also true with respect to the matter of business. It is impossible for an executive to completely communicate his or her intentions over a phone. If you can judge your client's demeanor, ascertain business, or transfer necessary data online, however, mutual communication is made easier. Such communication can be implemented through services offered by PictureTel. PictureTel is not just in the business of selling videoconferencing systems or MCUs; it aims to exploit technologies and provide better encounters between people. PictureTel executives say that by making PictureTel's state-of-the-art technology and NTT's up-to-date network technology and communication infrastructure widely available, the world's largest multipoint connection network service can be offered to a large number of customers.

NTT introduced the multimedia communication infrastructure known as ISDN, which is readily available today, for a wide range of customers and for uses extending beyond the business sector to the fields of education, medicine and welfare. In the telecommunications sector, the world's carriers urgently needed to shift from a diminishing returns-type business model centered on conventional analog telephone traffic to a stepped-up return business model of non-telephone traffic centered on digital video and data. In the area of cyber businesses supported by multimedia which merges networks, content and a variety of applications, there was a strong potential for creating new businesses spawned by diverse alliances concluded among companies and organizations in different lines of business. As an NTT executive put it:

> Our desire and mission was to implement an environment accessible across time and space by virtue of multimedia and networks. From the viewpoint of customers, the video network service should be neither expensive nor difficult to use. The most crucial task was to provide customers with high-quality, user-friendly network services plus the best cost-performance. From such a standpoint, PictureTel was the best partner.

Alliance in the multimedia arena adopts a style wherein individuals in organizations with mutually unfamiliar corporate climates form a community where they liaise and empathize with each other to fulfill their business. The leaders involved in this project are required to be innovative at all times and to possess a strategic concept and energy.

Moreover, the project leaders at NTT came in contact with the in-house and external leaders of Otsuka Shokai, Canon Sales, NOVA and NTT group companies or endeavored to take part in politics, depending on the circumstances, for the sake of implementing their new business proposals. Then the stakeholder leaders reached an agreement on the incorporation of a new joint venture business. This agreement was also based on empathy and resonance for the sense of value envisaged by each leader of the stakeholder companies, and was determined by the intention of the leaders, who were resolved to create and innovate a market for new video-based multimedia business. The enterprise strategy for leading-edge technological innovation had a particularly urgent need for project leaders to step forward in demonstrating original thinking and strategic behavior.

In this way, a strategic community was created comprising heterogeneous lines of business (NTT, NTT group companies, PictureTel, Otsuka Shokai, Canon Sales and NOVA) represented by telecommunications carriers, line maintenance agents, videoconferencing system development and production vendors, system integration and sales agents, and education-related operators, and an uncontested partnership was built up for the sake of creating a new venture business.

6.8   CORE COMPETENCIES OF NTT PHOENIX

Figure 6.2 shows the formation of a multipoint connection service which reflects the following core competencies of each stakeholder company that participated in the foundation of NTT Phoenix:

- NTT provides core network technology such as ISDN.
- PictureTel provides core technology relevant to MCU video.
- Otsuka Shokai and Canon Sales provide the expertise that serves as the rich core for forward-thinking sales of videoconferencing systems and other video systems.
- NTT-TE provides the expertise and core technology needed for the operation and maintenance of MCUs and network facilities.
- NTT-PC provides the expertise and core technology needed for the building of the leased lines for the inter-MCU network.
- NOVA provides the expertise and content for remote language education.[2]

Thanks to the integration of the core competencies provided by each member company, including technology potential, serviceability and expertise, NTT Phoenix, representing new business communities, has become capable of building new core competencies, which are expressed as a new service.

6.9   ADVENT OF THE WORLD'S LARGEST MULTIPOINT CONNECTION SERVICE AT IMPRESSIVELY LOW CHARGES

NTT Phoenix opened 52 access points across the country and enabled video conferences to be held by linking up to 1000 terminals. In addition, the nationwide flat rate of 40 yen per terminal for 3 minutes (about $7 per hour) is by far the cheapest in the world. By the end of March 1999, 1000 companies were already included on the list of users. The multipoint connection service not only boosts the availability of video conferences but also significantly contributes to the increase of NTT's ISDN traffic (see Figure 6.3).

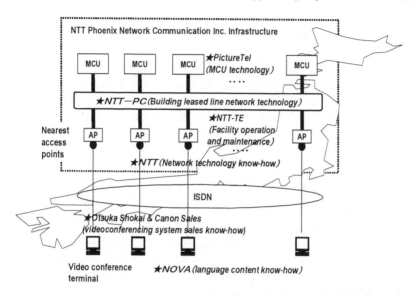

Note: ☆ Core competencies of stakeholder companies

Figure 6.2   Composition of NTT Phoenix Network Communication Inc. multipoint connection service

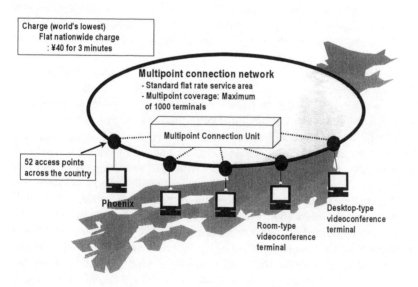

Figure 6.3   World's largest multipoint connection service

6.10 PROGRESS AND RESULTS OF MULTIPOINT CONNECTION SERVICE

After its founding in July 1997, the company continued to build communication lines and facilities, write contract covenants and accept applications for subscription, and prepare to open the service. Pre-services began in August, and then the full-fledged service began operating in September.

6.10.1 Development of Sales Arm

Initially, with the assistance of PictureTel, Otsuka Shokai, Canon Sales Co. and NTT, sales activities focused on existing video conference users, and then new videoconferencing system users were also recruited to the list of subscribers while an intensive sales effort was directed at corporate users, resulting in steady growth in membership. This included companies that already had their own MCU equipment, by virtue of the scale of the service and the reasonable service charges.

Otsuka Shokai and Canon Sales, stakeholders in the venture business, were sales agents for PictureTel in Japan and had their own proprietary sales channel and expertise with regard to sales of PictureTel products. In the past, the drawback to the sales of videoconferencing system-related products was the MCU. This was so expensive that a considerable number of potential users who were interested in purchasing a videoconferencing system bundled with MCU were deterred from investing in corporate ICT development. The costly MCU had a strong impact on sales of videoconferencing systems.

On the other hand, sales of the low-priced multipoint connection services from NTT Phoenix Network Communication Inc. bundled with the videoconferencing system provided an offering at a price acceptable to prospective users. This strategy allowed Otsuka Shokai and Canon Sales to boost sales of the videoconferencing systems, and for NTT Phoenix it also had a synergistic effect on the increase in multipoint connection service membership. Moreover, this held true with NTT with regard to sales of videoconferencing systems sold under their proprietary brand name.

This sales strategy was also employed by several videoconferencing system vendors other than the stakeholder companies. As a result, the partnerships spawned by the strategic alliance for NTT Phoenix's multipoint connection service evolved to capitalize on the synergistic effects to the utmost extent, aiming for impressive growth in profits raised between the group of videoconferencing system vendors and the venture business group. In this way, the stakeholder companies not only created a strategic sales alliance with NTT Phoenix in pursuit of their own sales profits, but also offered strategic support to NTT Phoenix from the viewpoint of breathing life into Japan's video communication market.

6.10.2   Development of Operation Technology and After-Sales Services

In response to MCU technical issues or network facilities and maintenance, NTT Phoenix was backed up by a strategic technical alliance with such stakeholders as PictureTel, NTT and NTT-TE. As above, NTT Phoenix was assisted through a strategic alliance with the stakeholders with regard to sales, operation technology and after-sales services and the strategic support of the stakeholders. Triggered by the New Year address of the presidents of each company in January 1998, the videoconferencing system rapidly found its way into corporate use and became available for annual meetings, in-house communications and non-conference applications such as remote education and franchise store management. By the end of March 1998, a total utilization time of nearly 200 000 hours was achieved. Customer feedback suggested favorable acceptance with regard to the handiness of the videoconferencing system and its low cost. Business deployment was achieved as projected in the first year of the start-up of business (July 1997 to March 1998). As of the end of March 2004, 2500 corporate members have intensively utilized multipoint connection services.

6.11   INTEGRATED STRATEGY OF NTT PHOENIX AND NTT

The rapid expansion of the market for a range of multipoint connection services and video terminals resulted in integration strategies of companies in both businesses. This integrated strategy was generated by the strategic innovation communities of both NTT Phoenix and NTT based on a strategic partnership between the two companies. As shown in Figure 6.4, these companies followed an integrated sales strategy whereby they offered an aggressive 'product + service' package bundling the Phoenix series (see Figure 6.5) sold by NTT and the multipoint connection networking service offered by NTT Phoenix.

By selling the low-cost multipoint connection service bundled with the Phoenix series, both companies were able to provide a new value to their customers, namely the ability to use video terminals at multiple points, at low cost. The synergy from this integrated strategy enabled NTT to improve its sales results for the Phoenix series, and NTT Phoenix to boost the number of subscribers to its multipoint connection service.

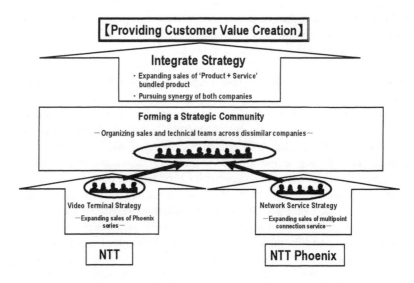

Figure 6.4   Integrated strategy by strategic community

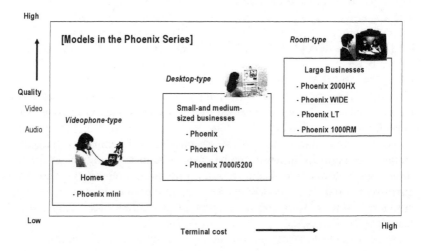

Figure 6.5   Phoenix series vitalizes Japanese video terminals market

Meanwhile, the technical teams within the strategic community of both companies could devote all their energies to improving customer services. The videoconferencing system flexibly accommodated applications for holiday or night conferences and adding to or changing reservations for conferences, and the quality of service was maintained through a purposeful daily routine to deal with fault prevention or facility line management upon setting up a conference. When a claim arose, the response was fast and careful, while courteous care was extended to users with regard to the terminal operation guide and maintenance of the availability environment. This careful attention to the start-up phase of the videoconferencing system helped retain the favorable impression felt by customers as the most important factor upon the launch of the system. The business was promoted by the strategic community consciously and strategically formed by NTT Phoenix and NTT, with the consequence of growth in the use of the Phoenix series and the multipoint connection service over the past four years.

6.12   INNOVATION BORN FROM THE CREATION OF STRATEGIC COMMUNITIES

6.12.1   Establishing Strategic Partnerships

The expansion of the video multimedia business mentioned above was achieved through the synergistic effects of an integrated strategy combining NTT's video terminal strategy and NTT Phoenix's network services strategy. Both companies' project leaders achieved a resonance of values (Kodama, 2001) toward the vision of creating a culture of video communications in Japan. This enabled them to promote this business from the viewpoint of advancing group corporate management as it cultivated the new business area of video multimedia.

To create the organizational structure, the two companies formed a strategic business community made up of a team from each company (a project group of about 10 members from NTT and a venture company of 13 employees from NTT Phoenix) who could work together as a single, seamless entity. This strategic innovation community was formed of a technical team and a sales team that crossed between dissimilar companies. They used the knowledge and core competencies within the community to cultivate new markets and gain customers.

While formally we each belong to different companies, colleagues sharing identical values and a sense of purpose got together and made it their common ground to think together and work together. The solid vision that binds them is to create a video communications culture in Japan. Each member embraces a strong passion and interest in the video multimedia business, and each possesses the spirit to act on their intentions and ideas to cultivate new customers (Interview with NTT and NTT Phoenix management).

A vital point is the resonance of values among community leaders (the project leaders who form the business community). This resonance establishes the strategic partnership for creating the strategic community. Furthermore, the innovative leadership of the community leaders unifies the values and sense of purpose of community members, and the community leader continuously empowers and motivates for the strategies and battle plans that need to be followed. As a result, community knowledge such as new knowledge and expertise within the strategic community can continue to propagate.

6.12.2 Issues in Strategic Communities Among NTT Phoenix and NTT

At the beginning, there were two strategies that the company felt it should adopt to start this business: one mirrored that of companies in the United States and Europe, and the other was unique to Japan. These are described in the next two sections.

Risks and future outlook for large-scale investment in equipment

NTT Phoenix's business was a typical example of the equipment industry needing future capital. The company invested freely in equipment (several billion yen over two years) from the time of founding, and the larger the scale of communications networks, the more valuable and convenient it became for customers to use. It was the largest multipoint connection service provider in the world, and in the two years since its establishment, the company focused on constructing communications networks and equipment. In order to hold down costs to customers, however, the rate structure featured extremely low fees and led to losses in 1998 and 1999. The expansion of the customer base starting in 2000 is now steadily lifting revenues.

An important issue was to define the future business outlook for the multipoint connection service, something that had yet to appear in the Japanese market. If the company learned the lessons of the companies in the U.S. and Europe that were already offering this service, its basic approach would have been to set fees that reflected the investment in equipment linked to the demand from users and suited the services being offered. However, NTT Phoenix adopted an opposite strategy, which was to make large-scale investments at the beginning and then to improve conveniences to customers while holding usage fees at a minimum. This strategy aimed to propagate wider awareness of this service among customers and promote usage. To achieve this aim, the first big issue facing the strategic community was to negotiate with the finance division of NTT headquarters, the parent company, and obtain the capital for large-scale investment in equipment. The basic philosophy of the strategic community in approaching the negotiations was 'customer value creation'. Through the products and services it supplies, the enterprise gives customers new value and satisfaction so that those customers become 'repeat users' of the products and services.

Peter Drucker points out that it is a big mistake to understand business or corporate value from the viewpoint of a pursuit for profit (Drucker, 1954, 1985). Drucker also emphasizes that the mission and objective of businesses operated by corporations is to create customers. In other words, no matter how competitive a company's product or service might be, if a customer does not ask for it and pay money for it, that product or service cannot possibly exist. The essential mission of an enterprise thus does not place priority on shareholders in a pursuit for profit. The viewpoint of 'customer value creation' is also a vital long-term issue for corporate management.

The strategic community strongly emphasized these concepts to NTT headquarters. The headquarters carefully weighed the investment risk in expanding the multimedia business in the future, evaluated the outstanding spirit of challenge and proposals from the project side (in this case, the strategic community), and decided to provide capital for establishing the new company and to increase the capitalization after that. As a result, the strategic community obtained the capital required to carry out the project.

Conflicts and negotiations

The second issue in the strategic community concerned how conflict and negotiation within the community were to be handled. Conflict affects the daily business process of conventional and strategic communities alike, but in the strategic community, conflict was recognized as a constructive process. In the community knowledge inspiration stage in particular, the variety of knowledge possessed by community members became mutually inspired and multiplied through dialog and discussion, and any conflicts that arose at this stage actually served to enhance the quality of community knowledge, stimulate creativity and innovation that could become the foundation for the strategic community's emergent strategy, and foster the creation of new community knowledge. In other words, it was possible for conflicts within the strategic community to become catalysts for productive and constructive dialog and discussion. This is consistent with the 'mutual utilization' logical view of conflicts in groups reported on in the past

(Robbins, 1974). If we explain the evidence qualitatively, the manner in which the visions and concepts of the community leader realized the strategic community principle of 'customer value creation' depended on the effect of the resonance of the values of all community members.

On the other hand, negotiations also occur frequently among community members as they go about their daily business. The difference is that the strategic community shares and understands the visions and concepts rooted in the common value of 'customer value creation', and the sharing of information and knowledge is constantly fostered by dialog and collaboration. As a result, firm relationships of mutual trust are built among strategic community members. In the event that negotiations occur, the strategic community members, as representatives of the overall strategic community, would never regret their hard work to uncover a desirable trade-off that would maximize profits and merits. In other words, a rational negotiating framework that always produces integrated agreements is built into the strategic community. This integrated agreement (Bazerman and Neale, 1992; Walton and McKersie, 1965) in the negotiating process is a vital element for building and maintaining the long-term relationships of the strategic community. Thus, while the elements of conflict and negotiation are unavoidable issues in group activities, in the strategic community, these issues can be considered a constructive plus that emerges from the resonance of values.

6.13 EXPANDING AVAILABILITY OF MULTIPOINT CONNECTION SERVICES AND DISTRIBUTION OF NEW SERVICES

The multipoint connection service offered by NTT Phoenix appeared in a number of newspaper and magazine articles, including the following:

Seminar Relay Service

- Konetto seminar (Simultaneous hook-up of 1000 elementary, middle and high schools throughout Japan)
- Seminar relay (IDG Communications Japan Inc.: Live relay via network) (Nihon Keizai Shimbun, 1998b; Nihon Kogyo Shimbun, 1998b)
- Remote extension lectures (Mitsubishi Research Institute, Inc.) (Nihon Keizai Shimbun, 1998d)
- Supply chain forum (Nikkei Business Publications, Inc.)
- Relay for the Japan Society of Anaesthesiologists

- Communication Japan relay (sponsored by the Communications Industry Association of Japan).

Large-scale Multipoint Meetings

- NTT (connecting approximately 300 branch offices and branch stores throughout Japan: mobile innovation through the use of intranets) (Hodo and Nakazono, 1997)
- Internal communications (Noevir Co. Ltd, a large cosmetics manufacturer) (Videoconferencing network connects 56 locations: speeds information and curtails expenses) (Nikkei Ryutsu Shimbun, 1997)
- Kirin holds a videoconference spanning all its offices (Nihon Keizai Shimbun, 1998c)
- Tokin (The installation of a videoconferencing system to link locations domestic and foreign) (Nikkan Kogyo Shimbun, 1999a)
- Tanabe Seiyaku directs its efforts toward computerizing sales (links 50 locations via videoconference) (Nikkan Kogyo Shimbun, 1999b)
- Anabuki Construction Inc. (Installing a videoconferencing system into all sales locations) (Nikkei Sangyo Shimbun, 1997c)
- Management communication (Videoconferencing relay networks: presidents prosper through New Year's greetings) (Nikkei Sangyo Shimbun, 1998a).

Other Services

- Wedding ceremony relay (Shidax Foodservice Corporation: live relay of a wedding ceremony spans the Pacific, bridges Hawaii and Japan) (Yomiuri Shimbun, 1998b)
- Franchise management (Gulliver International Corporation: Zero inventory used car sales) (Nihon Kogyo Shimbun, 1998c)
- Distance learning at a cram school (Shugakusha Co., Ltd: distance learning by videophone: 23 classrooms linked in Tokyo and throughout Japan) (Nihon Kogyo Shimbun, 1998b)
- Marketing research (Dentsu Research, Inc.: group interviews by videophone) (Nikkan Kogyo Shimbun, 1998).

With the introduction of (Phoenix) videoconferencing systems distributed nationwide to a total of 1000 primary, junior high and high schools, the Ministry of Education project (Konetto Plan) was set up to promote information exchange between schools by connecting them via video terminals. This has caused a new video communication culture to root.

What is more, in response to customer demand for more diversified, high-quality conferences, new services are beginning to take shape that are centered around a variety of video content distribution services utilizing multipoint connection services and video-on-demand (VOD). Specifically, those new services include the multiple split-screen/high-speed multipoint connection service (Nikkei Sangyo Shimbun, 1998b), the karaoke distribution service (Yomiuri Shimbun, 1998a), and other services designed to appeal to videoconferencing system users.

To quickly and accurately respond to a constantly changing business environment, high-level information sharing, along with speedy decision making and communication are indispensable. The most common way of achieving these conditions is to hold a meeting. But because meetings have the limitation of requiring all participants to assemble in a common location, effective tools such as email and groupware have been introduced and become widespread. However, because these tools are text-based and therefore make sufficient communication difficult, there are limits to how much they can speed decision making and communication.

So NTT Phoenix commenced new services using its video terminal multipoint connection service as a new multimedia tool to solve these kinds of problems and invigorate communication within companies. NTT Phoenix's offerings were not limited to the mere sale of products and services. Customers could use the multipoint connection service to become businesses in the new field of multimedia and offer services such as seminar relays, wedding ceremony relays and distance learning to end users. From this point of view, the multipoint connection service provided customers with new value. Moreover the multipoint connection service is now making a large contribution to customers' businesses as a management innovation tool by improving large-scale in-house meetings and internal communication, and in this way, customers are finding new value in NTT Phoenix's services. (NTT Phoenix management)

Many of the modes of use of the NTT Phoenix multipoint connection service are unique in the world and unique to Japan. Multipoint connection service providers in Europe and North America report that the multipoint connections used by customers usually link between four and eight locations. In comparison, Japanese customers link connections in multiples of 10 or 100, and there are many innovative, rapidly growing small and medium-sized companies, including venture companies, among multipoint connection service customers in Japan. Furthermore, customers continue creating and offering new services to end users, including seminar relay services, wedding ceremony relay services and distance learning services.

These NTT Phoenix business innovations were the result of wisdom and effort born in the course of dialog and collaboration with various customers.

6.14 NTT PHOENIX'S FUTURE BUSINESS STRATEGY

In order to expand its customer value creation business, NTT Phoenix added to its repertoire a business strategy of attracting customers who use video terminals over the Internet. Furthermore, with a market expansion from ISDN video terminals to mobile videophone terminals on its radar screen, NTT Phoenix also had its sights set on winning customers who would use mobile videophones utilizing a high-speed mobile communications network-based W-CDMA (third-generation mobile phone system), which was slated to go into service at the beginning of 2001. Expected to be in particularly high demand were an interconnected video communications service (gateway service) for customers using the Internet or W-CDMA and customers using ISDN, and a mixed platform multipoint connection service (ISDN, Internet and W-CDMA) (see Figure 6.6). (As of the end of the fiscal year 2005, NTT Phoenix has realized all of its initial concepts of new services.)

> NTT Phoenix would like to achieve an environment that permits video communication anytime, any place and with anyone, using platforms ranging from ISDN to Broadband Internet and mobile communications. So as to be able to offer new value to a great many customers, including general companies, small office/home office users, general households and individuals, in fields including business, education, insurance, social welfare and leisure, it would like to offer customers services that have the greatest possible merit. Finally, NTT Phoenix would like to construct a new culture of video communication on a global scale. (NTT Phoenix Executive)

For multipoint connection services centered on video communication, unlike regular telephone, fax, and electronic mail services, the customer's manner of using and applying the services is key. In particular, to create mobile videophone terminal-based video services, NTT Phoenix's offerings must be new value services that are not unilaterally proposed as a solution by NTT Phoenix, but also reflect the desires and will of customers. To achieve this, a sufficient process of interactive dialog and collaboration with the customer is important, and the continuous innovation of new community knowledge with various customers is essential. At the same time, this innovation of community knowledge gives rise to precious expertise and wisdom, and advances and promotes NTT Phoenix's own core competencies.

Customers using Internet-compatible video terminals: IP-based videophone)

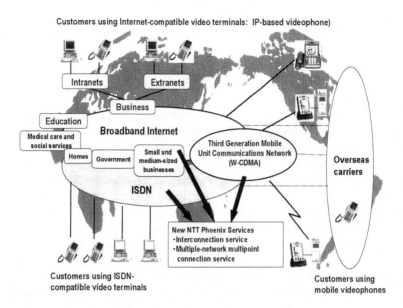

Figure 6.6   NTT Phoenix's business strategy

6.15   NTT PHOENIX'S ORGANIZATIONAL STRUCTURE AND STRATEGIC COMMUNITY

NTT Phoenix's organizational structure as a venture company (see Figure 6.7), is a flat set-up with three general layers ranging from president to general employees. The functions are organized simply: marketing and sales; service development; technology services; and planning, general affairs and accounting departments. In order to deal swiftly with individual customer solution sales and customized business, information sharing between departments is closely linked. Almost all important decisions are taken swiftly through meetings and informal discussions held each morning. At NTT Phoenix, the strategic community is usually formed to transcend the boundaries of each community (see Figure 6.7), to share closely information and knowledge, and to create new knowledge (Brown and Duguid, 1998; Spender, 1996a; Tsoukas, 1996; Carlile, 2002, 2004).

Boundaries of knowledge difference (Brown and Duguid, 2001) exist during interaction among actors belonging to different departments. Standard operating procedures (Grant, 1996b; Nelson and Winter, 1982) and common lexicons (Carlile, 2004) are established to facilitate information sharing among actors, and efficient coordination is implemented (Lawrence and Lorsch, 1967; Galbraith, 1973) among departments (communities) centered on the gatekeepers (Allen, 1977) that integrate diverse knowledge. New issues (such as an urgent response to customers) arise daily among actors, however, and the knowledge difference and inter-departmental dependency grows along with the degree of novelty and uncertainty in the issue content (Carlile, 2004). Actors promote creation of new meaning and learning with the aim of understanding the mutual knowledge difference and solving problems. Here, the existence of individual department leaders as boundary spanners (Brown and Duguid, 1991), translators (Yanow, 2000), and brokers (Hargadon and Sutton, 1997; Pawlowski and Robey, 2004) plays an important role. Moreover, the actors in the individual departments work on the same floor (positioned close together), so have the leeway to share closely tacit and explicit knowledge, and share meaning as regards new issues (Nonaka and Takeuchi, 1995).

However, the situation frequently occurs where knowledge transformation is required for new service development and large-scale customer support topics. This can lead to a clash of opinions between the customer side and technology services side. In the strategic community that has crossed the boundaries between each department, aiming at innovation to transform existing knowledge, actors form shared points of view, values and interests through concretizing the service image, service scenarios and simulations, prototypes and experimentation as 'common knowledge' (Carlile, 2004) and 'common ground' (Bechky, 2003). Close collaboration takes place within SCs through actors' constructive creative dialog and discussion.

From the viewpoint of organizational structures, each department possesses flexibility and autonomy, and the departments themselves are loosely coupled. Actors in each department carry out autonomous dispersal. Actors in the marketing, sales and service development departments, especially, construct purposefully networked 'adhocracy' organizations with external partners and specific customers, and aggressively promote emergent strategies (Nohria and Ghoshal, 1997). Meanwhile, each department's leader realizes the concepts, strategies and tactics set out by the president's leadership, while at the same time close cooperation among the leaders realizes new strategies and tactics. Visions and values are shared among the president and the leaders of individual departments, aimed at the mission of multimedia business promotion.

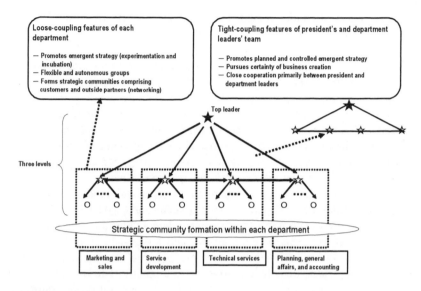

Note: ☆ Leader O Staff

Figure 6.7 Characteristics of NTT Phoenix's organizational structure

NTT Phoenix as a whole is strong in emergent strategy. However, the systematic, deliberate strategy elements of the department leaders and the organizational elements of close cooperation among individual leaders toward accomplishing the president's mission have the potential to link systematically and reliably to actual business as a result of experiment and incubation. The organizational structure essential for NTT Phoenix to develop this kind of novel, complex strategy has grown into an environmental adaptation system – a semi-structure of increasing complexity that possesses both the tight-coupling organizational elements strictly regulated by the executive team (president and individual department leaders) and the flexible and autonomous, loose-coupling organizational elements of individual departments.

Considered from the viewpoint of a strategic activity cycle, NTT Phoenix has made two cycles (A and B) integrated with different strategy-making processes (emergent strategy as future explorative activity and current deliberate strategy as exploitative activity) coexist in-house while operating as a venture company.

6.16 THE FORMATION OF NETWORKED STRATEGIC COMMUNITIES

A particularly important success factor in the business strategy established by NTT Phoenix is the assistance of each of the stakeholders in the venture business in providing, as much as possible, the core competencies relevant to both sales and technology. In general, multimedia businesses require unique and advanced technologies and sales expertise that involve diverse business communities; thus this business is rendered more complex in structure than traditional businesses.

At the start-up of the venture business, the most critical factor for success was the strategic support of the stakeholders. This beat out important issues such as vitalization of the market, forming strategic alliances with stakeholder companies in terms of the sharing of marketing and sales expertise, and providing access to distribution channels. The technical alliance with stakeholder companies having rich core competencies and the technical assistance combined with sales expertise from stakeholder companies were also important factors in maintaining a high degree of service quality and after-sales services in relation to technology and operation.

Although NTT Phoenix is basically an independent venture business, it needs to have business information that allows the greatest level of synergy to flourish. This leads to profit growth for the partnerships while maintaining the partnerships spawned by the strategic alliance with stakeholder companies that remain key to the success of the venture business. Business support-type ventures such as this will become a critical business model contributing to the start-up and growth of new businesses in the high-risk multimedia business sector.

An important element in establishing a large-scale enterprise-type venture business model is reinforcement of the partnership based on empathy and resonance of values envisaged by each leader of the joint venture businesses and the stakeholders, and the creation of a strategic community encouraged by strategic alliances between the joint venture business and the stakeholders. As shown in Figure 6.8, the strategic communities encompassing NTT Phoenix and individual stakeholders as well as the networking with the strategic community inside NTT Phoenix aim to share deep knowledge, sales and technical coordination.

The mission of the NTT Phoenix leaders is to achieve a collection of new businesses through stable alignment and solidarity with the leaders of the stakeholder companies in order to allow synergistic effects to be fully exhibited in each business community and to promote new business. The innovative leadership of each leader at NTT Phoenix and each stakeholder company made it possible to create strategic business communities, create new core competencies, such as the world's largest multipoint connection service aimed at customer value creation, and utilize videoconferencing systems in Japan to create and exploit a market for new video network services.

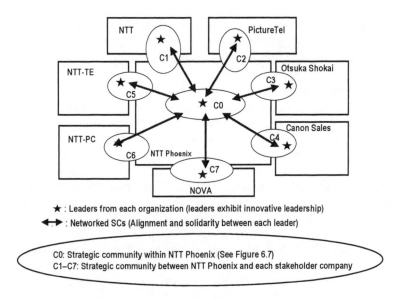

★ : Leaders from each organization (leaders exhibit innovative leadership)
◄►: Networked SCs (Alignment and solidarity between each leader)

C0: Strategic community within NTT Phoenix (See Figure 6.7)
C1–C7: Strategic community between NTT Phoenix and each stakeholder company

Figure 6.8   Creation of networked strategic communities between NTT Phoenix and stakeholder companies

6.17 CONCLUSION

This chapter has presented a case study in the multimedia area and dealt with the multipoint connection venture business of the world's largest videoconferencing system implemented by a joint venture business established through investment from U.S.–Japan heterogeneous businesses. The article also acknowledged the importance of an enterprise strategy encouraged by a large business-support-type venture business model in terms of the strategic alliance with the original stakeholders and venture businesses and the strategic support of the stakeholders being key factors in success.

To achieve the above goal, it is especially important for the leaders in each organization to possess a strategic philosophy that cultivates an entrepreneurial spirit, network outside connections to find the key person, share empathy and resonance for the philosophy, vision and values of the key person, and possess enough innovative leadership skills and energy to accomplish the creation of strategic communities.

NOTES

1. A server with a type of switching function that permits interactive video/voice communication through connection between multiple videoconferencing systems.
2. NOVA is Japan's largest language school. It is currently providing a service named 'Study abroad in your living room' (NOVA service brand name) using a videophone.

7. Customer value creation through knowledge innovation

In this chapter, I will discuss business processes that lead to the creation of new value with new customers and enable a company to create new knowledge among company and customers through the provision of new products and services. I will look at case studies from the Japanese business world where project teams in a high-tech company providing IT-based products and multimedia services have experienced the knowledge creation process with customers. The formation of strategic communities is key to creating customer value and succeeding with new markets in IT and multimedia. These communities are formed through close collaboration and dialectical dialog with diverse customers, based on the resonance of values, mutual trust and the innovation of new knowledge creation by integrative competences through dialectical leadership.

7.1 FORMATION OF STRATEGIC COMMUNITIES WITH CUSTOMERS

Since the start of 1995, Nippon Telegraph and Telephone Corporation (NTT), Japan's largest telecommunications company, has endeavored to promote and expand the digital network in a bid to break away from the old business model based on the analog telephones of the past. The public digital network enables high-speed access to the Internet and offers a fixed transmission speed and guaranteed speech quality, making it the optimum communications network for video communications such as videophones and videoconferencing. Examples of applications that NTT developed for digital networks are video terminals, including videophones, videoconferencing systems and multipoint video communication services. Nihon Keizai Shimbun announced these products in February 1996, and NTT started selling the products and services (hereafter, new systems) on the Japanese market shortly thereafter. Customer research was a necessary first step in promoting the acceptance of the new systems. Issues included the type of customers who would use the interactive video communication functions that the new systems could provide, how and in what fields they would use them, and what sort of value customers would receive as a result.

One of the targets for the NTT project teams was to develop uses for new system applications in the fields of business, education, medicine and welfare. The issue for NTT's project leaders was how to approach customers with the newly-developed systems and persuade them of their value. Back in 1996 the education, medicine and welfare fields in Japan felt that they had little need for new systems, and in other fields as well, including business, the need for new systems had barely taken root as a general social culture. The concept and vision of NTT's project leaders in creating a new culture of interactive video communication in Japan was very powerful. It predicted the promising markets in the fields of business, education, medicine and welfare, and the importance for society overall, from small children to the elderly.

NTT formed four project teams, dealing with business solutions, education, medicine and welfare. The issue directly facing these project teams was how to establish new business solutions and models using these new systems. NTT's project members were sales and technical experts, especially in the area of telecommunications, but there were no members from the education, medicine or welfare fields. The project teams therefore established the urgent task of obtaining new knowledge in new industries and fields. To accomplish this, potential customers had to be approached in different industries and fields outside NTT.

> It was felt that customer research could help provide the key to promoting new systems and the tools of interactive video communication. The new systems were generally used by businesses for virtual conferences, but an analysis of the future market suggested that demand in telemedicine and distance learning would increase. Since NTT was a telecom carrier, we possessed no knowledge or expertise in fields such as medicine or education, and we needed to learn from doctors and educators. (From dialog with the medical project leader)

What approach to customers would be needed? Should NTT target well-known universities, hospitals or medical welfare organizations? Would prominent scholars, researchers or managers be appropriate targets? The project teams contacted various customers, and after concerted dialog and discussion, the team learned that it was important to find and contact potential customers who were passionate about learning and embraced new ideas and visions. Potential customers had the spirit to look beyond the status quo and present the challenge of new work in their specialist fields. These customers also possessed strategic ideas and the power to act. The project teams became aware of how important it was for themselves and these potential customers to learn from each other through dialog and collaboration. And the project teams, through dialog with customers, generated empathy between themselves and the customers based on mutual values in visions and concepts, and raised awareness aimed at building new business solutions and business models. In addition, customers were brought virtually into the project teams, SCs were formed with customers, and concrete businesses were promoted. In the following sections, I will introduce case studies of project teams in the fields of education, medicine and welfare.

7.2 ESTABLISHMENT OF NEW BUSINESS SOLUTIONS AND MODELS WITH STRATEGIC COMMUNITIES

7.2.1 Examples of Business in the Field of Education

Adult education, lifelong learning and language study

Forming a strategic community with Shukutoku University In September 1997, Shukutoku University and an NTT educational project team formed a business partnership to create a trial 'cybercollege' business. The business was to conduct top management seminars, lifelong learning courses, and other educational activities using Shukutoku University content via a multi-site network linking businesses and adults throughout Japan. This partnership would harmonize the concept and vision of both project leaders expressed using the phrase 'nationwide lifelong learning through the use of multimedia', and greatly boost the study of actual businesses. The partnership involved opening a cybercollege aimed at general businesses and adults, launching trial services using the platform proposed by NTT, and offering interactive management seminars and lifelong learning courses via multimedia and video.

The term 'cybercollege' refers to a virtual university offering distance learning through networks that allow lectures and seminars to be attended from a company office or home, giving the student the sense of being in a university classroom or seminar hall. Encouraging people to 'Attend the latest business management or education course from your office or home', Shukutoku University aimed to offer courses that were a cut above most adult education and lifelong learning programs. Aimed at business managers, management staff and other adults, the specific content initially offered by the cybercollege included courses entitled 'Top management seminar', 'Communication in education', and 'People-to-people communication', which were provided over a multi-site network linking Shukutoku University with businesses and individuals throughout Japan.

The decision-making process for the two organizations involved in the first virtual education business was discussed from the perspectives of Shukutoku University's desire to establish a virtual education business for the future, and NTT's desire to develop a new multimedia business. On the university side, the decentralized nature of the organization, with its many departments and separate graduate school, required a consensus and decision-making process among top management, including the board of directors and department deans, when promoting and implementing a virtual education business as a university entity. The university's management, however, exploited its top-down decision-making process to move forward through active dialog. This partnership was an important trial for the fully-fledged creation of cybercollege businesses. First, it allowed Shukutoku University to acquire experience of this platform in various areas of expertise associated with the provision of distance learning. Second, it provided a critically innovative process of new knowledge creation for the NTT educational project team by forming an SC from the perspective of field-testing a platform developed for service, highlighting problems and areas for improvement, and receiving feedback to help in developing an enhanced platform.

This learning process was an active dialog and collaborative endeavor that shared and merged NTT's ICT and multimedia technology with the educational content, training and expertise of innovative customers in order to create new knowledge (known as 'virtual education services') accumulated as valuable expertise. The learning process within this close-knit SC provided greater educational opportunities for working people, and the SC activities utilizing this multimedia contributed greatly to promoting the interchangeability of academic credits among universities, deepening exchanges between universities, raising educational and research standards, and facilitating open education in other regions for the future.

The NTT educational project team developed further by expanding to other universities and educational organizations of all kinds that could become further customers, for example skills and expertise were accumulated in the SC with the Keio University business school (a potential customer). The fields of choice were lifelong learning and language study, which were expected to grow in importance alongside education for working people. To this end, an SC chain was formed with customers in a variety of educational fields.

In the field of lifelong learning, strategic communities were formed with universities and all types of educational organizations, including the following:

- June 1997: Launched a multimedia lifelong learning course service in partnership with Koriyama Women's University (news published in *Fukushima Minpo Shimbun*).
- September 1997 to March 1998: Launched a multimedia lifelong learning course service in partnership with the Ministry of Education's Media Education Development Center and five universities located throughout Japan (news published in *Kyoiku Shimbun*).
- September 1997: Opened a cyber college in partnership with Shukutoku University (news published in *Nihon Keizai Shimbun*).
- November 1997: Opened the Ishikawa Prefecture Distance Learning School. A videoconferencing system was installed in civic halls in Ishikawa Prefecture and open lectures from Kanazawa University and other locations were broadcast live to prefectural residents.
- March 1998: Launched a joint U.S.–Japan MBA program under the auspices of Case Western Reserve University of the U.S. in partnership with the Society and Economic Institute's Productivity Headquarters (news published in *Nihon Keizai Shimbun*).
- November 1998: Implemented lifelong learning programs and other educational programs at universities in Aichi Prefecture (news published in *Nikkei Sangyo Shimbun*).
- August 1999: Started development of a smart campus system and an experimental remote management seminar to cultivate entrepreneurs in a partnership between Mitsubishi Research Institute, Inc. and NTT (news published in *Nihon Keizai Shimbun*).
- August 1999: Started development of an entrepreneur cultivation scheme and an experimental remote evaluator training program aimed at management in a partnership between the Japan Productivity Center for Socio-Economic Development and NTT.

In the field of language study, SCs were established with large language schools, including the following:

- October 1996: Started a 'Study abroad in your living room' service provided through a partnership with NOVA, a major language school (news published in newspapers).
- August 1997: Launched a multimedia, distance language-learning service for businesses in partnership with Overseas Broadcast Center, Inc. (news published in *Nikkei Sangyo Shimbun*).

7.2.2   Examples of Business in the Field of Medicine

Home, remote, and emergency medical care

As the population continues to age, businesses are responding with a variety of services. One of these appeared after the medical insurance system in Japan was revised and the amount that the elderly were required to pay for medical expenses rose in September 1997, leading to the prediction that increasing numbers of elderly people would opt for medical treatment in their own homes rather than go to expensive hospitals. Against this sort of background, Otsuka Clinic, a pioneering medical company specializing in home medical care, started home visitation treatment services for the elderly in 1995. Service areas comprise four wards in Tokyo (Toshima, Bunkyo, Kita and Itabashi) and a segment of two additional wards (Nerima and Taito). For a monthly fee of 2000 yen, doctors and nurses make periodic visits by car to provide care. At present, they have approximately 200 patients.

Important items in home medical care are periodical checks on the patient's state of health and prompt measures to address any sudden changes. Videophones were thought to enable more thorough treatment, since they enable periodic 'visits' to patients' homes for tests, and enable a doctor to grasp a patient's condition effectively in the case of an emergency. An NTT medical project team utilizing new systems formed an SC with Otsuka Clinic (the innovative customer) and the 'Home Visitation Medical Care Support System', and launched distance home medical care (news published in *Nikkei Sangyo Shimbun*) (see Figure 7.1).

This series of incubations has led to remarkable results. Besides helping doctors perform routine diagnoses, the system can connect to a patient database, make judgments against a patient's history and state of health displayed on-screen, and send a doctor or notify supporting hospitals in the event of an emergency report (news published in *Nikkei Business* in 1998). Guidance for taking medicine is also provided from a visiting pharmacist, and the pharmacist can use the new system to confirm the medicine's provenance with the pharmacy. Since new systems are used to make diagnoses, patients and doctors have more occasions to 'meet', in addition to actual periodical visits from doctors, and this has helped to improve the reliability of the diagnosis. Since the new systems enable an accurate diagnosis of the patient's state of health when an emergency call is made, the dispatch of a doctor has become more efficient, the number of night-time emergency visits has reduced by 80 percent, and the staff spend less time moving from place to place, thus cutting personnel costs and enhancing efficiency.

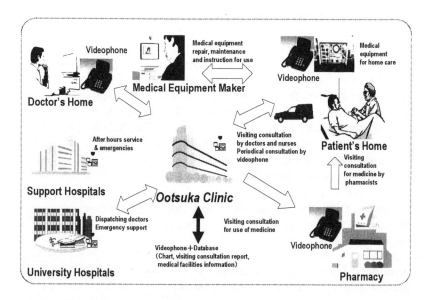

Figure 7.1   Home health care support by new systems

Through this series of incubations with potential customers, a distance home medical care business model exploiting the new systems was established through a learning process within the SC. In addition, an NTT medical project team extended the results obtained from the SC with Otsuka Clinic (a potential customer), to customers in similar areas including hospitals, medical treatment organizations and self-governing bodies. Specifically, businesses were developed on the basis of strategic communities with all types of customers in the remote-area medical care, emergency medical care and the health and medication consulting fields.

In the field of remote-area medical care, strategic communities were formed in many cities, towns and villages, including the following:

- February 1998: 'Government services by videophone: installation in every household in Katsurao-mura, Fukushima Prefecture' (news published in *Nihon Keizai Shimbun*).
- March 1998: 'Verification experiments using videophone in distance home medical care and home care in Toono City, Iwate Prefecture' (news published in many newspapers).
- March 1998: 'Verification experiments using videophone in remote distance medical care for the elderly and home care in Setagaya Ward, Tokyo' (news published in many newspapers).

- April 1999: 'Home delivery of medicine via videophone: doctors in Katsurao-mura, Fukushima Prefecture, making remote diagnoses' (news published in *Nikkei Sangyo Shimbun* and *The New York Times*).
- December 1998: 'Videophone-based village-level networks: Nosegawa-mura, Nara Prefecture', (news published in *Asahi Shimbun*).
- December 1999: 'Decision taken to select Yajima-machi, Akita Prefecture, as leading-edge model region' (news published in *Akita Sakigake Shimbun*).

In the emergency medical field, partnerships were made with university hospitals, including the following:

- December 1997: Partnership in the emergency medical field with Tokyo Women's Medical University using a videoconferencing system (news broadcasted on NHK).
- December 1997: Partnership in the videophone-based remote surgical procedure area with the Medical Department of Osaka University (news published in *Sankei Shimbun*).

In the health consultation and medicine consultation fields, strategic communities were formed with all types of medical care organizations, including the following:

- February 1997: Partnership with Tokyo-based T-PEC Corporation in videophone-based health care consulting (news published in *Nihon Keizai Shimbun*).
- February 1998: Partnership with Chukai Industries, Inc., in Kobe. Using videophones, remote diagnoses with a famous Chinese physician were carried out based on Western and Eastern medicine (news published in *Nikkan Kogyo Shimbun*).
- April 1998: Partnership in the herbal medicine consulting field with the regional herbal medicine chain store Kusuri Nihondo (news published in *Nikkei Sangyo Shimbun*).

7.3 CONCEPTS DERIVED FROM THE CASE STUDIES

In this section, I will use the crucial aggregated dimensions derived from grounded theory to consider what sort of impact the strategic communities with customers and the integrative competences through dialectical leadership of the project leaders had on new knowledge creation and the output of NTT project teams. First I will analyze the characteristics of strategic communities that triggered new knowledge creation between the customers and project teams. These characteristics, which were derived from grounded theory, consist of four broader dimensions, which I will refer to as close collaboration, dialectical dialog, resonance of values and building trust. Second, using three broader dimensions which I will refer to as dialectical leadership, integrative competences and the community knowledge creating cycle, I will discuss the integrative competences through dialectical leadership by which project leaders dialectically synthesize the various contradictions and paradoxical elements within the SC, and then exploit them through a community knowledge creating cycle with many customers.

7.3.1 Close Collaboration and Dialectical Dialog with Customers

In order to provide customers with the kind of new products and services that are represented in the fields of ICT and multimedia, it is important for companies to develop and market products and services from the viewpoint of the customer, and in cases where both new solutions and business models are sought, it is also important to absorb opinions, requests and criticisms from customers who are thoroughly familiar with related products and services. It is especially important to form the kind of SCs with customers and companies represented by the project teams in these cases, and to build new solutions and business models through dialectical dialog and close collaboration within SCs.

Collaboration has been studied in a wide variety of literatures. According to Gray (1989, p5), who is often credited with formally launching collaboration theory, inter-organizational collaboration is defined as 'a process through which parties who see different aspects of a problem can constructively explore their differences and search for solutions that go beyond their own limited vision of what is possible'. Learning and innovation literature (including Anand and Khanna, 2000; Larsson *et al.*, 1998; Kale *et al.*, 2000) emphasizes that collaboration can facilitate the creation of new knowledge, not just transfer existing knowledge (for example, Gulati, 1999; Powell *et al.*, 1996). Collaboration might also operate as a strategic tool for gaining efficiency and flexibility in a rapidly changing environment by, for example, targeting customers' fields and needs (Westley and Vredenburg, 1991). Thus collaboration theory, which builds on empirical and theoretical perspectives from a variety of research streams including resource dependence, learning and strategic management (Gray and Wood, 1991; Wood and Gray, 1991), is useful at interpersonal, intergroup and inter-organizational levels of analysis within strategic communities, such as the customer's relationship with the company as described in these case studies.

Especially noteworthy characteristics of collaboration in strategic communities observed in these case studies are: (1) the stakeholders are interdependent; (2) business solutions emerge by dealing constructively and dialectically with differences between customer needs and company technology; (3) decisions, such as trials and installation of new systems, are typically jointly owned; (4) collaboration is an emergent process in the daily routine of project activities; and (5) close collaboration can produce new capabilities for project teams, enabling them to provide the best new solution and business model with customers. Therefore, collaboration can produce new capabilities for organizations within strategic communities that they would not otherwise possess, and can aid organizations in innovating the new business solutions and business models described in these cases beyond an individual organization's presently bounded rationality, as well as being a way of spreading risk and pooling resources.

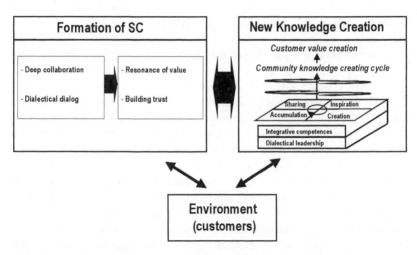

Figure 7.2   Characteristics of strategic communities and new knowledge creation in these case studies

Another important perspective is to promote close dialectical dialog within strategic communities through constructive approaches to customers. Rather than businesses unilaterally establishing new solutions and business models and providing them to customers, as was done in the past, new solutions and business models should be conceptualized through dialectical dialog with customers. In other words, customers should be considered as members of staff. An important point in this respect is that the visions, desires and other values leading toward the realization of new concepts and business models with the company project leaders and customers must resonate. The desire on the customer side lies in the ability of many customers (including themselves) to accept the high-quality, low-cost products and services through the new solution and business model. The mission of the company side, the role of the project leader, is to provide competitive products and services through the solution and business model to many customers and to obtain high customer satisfaction. Here, the project leader and the customers resonate each other's values through repeated dialectical dialog and establish a new concept. It then becomes vital for SCs to be formed among the customer and the company project teams. In these strategic communities, the resonance of values among all members, building of mutual trust, acceptance of the customer as a member of the project team, and the business process by which the customer thinks and acts together with the project members need to be encouraged. So creating an SC, dialectical dialog and close collaboration with customers are crucial factors by which the resonance of value and mutual trust, which are discussed in the next section, can be produced (see Figure 7.2).

7.3.2   Resonance of Value with Customers

Before new systems utilizing ICT and multimedia technology could be installed for corporate users, educational, medical and welfare institutions and other customers, the customers themselves needed to understand fully the new value that they would obtain with the installation of the new systems. For corporate users, this new value meant dramatic improvements in business processes, promotion of knowledge management linked to the sharing of information and knowledge among all employees, and rapid decision making. To educational and medical institutions, new value meant using distance learning and telemedicine methods to achieve their goal of implementing major reforms in their existing educational and medical systems. The majority of customers, however, harbored considerable resistance to installing new systems based on new ideas in ICT and multimedia. A big issue for NTT project teams has thus been how to dispel the entrenched values of these customers.

For NTT project teams, the first issue is to get customers to understand the new values associated with new system concepts. In other words, NTT project teams want customers to empathize with the thoughts, philosophies, beliefs, intentions and other aspects of the concepts underlying the new systems, to change customers' values regarding new systems, and to inspire them to resonate. Once NTT project teams and customers can begin resonating their values of new systems concepts, the new systems give customers new value, enabling them to receive innovations concerning improvements in their business processes, rapid decision making, and reforms in educational, medical and welfare systems.

Generally, when customers are corporate users, they belong to an information systems, planning or business operations improvement division. Users at educational institutions tend to be either in a planning division or members of a special project, organizational task force or conference group. Thus a single customer may consist of various types of members, and it becomes necessary to modify the values of each individual. To attain a resonance of values, strategic communities should comprise NTT project team members and numerous members representing the customer, and the two parties should engage in close dialectical dialog. The NTT project leaders consciously formed this sort of SC with customers with the aim of stimulating a resonance of values.

The process of resonating values between NTT project teams and customers was observed throughout these case studies. To stimulate the resonance of values among all members of the strategic communities made up of the NTT project team and customer members, customers had to shift from their existing (old) values to new values, and the resonance of values was achieved through a process of four steps: sharing, inspiration, creation, and resonance (see Figure 7.3).

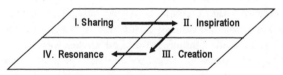

I.   Sharing Step

   Learning and understanding new value indicating direction in which SC should proceed

   (Customer members learn about and understand new values for new systems' concepts.   Customer

   members learn about and understand innovations that use ICT and multimedia technologies.)

II.   Inspiration Step

   Inspiring new value in SC aimed at the destruction of existing values of members and the fusion of visions

   and values of a different nature

   (Old values of customer members are destroyed; new values are inspired for customer members toward the

   goals of innovation that utilize ICT and multimedia technologies.)

III.   Creation Step

   New value is created toward the introduction of new systems within SC.

IV.   Resonance Step

   All members resonate their ideas, intentions and spirits toward innovation for new value within SC.

Figure 7.3   Process of resonating values with customers in an SC

The purpose of the first step, the sharing of values, is for members in the SC to study and understand the new values associated with the concepts of the new systems. Customer members learn about the differences between existing and new values through constructive dialectical dialog within the SC, and then they understand the essence of the new values. In these cases, in order to promote the use of newly-developed systems in a variety of fields, NTT project team members engaged in repeated dialectical dialog with customer members. The first lessons that NTT project teams needed to learn were to understand customer members' current problems and issues (which for corporate users were how to improve the business process, and for educational users were how the new education system brings about reforms). Customer members, on the other hand, needed to understand sufficiently the concepts of NTT's new systems.

In the second step, the inspiration of values, the existing values of customer members were given a jolt, and the concepts of new systems proposed by NTT project teams inspired new values in the customer members. One of the important triggers in this process of inspiration was the inducement of a sense of crisis or motivation among customer members concerning the breakdown of their current condition. The NTT project team's firm belief and confidence that their new systems were able to provide new value to customers inspired new value for individual customer members from the viewpoint of innovation.

The third step of value creation is where new value is created within customer members aimed at adding to the new systems concepts. In these cases, individual customer members applied themselves to creating new value within the SC aimed at reaching the new goal of innovation that utilized ICT and multimedia. The challenging goals of acquiring new business, operational, educational and medical skills as an organization required the installation of new business processes. Educational and medical systems that utilize the new systems were also established in this step.

In the final step of the resonance of values, all members, including customers, resonated their thoughts, intentions, mentality and other vectors of the mind aimed at newly-created values within the SC, and a sense of unity as a community was formed. A resonance of values in the SC was achieved through this process. In these cases, individual customer members became aware of a firm courage and confidence in disseminating and establishing new business processes or educational and medical systems inside their own organization aimed at acquiring new knowledge, skills and expertise regarding the installation of the new systems.

In this manner, by forming many SCs with a variety of customers, NTT project teams created value resonance platforms for each customer. Using this platform as a base, the company implemented trials aimed at installing the new systems; and, as indicated in the next paragraph, worked at the innovation of diverse knowledge within the SC.

7.3.3 Building Trust in the Strategic Community

The project leaders regard potential customers as members of the company, and they create an organizational SC rooted in resonance of values and mutual trust. In this SC, all corporate team members including customers share the same values, and they build mutual trust that embraces all potential customers. The project leaders promote a dialectical dialog and deep collaboration in resonating the values of all project members and building mutual trust.

Theories on trust are based on the notion of interdependence between the party who trusts and the party who is trusted (Dasgupta, 1988). Trust is an enabling condition which facilitates the formation of ongoing networks (Ring, 1994), and some trust is required to initiate collaboration (Webb, 1991). Thus, dialog in collaboration helps to build trust because it provides the basis for continued interaction with customers as described in these case studies (Leifer and Mills, 1966). From the analysis of these cases, it was found that trust could be gained through close collaboration and dialectical dialog within the SC, where it serves as an important element in new knowledge creation relating to new business solutions and models, and later in formal contracts for the new systems installation and sales to customers (Bradach and Eccles, 1989; Gulati, 1995). Therefore, the presence of trust in the SC is essential for collaboration to be successful.

Trust is best understood in terms of the ability to form expectations about aims and partners' future behavior in relation to those aims (Gulati, 1995; Rousseau *et al.*, 1998; Sitkin *et al.*, 1998). A necessary condition for trust in these cases is that expectations for the new business solutions and models using IT and multimedia technology can be formed and fulfilled through deep collaboration and dialectical dialog based on members' resonance of value. Trust enables actors to establish mutually specific expectations about their future-oriented perspectives and behaviors (Lane and Backmann, 1998). Thus, creation of trust can be rooted in anticipation that something will be forthcoming (Lane and Bachmann, 1998; Vansina, Taillieu and Schruijer, 1998). In these cases, the objective of both parties is to make a large contribution to business, educational and medical fields using a new ICT and multimedia system.

7.3.4   Integrative Competences Through Dialectical Leadership of Project Leaders

Struggles and conflict are a common occurrence within the SC. These elements are harmful factors in the effort to create new knowledge. This new knowledge creation is thus promoted by dialectical leadership of project leaders, which we describe below.

The role of the project leaders is to create new knowledge within SCs that were formed by project and customer members and to generate integrative competences (Kodama, 2004) through dialectical leadership. The project leaders need to balance the various paradoxical elements and issues within the SC in order to realize these integrative competences. The project leaders also need to consciously promote dialectical leadership and engage in dialectical dialog to resolve the various differences and issues within the SC. The result will be that the project leaders actively analyze problems and resolve issues, form an arena for the resonance of new values, build trust, and create a higher level of new knowledge. Dialectical management is based on the Hegelian approach, which is a practical method of resolving conflict within an organization (Kodama, 2003a).

The balancing of paradoxical elements and issues involves the synthesis of mutually divergent views among project and customer members coming from different corporate cultures on the one hand, and the synthesis of a variety of divergent business issues (such as the organization's internal resources and the environment of a customer's needs) on the other. In these case studies, for example, syntheses were required in two areas: (1) the values of many members possessing a broad diversity of viewpoints and knowledge shaped by different corporate cultures to which they belonged, whether business-oriented companies or educational and medical institutions, and (2) balancing social customer viewpoints and needs derived from the environment based on the positioning-based view and new systems technology acquired by the internal resource of the organization based on the resource-based view. The project leaders play a central role in synthesizing the paradoxical elements and issues in the specific areas of culture and business. The dialectical leadership, with the new ideas and approaches of the project leaders who have adopted the methods of dialectical management in their efforts to integrate and synthesize paradoxical elements and issues, makes new community knowledge creation and innovation possible (see Figure 7.2).

The SC promotes dialectical dialog and close collaboration among project and customer members in order to cultivate a thorough understanding of problems and issues. By communicating and collaborating with each other, project leaders and members become aware of the roles and values of each other's work. As a result, they are able to transform the various conflicts that have arisen between customer members into constructive conflicts. This process requires project leaders to follow a pattern of thought and action in which they ask themselves what sorts of actions they themselves would take, what sorts of strategies or tactics they would adopt, and what they could contribute toward achieving value creation for the customer and the innovation of a new business and solution. And in achieving this innovation, the project leaders promote the sympathy and resonance of the project target's values and build mutual trust within the strategic community, while the dialectical leadership of the project leaders results in the high levels of integrative competences that have enabled NTT project teams to create new community knowledge, realize customer value creation, and form new business solutions and business models (see Figure 7.2).

7.3.5   Innovation Process of New Community Knowledge Creation with Diverse Customers

This section takes the example of the Society for the Promotion of the Konetto Plan Council, the first of many customers to install new systems, to describe how the NTT educational project team pursued the innovation of knowledge with the customer and how it provided new value through the new systems. In one noteworthy case, the videoconferencing system was installed in 1000 elementary and middle schools throughout Japan. The Ministry of Education is now promoting a project (the Konetto Plan) under which the video terminals of this videoconferencing system are simultaneously connected for large-scale seminar relays (known as Konetto seminars) and inter-school exchanges. A new culture of communication is taking root through this project (see Figure 7.4).

The Konetto Plan Council, which is charged with promoting the Konetto Plan, is the NTT educational project team's largest customer, and the project team saw the scheme as a big opportunity. At first, it encountered some major hurdles to actualizing and making a success of these large-scale seminar relays and inter-school exchanges. First among the sets of issues encountered was that of connecting 1000 video terminals to provide bidirectional video and voice communication accurately for the first time ever. The second set of issues facing the Konetto Plan involved the human aspect of carrying out a seminar in a satellite assembly hall comprising 1000 locations, including the main hall where the lecturer was present.

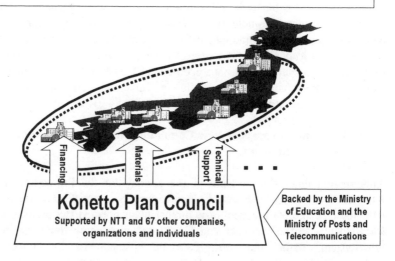

Configuring a Digital Environment in 1 000 Schools Throughout Japan

(1) Supporting personal computer education
(2) Offering educational opportunities, beginning with
   the Konetto Seminars
(3) Providing a multimedia environment (digital network/Internet)

Financing　Materials　Technical Support　■ ■ ■

Konetto Plan Council
Supported by NTT and 67 other companies,
organizations and individuals

Backed by the Ministry
of Education and the
Ministry of Posts and
Telecommunications

Figure 7.4　Composition of the Konetto Plan

Behind the success of the first Konetto seminar was the innovation of knowledge within the SC formed by the NTT educational project team and the Konetto Plan Council (hereafter, the Council). This took place through the dialectical dialog- and close collaboration-based processes of sharing, inspiring, creating and accumulating. The first process, that of sharing, refers to the step where both sides sufficiently understand their shared vision and objectives, and in so doing, share their tacit knowledge. Specifically, in order to hold seminar relays and inter-school exchanges, a system was required in which 1000 locations are connected simultaneously, and the scene shown on the screen naturally switches from the hall where a question is asked of the lecturer to the hall where the lecturer is speaking, as well as high-quality, bi-directional video and voice delivery. The NTT educational project team suggested the use of its core business multipoint connection service solution to the council. Through discussions with the council, the NTT team made the specifics of its service understood and ensured that it sufficiently understood the council's needs. Discussions between the two sides lasted several weeks, and this interactive process was an important step in the mutual sharing and understanding of the knowledge possessed by each side.

The second process, that of inspiration, is the step where the two sides mutually inspire and promote diverse community knowledge. Through dialectical dialogs among individuals, the actors' contradictions and problem points were gradually solved. This involved working from the basis of the two partners' shared and created community knowledge to discover the problems and issues hindering the realization of the world's first large-scale seminar relay, and the means of addressing and solving these problems and issues. Specifically, it involved repeatedly performing demonstrations using the actual equipment to ferret out technical and operational problems and establish strategies for solving them. During this process, the parties were able to create an operations manual as explicit knowledge in which expertise relevant to correctly managing seminars would be concentrated.

The third process, that of creation, is the step where the two parties create new, advanced community knowledge based on the knowledge they have inspired and promoted. Specifically, this consisted of solving technical and operational problems and establishing firm standards for the seminar relay service. Methods for solving technical problems included establishing strategies for eliminating video and audio noise on the video terminal side, and the simultaneous completion of the operations manual, which serves the function of a paper expertise repository, as a solution for human-side problems in the operational realm. With this manual, it became possible for the individuals in charge of each of the 1000 venues to conduct the seminar accurately.

The fourth process, that of accumulation, refers to the step where the seminar relay service, which is based on newly-created community knowledge, was established. The diverse community knowledge acquired in the processes of inspiration and creation was systematically accumulated as precious expertise, and the NTT team's core knowledge was established and advanced. Specifically, this process consisted of systematically accumulating the various technical and operational skills and expertise as new community knowledge in the course of establishing the seminar relay service, and working to enhance the professional skills of each member and in other ways advance the core knowledge of the NTT team. Furthermore, in the course of providing specific services, the NTT team received feedback and suggestions for improvement from the council and added these comments to its expertise in order to improve further the quality of services. The council also enabled delivery of precious content through the seminar relay service, which arose from the creation of new community knowledge, to end-user elementary, middle and high schools throughout Japan, and enabled inter-school exchanges among elementary, middle and high school students. In effect, the new value of realizing the world's first large-scale seminar relay was provided to the council via NTT's multipoint connection service.

As shown in the preceding paragraphs, NTT's educational project team, by making a success of the Konetto Plan seminar relay service, accumulated within itself a variety of skill, know-how, and expertise related to this service as new community knowledge, while further establishing its own core knowledge. At the same time, it promoted customer value creation using the sort of community knowledge innovation based on the resonance of values described in this chapter.

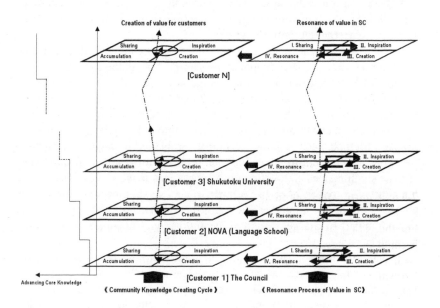

Figure 7.5   Spiral process of new community knowledge creating cycle based on resonance of value in SC – activities of educational project team

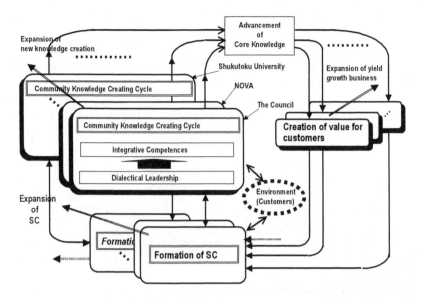

*Figure 7.6   Promotion of customer value creation through new knowledge
creation within SC – activities of educational project team*

7.3.6   Continuous Community Knowledge Creation with Customers

For the NTT educational project team, the success of the Konetto seminar
became the motivational power behind the acquisition of new customers,
such as the NOVA language school, Shukutoku University, Keio University,
Koriyama Women's University and the Ministry of Education's Media
Education Development. Through the formation of SCs based on resonance
of value with new customers, the NTT project team repeated the innovation
process of the community knowledge creating cycle and endeavored to
enhance its core knowledge. The NTT team repeated this community
knowledge creating cycle continually in a chain-like manner for each new
customer, and in so doing established the new systems even more firmly,
and further promoted customer value creation businesses (see Figure 7.5).

The connection between SCs and the community knowledge creating
cycle is extremely important in order to create businesses successfully that
generate value for the customer while the project teams continuously interact
with the environment (customers). The first key consideration is to form SCs
using the dialectical dialog and close collaboration ability of the respective
NTT project leaders and their customers, based on the resonance of values
and trust-building between the project and customer members. The second is
to initiate the community knowledge creating cycle through integrating

competences through the dialectical leadership of the project leaders, so as to offer new value to the customer. By repeating these processes in its relationships with customers in a spiral pattern, NTT project teams are able to advance their own core knowledge while finding new customer value creation business markets (Figure 7.6).

7.4 IMPLICATIONS

Developing new systems in the ICT and multimedia fields entails considerable risk for companies. No matter how functional or competitively priced a system might be, it does not necessarily mean that customers will readily accept it. Numerous companies have developed and marketed new systems that reflect the results of market surveys among their many customers, but many of these companies used business solutions and models from the 'seeds' they themselves produced as a base for generating marketing and sales strategies.

In the new perspective obtained through the case studies in this chapter, customers were accepted as corporate members, SCs were formed with customers, and a new business process that featured thinking and acting with customers was built. The following four points are important in this business process for practitioners.

7.4.1 Formation of Networks with Customers

Face-to-face dialectical dialogs with customers are important in building completely new business solutions and models utilizing the company's products and services. Customers are heard in their own voices, and innovative ideas for improving products and services and for building new solutions and business models are absorbed. To this end, it is prudent to hold regular forums focusing, for example, on the customer, customer appreciation or services usage. Another tactic is to form virtual forums on the Internet where ideas for new business solutions and business models can be solicited. A corporate stance that actively gathers critical yet constructive opinions and requests from customers by maintaining multiple contact points with them and further expanding human networks is important (Lipnack and Stamps, 1997). It is the first bold step to uncovering a precious vein of gold from the mine.

7.4.2 Innovation of Community Knowledge Creation Based on Resonance of Values and Building Trust with Potential Customers

The next issue is to discover and cultivate potential customers from the networks formed with them and to create constructive connections with these potential customers. Potential customers have their own unique visions and desires, and they express constructive opinions concerning companies' products and services, although the majority of their opinions are critical, and companies are taken aback by their excessive expectations and requests. Nevertheless, their new ideas, born from detailed knowledge based on learning experience, are valuable, and project leaders need to understand their desires through sufficient dialog with these customers. Patience and tolerance are sometimes necessary when fielding the excessive criticisms in order to understand and empathize with the desires and visions of these potential customers. It then becomes possible to resonate value between the potential customers and the project leaders, and to create new business solutions and models based on the new ideas.

The project leader regards the potential customers as members of the company, and they create SCs as an organization rooted in resonance of values and mutual trust. In an SC, all project members share the same values, and build mutual trust that includes all potential customers in the SC. The project leader plays a vital leadership and organizational role in resonating the values of all project members and building mutual trust. In SCs built on a foundation of resonated values among all members (including potential customers) and mutual trust among members, it is important to promote actively an organization-wide learning process of knowledge creation. In trials, dialectical dialog and close collaboration among project members, including potential customers, have created new community knowledge and promoted the knowledge possessed by individual members, and great expertise, skills and other resources are accumulated by organizations through this process.

7.4.3 Chaining Creation of Strategic Communities with Many Customers

The mechanism whereby an SC success with potential customers forms other new strategic communities and creates a business is an important process for achieving continued innovations in corporate activities. It is like a spiraling knowledge creation system in which the success of a large project with a customer whose aim was to develop strategic products and services for their company leads to similar expansion with other customers.

The objective of these case studies was to promote and extend the results of strategic communities consisting of NTT project teams and potential customers in the fields of business, education, medicine and welfare to other customers throughout Japan. By taking maximum advantage of ICT and multimedia, exploiting the core knowledge of the project team's own company, and chaining the formation of strategic communities with customers from different industries, it is possible to establish the validity of new business solutions and models using new systems in the various fields while also providing new value to customers.

7.5 CONCLUSION

This chapter addressed new business solutions and models created through collaboration between a company and customers in different fields as business case studies in ICT and multimedia technology. It indicated the key factors in creating and succeeding with new markets in the fields of ICT and multimedia: of forming SCs through close collaboration and dialectical dialog with customers based on the resonance of values and mutual trust; and creating customer values based on the innovation of new knowledge with customers within SCs. The essence of customer value creation is providing customers with new values through innovation of new knowledge in SCs formed with numerous customers based on the resonance of values and mutual trust while simultaneously advancing core knowledge. In this connection, it is critical that the project leaders of the corporate organizations wield their dialectical leadership to produce new knowledge through integrative competences and then foster diverse, spiral-shaped chains of SC arrangements. To realize this, project leaders must work to harmonize the philosophies and visions of various heterogeneous customers. They must also exhibit dialectical leadership while recognizing the importance of amassing even higher levels of new knowledge through a spiral, community knowledge creating cycle within many SCs.

An image of leadership reflecting a brand-new format will be demanded of project leaders that promote customer value creation, both inside and outside the corporate organization. Against a backdrop of future multimedia and cyber companies, the most important element of the forthcoming corporate organization is the cultivation of excellent project leaders who will shoulder the burdens imposed by the corporate revolutions expected for the twenty-first century, and the promotion of SC formation.

8. Customer value creation through community-based information networks

In each chapter so far, I have used in-depth case studies to discuss the importance of knowledge possessed by individuals, groups and organizations, and the importance of creating SCs and NSCs to help companies formulate and implement strategies. In this chapter, I will describe cutting-edge ICT (Information and Communication Technology) tools to support the actions of the organization's players and accelerate knowledge innovation from the creation of SCs and NSCs. Then I would like to use case studies from strongly performing companies to discuss the mechanisms actors use to exploit fully these tools while achieving management reform and customer value creation.

With recent, rapid technological innovation in multimedia digital networked ICT, it is now possible for strategic communities within and outside a company's structure to develop businesses in a new customer value creation model, exploit the latest ICT to bolster strategic community management, and promote management characterized by speed and excellence. This chapter will point out that fully utilizing community-based information networks based on multimedia digital networked ICT makes it possible to formulate a new customer value creation business model. Aggressive ICT investment by top management to build community-based information networks (a support tool for this future network strategy) will permit business innovation based on strengthened competitiveness and enhanced customer service.

8.1 A GRAND DESIGN FOR ORGANIZATIONAL MANAGEMENT AND THE SPREAD OF INFORMATION NETWORKING

Amid dizzying changes in the business environment, aggressive application of ICT is essential in order to make future management more strategic, continually increase the productivity of individual employees, and endeavor to raise the management profile of the overall company organization. Prominent examples include recent cyber-businesses that use the Internet and companies that have brought efficiency to their business operations through the active use of intranets and extranets.

First, I will describe a grand design for the future of organizational management in the corporate structure, and the spread of information networks, which is likely to influence it significantly (see Figure 8.1).

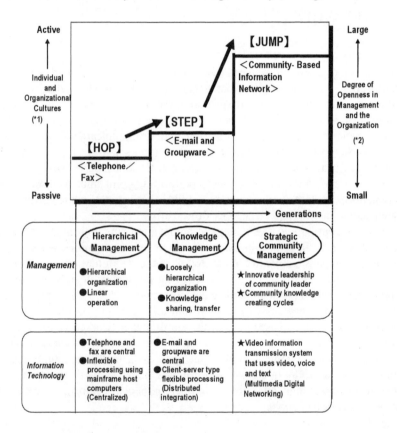

Note: (*1) Culture that facilitates the active adoption of ICT for business management, organizational evolution and innovation

(*2) Extent to which a business that openly adopts outside resources, including customers, is developed

Figure 8.1 A grand design for organization management and the spread of information networking

8.1.1   The Hop Process

Before the development of international digital networks such as the Internet, most companies accomplished their daily business operations using telephones and facsimile (fax) machines for both internal communications (between and within departments) and external (with business connections and customers). The various types of business processing performed by computers consisted mainly of centralized, fixed processes, typified by accounting and performed on general-purpose, mainframe host computers. On a time axis, this process is defined as the Hop stage.

This stage, described from an info-com technology perspective, was a world based on analog networks and low-speed transmission digital networks in which voice communications and data transmission played a central role. The organizational form was hierarchical, management-based, administrative and pyramid-shaped. Operations were carried out vertically, through lines of command. Within a company, information flowed from high to low organizational rank.

8.1.2   The Step Process

Trends of decentralization and integration through the large-scale downsizing of computer systems mark the next stage, known as Step. During this time, against a backdrop of Internet and intranet network technology, more and more companies make progress with the configuration of intra- and extra-company networks that fully exploit digital technology.

The Step process establishes an environment in which communication and collaboration play a central role through electronic mail and groupware that fully utilize digital networks. Progress in improving organizational work flow is a step above the Hop stage, and external communication and collaboration flourish.

Due to a loosely hierarchical organization in which flattening proceeds more smoothly than in the Hop stage, this stage better facilitates rapid decision-making and delegation. As for organizational management, the climate of the Step stage better lends itself to promotion of so-called knowledge management based on knowledge sharing and transfer, so more individual and organizational activity can be anticipated.

Many companies are currently moving from the Hop process to the Step process, and cases of companies actively adopting email or various types of groupware to facilitate inter-organizational communication and information sharing are common. Many companies are using methods like these with the goal of promoting company efficiency, thus taking knowledge management to the next level.

Another truth about the Step stage is that for companies that have already carried out cultural reform by adopting new tools like email and groupware, it is becoming apparent that these alone do not allow them to strengthen communication sufficiently or expedite decision-making, whether inside or outside their organizations.

In short, problems related to the one-directional, non-real-time nature of contact and consultation by email are being raised as the largest obstacle to making important judgments and decisions quickly. The reason is that the most important element in organizational communication is the empathy and solidarity between individuals that comes with face-to-face communication.

Accordingly, the next process, known as Jump, will require eradication of the stifling feeling experienced when using email or groupware that one cannot adequately convey his or her thoughts or intentions. It will also demand the ultimate communication tools to lead corporate organizational reform.

8.1.3 The Jump Process

For the business models of the future mentioned above, we can increasingly expect to see the pattern of business development by SCs inside and outside the company organization that have openly incorporated external resources, including customers. Compared with Step, this process will demonstrate flatter and more flexible organizational composition together with more open management.

In the Jump process, community leaders must exercise innovative leadership and leverage SC management to promote business strategies dynamically within and among strategic communities. Furthermore, network strategy support tools to back up this new management will be essential.

Specifically, these tools will comprise a system that supports community leaders and the sharing, inspiration, creation and accumulation of community knowledge. In concrete terms, it will be a new, multimedia image-based information network system that emphasizes interaction among individuals and the high-quality collaboration needed for decision-making by community leaders (in this book, it is referred to as a community-based information network, hereafter, community net). In this step, dynamic reform of individual cultures and overall organizational climates, and the active adoption of multimedia, digital networked ICT-based community nets, will be important to further the Jump process transition that is already underway throughout the world. It will also be important to promote dynamic businesses by making management and organizations transparent throughout the various SCs, both within and outside the organization.

8.2 THE COMMUNITY NET CONCEPT

The community net is networking that takes the one-to-one, text-based communication and collaboration represented by email and groupware to a new level to allow interactive communication and collaboration, fusing the three multimedia elements of images, voice, and text. It uses technologies spearheaded by broadband Internet, high-speed mobile communications networks and ISDN (Integrated Services Digital Network) that are continually being realized through network development and technological innovation. As for applications, interactive real-time models and storage-type, non-real-time models both exist.

	Voice	Data	Video, Voice and Data
Real-time model	- Telephone	- FAX	- Video conferencing - Videophone - Mobile videophone
Non-real-time model (Storage system)	- Voice mail	- Electronic meeting - Email - Groupware	- Video-on-demand(VOD)

▭ : Province of Community Net

Figure 8.2   The community-based information network concept

8.2.1   Use of Community Nets in the Interactive Real-time Model

The first application, as shown in Figure 8.2, is an interactive real-time model that allows simultaneous exchange of information from different locations. Typical systems are desktop personal videoconferencing systems (DTC: Desktop Video Conference) and video terminals such as videophones and mobile videophones, which are more personal, easier to use, and more suited to the general user than single-use, room-based videoconferencing systems. These systems allow interactive, real-time transmission of voice and image while supporting the sharing of textual information through, for example, two-way collaboration on a data sheet. Video terminals allow content-rich debate and rapid decision-making, overcoming the email and groupware disadvantages of neither being real-time nor facilitating easy communication of thoughts and intentions.

This enables decision-making support by community leaders and contributions to the inspiration and creation of community knowledge in know-how, expertise and conceptualization, both within and among strategic communities. The use of video communication with business contacts and customers further enables a new customer-creation business model.

8.2.2   Use of Community Nets in the Non-Real-Time Model (Storage)

The second application is storing community knowledge such as know-how and expertise, which are not real-time in nature, in storage systems from which they can be searched and extracted on demand. A typical system is video-on-demand (VOD).[1] VOD systems allow image databases (as well as voice and textual information) to be accessed and searched using the video terminals of devices such as videoconferencing systems, videophones and mobile videophones.

VOD allows knowledge and expertise (community knowledge) gained from organizational learning, which does not lend itself to text-based communication, to be stored in visual form and then shared within or among strategic communities. R&D, design, manufacturing and personnel training applications will be particularly useful.

8.3   THE COMMUNITY NET AS A NETWORK STRATEGY SUPPORT TOOL

8.3.1   Superiority of Community Nets over Groupware and Email

Mainframe host computers are a type of information system that has changed little over time. These numeric processing-based machines are positioned as management control systems for work involving routine operations. With the arrival of email and groupware, however, many companies are clearly supporting decision-making by community leaders and collaborating within and among strategic communities to promote knowledge management over older models. But our survey results show that community nets are a stronger strategic network support tool than email and groupware, in the light of the trend toward the management innovation and the customer value creation models (see Figure 8.3).

Figure 8.4 shows the results of a survey of 100 leading companies in Europe, the U.S. and Japan that are already actively using community nets in individual business processes such as planning, design, development, manufacturing, sales, physical distribution and support. It summarizes the results of a conventional and informal survey of the project leaders, group leaders, team leaders and other upper-level managers whose roles correspond to that of community leader. Using these results, we compared community nets to conventional tools such as email and groupware, and found that community nets are superior for promoting strategic community management in the company setting.

First, take the community net's superiority in bringing efficiency to business processes by expediting the decision-making of community leaders in order to promote strategic business, and by fostering the high-quality collaboration within and among strategic communities that is embodied by interaction among individuals. Take also the community net's superiority for sharing, inspiring, creating and accumulating community knowledge such as know-how and expertise, a process known as learning and further innovation.

Second, in the realm of marketing strategy, including service improvements and enhancement of after-sales service, community nets are superior in customer value creation. From the standpoint of management innovation and customer value creation, community nets can assume the job of supporting SC management and expediting innovation in company business. In section 8.4, a Japanese case study demonstrates the value of community nets as a network strategy support tool that bolsters SC management in companies.

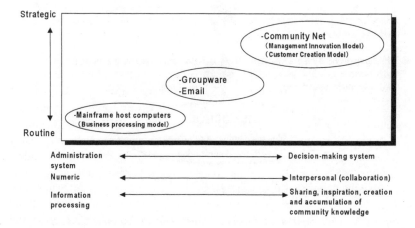

Figure 8.3   Positioning of community-based information

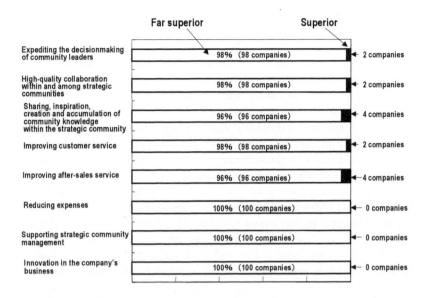

Figure 8.4   Superiority of community nets over groupware and email

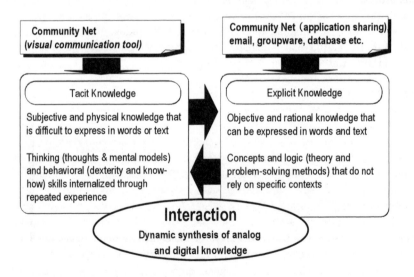

Note: Adapted from Nonaka and Takeuchi (1995)

Figure 8.5   The connection between human knowledge and ICT tools

8.3.2   Community Nets Inspiring Actors' Creativity

A company's knowledge-creating activity has a great impact on the consolidation and efficiency of explicit knowledge (including knowledge already completed as documents) such as email, all kinds of groupware, application sharing (including added functions of community nets), and databases. Visual communication through community net images, however, fuses the worlds of cyberspace and real space for dialog and collaboration on a level of tacit knowledge (such as knowledge that cannot be articulated, including people's trust, feelings, sensations and images). This can trigger new concepts, thoughts, sensations and feelings (see Figure 8.5).

Accordingly, a community net gathers, analyzes and links unevenly distributed information and knowledge, and can be considered as achieving a creative age that produces new wisdom and values, such as the creation of rich tacit knowledge and its transformation into explicit knowledge. Realistically, in the generation of corporate innovation (new products, services and business models), the tacit (analog) knowledge possessed by people, groups and organizations and the spiraling synergy (dynamic synthesis) of explicit (digital) knowledge is indispensable (Nonaka and Takeuchi, 1995). The community net is one of the ICT tools that supports this process.

8.4   CUSTOMER VALUE CREATION MANAGEMENT (IBIZA, INC.)[2]

8.4.1   The Starting Point for Customer Value Creation

IBIZA, Inc.,[3] a Japanese manufacturer of high-grade women's leather bags, won the Japan Quality Award in 1998[4] and represents Japan at the top of its industry. IBIZA has established a production system incorporating every stage of the bag-production cycle, from careful selection of the leather through manufacture, wholesaling, retailing and after-sales service. By establishing sales channels that by-pass wholesalers to deal directly with retail outlets, and by designing, manufacturing, selling and repairing its bags, IBIZA has developed a highly profitable management style that has seen a 20 percent increase in nominal profits over the past five years.

An unusual feature of the company pointed out by observers is that it manufactures and sells its original designs of 'warm, all-natural, hand-made bags' in various styles and small lots, with a lifetime guarantee. IBIZA also offers a range of substantial after-sales services to reflect company management in the customer value creation model, and to further win over its customers.

IBIZA's attention to these after-sales services, in particular, has created a new kind of business that wins intense loyalty from customers. IBIZA not only offers informational services that include sending more than 50000 direct mailings and copies of *IBIZA Magazine* to fans of the IBIZA brand each year, but also impresses each customer who purchases a bag by sending a personal letter of thanks from the company president.

8.4.2   Past Issues

The concept and value behind IBIZA come from making products that utilize nature in its original state. In practical terms, this means using animal leather that has been affected by changes in the natural environment. The fact that a piece of leather from an animal's abdomen differs greatly from one from its back makes each IBIZA product a little different from the others, despite being produced as a standardized article.

The company has been searching by trial and error for a way to communicate with its customers and salespeople about products while remaining faithful to each individual article. A similar situation exists with repairs. IBIZA products come with a lifetime guarantee. The company used to take repair requests by telephone and fax, but customers were somehow unable to get across the subtle nuances of their requests. So it was important to contrive a way for repair staff members to communicate with customers located far away as though they were holding the product in question in their hands.

As a company based on direct sales that by-passes wholesalers, IBIZA pondered methods of direct communication with its customers and dealers that Mr Yoshida (the Chairman) himself could oversee. Under the constraints of time and distance, voice and text-only systems such as telephone, fax, email, and groupware were somehow unable to solve these problems. The company needed to create a 'take a look and you'll see what I mean' environment with the feel of television or video.

8.4.3   ICT Investment for the Customer

So the company undertook a large-scale ICT investment project to construct a community net focused mainly on connecting IBIZA (its headquarters and factories), with dealers throughout the country using videoconferencing systems, videophones, or similar devices.

The combination of a company with a slogan like 'Warm, all-natural, hand-made bags', and multimedia video information distribution may seem paradoxical. From the standpoint of customer value creation and management innovation, however, it suggests an important element in IBIZA's unique brand of company management.

The company's reason for taking the plunge into ICT investment was not simply to bring efficiency to its business operations using the latest multimedia, but to innovate, share and develop the concept and value of each individual product (or 'composition' – the company goes so far as to call each individual product a composition) with employees, customers and dealers, using video information. Mr Yoshida's customer-oriented ideas and superior leadership were the basis of this investment in 'ICT for the customer'.

8.4.4   Community Networks Supporting Customer Value Creation Models

At the end of January 1996, IBIZA had built a network on its own premises and those of its dealers, and was using it to send product information, take orders and carry out maintenance. In this way, the SC comprising IBIZA and its dealers and that comprising the company and its customers were put to use. Specifically, the community net had two broad objectives. The first was to win orders by sending information on newly-created products to dealers throughout the country without delay. The second was to take orders and check inventory quickly and accurately.

In the past, methods for announcing new products were limited to exhibitions, private viewings and the semi-annual publication of a catalog, but by introducing a community net into a segment of the dealers in Japan, IBIZA was able to offer those shops detailed information on new products easily without a moment's delay, and to obtain purchase orders on the spot using bi-directional video communication. Using the community net to make product announcements eliminates decorating and traveling expenses incurred in preparing venues for conventional product announcements. Because each piece of the leather used for making bags looks different, dealers like to inspect products and get detailed inventory information when placing orders. This is another area where the community net is demonstrating its power. This application of the community net in the strategic community of IBIZA and its dealers is garnering attention as a new method of marketing through one-on-one interaction.

The application of the community net to respond properly to customers' product maintenance needs is another important business process. IBIZA products carry a lifetime warranty. Connecting IBIZA factories with dealers by means of a community net allows repair staff members to directly observe images of the repair locations, check work and respond to inquiries, permitting an accurate response to all the nuances of customer requests with no misunderstandings. There have also been cases of a product planner or factory supervisor giving a direct product demonstration to a customer at a dealer's shop over the community net, with the demonstration leading to a new order. This can be seen as a new form of SC management that includes not only IBIZA and dealers, but also customers. It consists of virtual, real-time contact between the IBIZA corporate organization and customers over the community net, and is also an example of a customer value creation model eliciting trust and security from a customer.

With strategic communities comprising a company and its dealers like that mentioned above, the sharing, inspiring, creating and accumulating of new community knowledge and the ability to earn the empathy and trust of customers through communication and collaboration are great assets.

8.4.5 Continual Sharing, Inspiration, Creation and Accumulation of Community Knowledge

As the first step in configuring a community net, IBIZA promoted SC management with customers and dealers. As the second step, to enhance the sharing, inspiration, creation and accumulation of community knowledge within the company, it built a cutting edge community net that uses product images to function as an order placement and reception system on a high-speed, wide-band, fiber-optic ATM network.[5] While promoting communication and collaboration among individuals in the SCs operating between the headquarters and factories, IBIZA also aims to store community knowledge, such as new product planning and shop expertise, in the form of video information, share it, and engage in new competency creation and innovation. See Figure 8.6 for the structure of the community net at IBIZA.

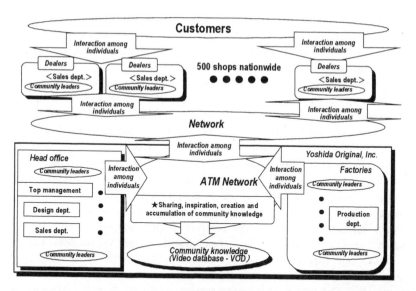

Figure 8.6   The community net at IBIZA, Inc.

Communication and collaboration using high-quality video information

To respond quickly and accurately to rapidly changing market needs and diverse customer demands, businesses must raise the level of their customer service through such means as shortening the new product development period. For these purposes as they relate to development, there is a need to carry out design, development and manufacturing-related interaction more quickly, accurately and frequently. High-quality video information used over a community net offers an environment that gives the impression of holding a consultation in the same location, even when the headquarters and factories are separate. IBIZA is aggressively carrying out communication and collaboration in the strategic community among its design, development and manufacturing departments.

On-demand searches of shop and new product information

In the past, there was a problem with product planners at headquarters being unable to convey accurately their intentions to the sales department. As a result, products often went to market without clear explanations of the ideas behind them. The new product information stored in the VOD system contains images of the products from all angles, as well as the developer's comments and concepts. A user can gain a clear understanding of information, such as the new product's features and the ideas behind its development, by merely pointing and clicking on a personal computer screen. This form of the community net permits the spectrum of information, knowledge, expertise and ideas that make up community knowledge to be stored in the form of video information and then developed through further creation and innovation.

Salespeople used to make the rounds of their assigned shops, and then include detailed written information on product displays and the situations in stores in their daily sales reports. But these reports were somehow unable to convey an image of the customers and bags in the shops, and when personnel changes brought a new salesperson, background information that could not be found in figures and written reports, such as scenes of communications with customers, would disappear with the old salesperson. Today, the newly configured VOD system enables a user to take in at a glance scenes such as a store's layout, manager and product display, and enables headquarters to give stores detailed guidance on matters such as product display changes. This mechanism is an application of the community net that makes possible constant contribution of novel, front-line sales styles that are in harmony with the new strategies of IBIZA's sales department. The goal is to enhance further customer service related to on-site sales.

Moreover, IBIZA endeavors to share knowledge with customers who use mobile videophones (third-generation mobiles) with the aim of further direct marketing with the customer (see Figure 8.7).

As a support link with the customer, IBIZA implements the policy of using mobile videophones and communicating the repair location by image with the factory. Supervisors use it as a support tool to check displays and inventory in the store, even from remote locations. Recalling IBIZA's motto of 'Whenever, wherever, whoever', we would like to thoroughly undertake direct marketing using mobile videophones as an ideal. A service currently on trial supplies images of new product and entertainment information to customers' mobile videophones, not just in-house but also to members through IBIZA's broadcasting office. Although there is the practical issue of whose names the phones would be in, it would be desirable to distribute mobile videophones to all customer members and enable them to communicate visually without the mediation of stores as soon as they have made up their minds to do so. (Mr Oguchi, general manager and director)

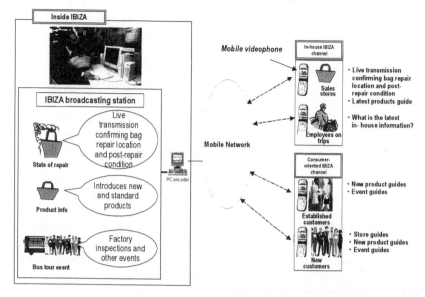

Figure 8.7   Direct marketing with customers using mobile videophones

8.5   CUSTOMER VALUE CREATION AND KNOWLEDGE INNOVATION

8.5.1   Customer Value Creation

Companies impart new values and feelings of satisfaction to customers through the provision of products and services. This concept of 'customer value creation management', which emphasizes the customer values that turn customers into repeat consumers of products and services, drives high-quality corporate management, and becomes an important focus leading to concrete results. This is a very different way of thinking from 'value-based management' (Reimann, 1989; McTaggart *et al.*, 1994; Knight *et al.*, 1998), and 'cash-flow management' (see, for example, Black *et al.*, 1998) comprising business-created cash flow, where corporate value is simply investors' profit. This 'shareholder value creation' was brought about by the shareholder-focused corporate culture prevalent in the U.S. Drucker (1954, 1985) points out the big mistake of understanding business or corporate value from a profit-pursuit perspective, and emphasizes that a company's business mission and objective is the creation of customers. In other words, even if a company provides competitive products and services, if customers do not want and pay for them, they cannot exist. The important focus is how much the customer is prepared to pay for these products and services, what they do for the customer, and whether they are right for the customer – in other words, whether they have value for the customer. Moreover, Barnard (1938, 1948) also thinks that the corporate aim is not profit but customer service, and emphasizes the importance of collaboration with the customer. Considering these as background, a company's fundamental mission is not to prioritize shareholders through a profit-pursuit model, but to focus on customer value creation as a long-term corporate management theme.

IBIZA is one of the few Japanese companies to have gained major results from the perspective of customer value creation. When companies systematically rationalize and pursue cost efficiencies for profit output, there is a tendency toward cheap customer value creation. Accordingly, maintaining committed investment for long-term customer satisfaction rather than short-term, near-future profit enables a company to create customer value and a sustainable competitive edge. At IBIZA, creating and sustaining opportunities for a range of dialogs with customers and capital investment in areas such as community net aimed at customer satisfaction is essential for building a customer base determining future business. (Such dialogs include factory inspection tours, *IBIZA Magazine*, IBIZA fair, after-sales maintenance visits, exhibitions, parties and postcards.) The essence of customer value creation is to provide goods with value to the customer at all times, share values with the customers and employees, and to confirm the companies' values by continually responding to these matters. Chairman Shigeru Yoshida firmly believes in targeting customer value creation.

Japan's handbag industry is on the verge of an era of tough competition as branded goods arrive from Europe and the U.S., and cheap goods arrive from Southeast Asia. To survive in such a climate, we are doing what other companies don't do, working earnestly with leather while adjusting to the customer's viewpoint through trial-and-error. Moreover, the company acknowledges that its aims are not simply to increase sales, but to provide a bag that pleases the customer. But the company's customer focus does not end with providing goods of value to the customer, sharing a sense of values with the employees, and building customer trust and satisfaction by continually responding to expectations. In the future, too, we would like to pursue customer satisfaction through mutual cooperation with employees, not just through satisfaction of purchase but also through their continued use of the bag.

Enhancing employee understanding by any amount will improve the company as a whole. The emphasis on the customer cannot come from the chair alone – it must come from everyone. When I was serving, salaries were low, so the 'profit distribution system' was launched with the idea of raising the salaries only of those around you. With this system of distributing to all employees the necessary amount withdrawn from the company, the amount differs depending on the ability of the employee. The department or section manager makes an evaluation depending on how much the employee has contributed to the company. Each department's share is first determined, and then the department and section heads make assessments depending on their share. Other sections are consulted to help determine employees' contributions. I have my own evaluated amount. Since ordinary income was determined as a percentage of the principal, it has never fallen very much. We have continued like this ever since the system was established. However, it isn't just about money-making – a contribution to the community was also important. We are doing a job that makes customers happy through the medium of bags. I was continually talking to customers and young people about this. (Shigeru Yoshida, Chairman)

As with IBIZA, the aims of companies involved in customer value creation are to maintain focus on a constantly changing management environment, and for employees to work together as one, and to commit themselves and always pursue new value for the sake of the customer.

8.5.2   IBIZA's Knowledge Innovation

Creating a sense of unity among employees through sharing tacit knowledge

IBIZA's corporate vision is to enable even one more person to feel 'I'm glad I have an IBIZA bag' by aligning with the customer's vision, cherishing contact with the customer and swiftly responding in good faith. At IBIZA, each employee shares the concept of this corporate vision, and works hard to create new knowledge constantly by dialectically achieving compatibility of customer values (satisfying customer needs) and management efficiency (cost efficiency). IBIZA's in-house activities involve the frequent formation of informal projects from SCs and NSCs operating cross-functionally among departments (see Figure 8.8).

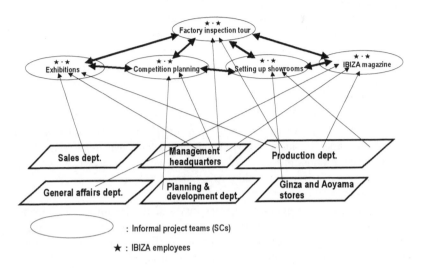

Figure 8.8   IBIZA's networked strategic communities

Young people in each post, whether at management headquarters or in the sales, production, planning and development or general affairs departments, are the mainstay of temporary project teams formed around important proposals (including factory inspection tours, in-house competitions, exhibitions and setting up showrooms). The commitment to and pursuit of these missions is a great motivation for the employees. For example, all IBIZA members participate in the in-house competition projects around the core of the young employees. At IBIZA, a bag creation competition is held once a year, and all sections take part, general affairs and sales as well as design and production. Employees who are not involved in bag production on a daily basis get to grips with production while asking questions of knowledgeable staff. This improves communication among employees naturally. The competition raises employees, understanding and interest regarding handbags and the spirit of production, and becomes a valuable opportunity to build collaborative connections across department boundaries. In other words, by producing handbags, in-house tacit knowledge is shared. The prize-winning creation is featured in *IBIZA Magazine*, along with a picture of the prize-winner holding the bag and a comment from Chairman Yoshida. As specific examples, Mr Yoshida uses short sentences to note his technology-related thoughts, such as 'an elaborate patchwork product of gathered leather', and thoughts that reflect the employee's feelings, such as 'Please maintain the gentle feel that went into this handbag'. The employees' thoughts, too, express happiness in ways such as this: 'Winning the prize for excellence is like a dream', 'My target was to perform all work myself, from pattern paper to selecting the leather and sewing. Achieving this target and even winning the prize has inspired me deeply.'

> Since we are a bag-making company, we have undertaken this competition every year throughout the company, involving even the clerical sections in order that all employees recognize the spirit of production. It brings out the employees' diverse abilities, which is positive for the company, and creates a forum for communication. Recently, we made a bag together with the clerical staff, and this gave us opportunities to talk that we don't ordinarily get. It led to good communication. The employees, too, seem to enjoy putting a shape to their own imagination. It has continued for more than ten years, and some of the creations have been made into products. (Shigeru Yoshida)

Absorbing and applying customer knowledge

Another feature of IBIZA is a continuous range of activities (including factory inspection tours, the *IBIZA Magazine*, IBIZA fairs, after-sales maintenance visits, exhibitions, parties and postcards) created through close dialog with customers. The structural concept of the community knowledge creating cycles that support IBIZA's strategic management are as follows. IBIZA is grappling internally and dialectically through the medium of diverse customer knowledge (tacit and explicit), including the management environment and customer needs, which it has consolidated in stratified SCs operating within and outside the company (including various customers) in a dynamic context. IBIZA is acquiring and expanding new customer and fixed repeater business through linking customer vision (customer value creation management), strategic targets (customer-first principle), forming NSCs, dialog (in-house collaboration and close dialog with the customer), and application (applying customer value creation management). A conspicuous practice at IBIZA is that important proposals and issues are always discussed deeply among employees relating to the questions of 'Who', 'Why', 'What', 'When', 'To whom', and 'How' posed by the IBIZA employees. At companies where customers' lifestyles and satisfaction levels vary, dialogs with customers are essential. The employees at IBIZA are continually applying new knowledge creation activities through close dialog involving customer-inclusive SCs. IBIZA's knowledge innovation is not the same as the narrowly-defined 'knowledge management' term so often used in ICT. Employees ascertain customer needs through the formation of SCs, which provide a great deal of the interaction with the customers, and the knowledge thus acquired is quickly shared by employees and returned to the customer. This mechanism accounts for a high 20 percent of the ordinary profit ratio.

NOTES

1. The system sends stored video data when a request is sent from a remote location. It is generally used for delivering entertainment such as movies and television programs to homes, but recently it has been used at universities for distance learning and at companies as a training tool.
2. When this chapter was drawn up, it received great support, and I would like to express my appreciation to Mr Yoshida, the Chairman, Mr Oguchi, general manager and director, Ms Miyagi at management headquarters, and a great many IBIZA employees. The content here has accrued from around a decade of association with IBIZA, and reflects the various human and management philosophies that I myself have learned from IBIZA. My association with IBIZA began in August 1996. At that time I was working for NTT, and IBIZA was a progressive customer that swiftly introduced and activated the PHOENIX multimedia conference system that my project team developed and commercialized. At that time, Mr Oguchi asked me whether a videophone could convey the color of a handbag. I carried out a number of trials down at the IBIZA head office, and after showing the results to the IBIZA staff, suggested that there would be ways of achieving it. As head of the project to develop new models of use for videophones, I learned from IBIZA. Later, in 1998, we introduced an image data network exploiting the world's most advanced fiber-optics with the aim of accumulating bag-making expertise through images. I was moved when Chairman Yoshida said that the investment was made for the customer. Moreover, we have recently been putting our efforts into direct marketing with customers using third-generation mobile phones. Every day, I feel that IBIZA is a continually innovative company that works hard to apply customer value creation management.
3. The company's product brand name is the name of the Spanish island of Ibiza, and it has earned 780 000 devoted customers throughout Japan. It has won numerous management awards, prominent among which are the '13th Nikkan Kogyou Shimbun Excellence in Management Award', 'The Corporate Small Business Research Center Award for the Kanto District', and 'The 1995 Saitama Prefectural Sai no Kuni Factory Designation'.
4. 'Determination of the Japan Quality Award in 1998', *Nikkei Shimbun*, 19 November 1998, p. 26. The Japan Quality Award is an annual award which recognizes excellence of management quality. Award winners are companies which are managed from the viewpoints of customers (the source of business profits) and which have a management framework to continually create new values. The purposes of this award are to innovate the whole industry, change economic structures and improve living standards in harmony with international situations. This award system was established in December 1995, and has seven central concepts. The evaluation criteria ('Japan Quality Award Criteria') have eight categories. Applying companies submit their management quality reports, and are evaluated in four stages by the reviewers. They must finally be judged by the Japan Quality Award Committee.
5. 'Product Information Sending and Receiving System Configuration (IBIZA: former company name is Yoshida Original)', *Nikkei Sangyo Shimbun*, 18 February 1998, p.3 (the text of this article also appeared in *Nikkan Kogyo Shimbun* and *Nihon Kogyo Shimbun*).

9. The innovative leadership of the community leader

Leadership is about setting corporate direction, motivating and inspiring actors (Hooper and Potter, 2000), and leading continuous organizational learning and innovation. Leadership in a knowledge-based organization is most important because new products and business arise out of the inspiration of knowledge from the actors themselves and the boundaries between actors. What enables this process is the leadership of the actors (Popper and Lipshitz, 2000). Important attributes of SCs and NSCs include an organization's skills and expertise in constantly stimulating knowledge sharing, and inspiring, creating and accumulating community knowledge (as shown in Figure 2.3), which is a vital issue in promoting knowledge management and innovation. When knowledge creation and thus innovation is a crucial issue, community leaders must devote time and attention to activities in the community knowledge creating cycle, such as new products and service development and other important business issues. Community leaders must also manage many actors (such as knowledge workers) with specialized expertise and skills, and become role models of the desired behavior for knowledge workers (Pan and Scarbrough, 1998; Burtha, 2001). Leadership in a knowledge-based organization is thus of great importance, and the different leadership styles and roles of instructors, coaches, servants, stewards, mentors and others who encourage, motivate and support knowledge workers to learn have been recognized as appropriate for leading a knowledge-based organization (Maccoby, 1996; Marquardt, 2000).

In this chapter, I will discuss the leadership that corporate top and middle management should adopt in industries where the competitive environment changes rapidly. Over the past ten years, I have derived numerous new frameworks from in-depth qualitative studies at the business workplace on the question of thinking and action from the perspective of top and middle management leadership regarding 89 new products, services and new business processes.[1] In this book, I use the term 'innovative leadership' to describe the essential leadership for community leaders (defined in this book as partner companies and corporate top and middle management, including customers).

In Chapter 2, I described the strategic activity cycle as a framework related to strategy formulation and implementation. Multiple strategic activity cycles function within the company, and the aggregate of these individual strategic outcomes is reflected as corporate results. From a practice-based view of strategic management, various actors, including customers and external partners, are connected to business through these individual strategic activity cycles, and the results vary greatly depending on the formulation and implementation of the 'Who', 'Why', 'What', 'When', 'To whom' and 'How' strategies. Various practical issues exist, such as the kind of leadership actors should display in order to function successfully in a strategic activity cycle, and especially, the kind of relationships that top and middle management community leaders should have with superiors, juniors, partners and customers, and the leadership style to be assumed.

A number of core concepts have become clear from the huge database relating to leadership that I have collated through participant observation and ethnography over a long period. One element is 'value-based leadership', which comprises the elements of 'resonating leadership' and 'practical knowledge leadership'. Another element is 'dialectical leadership', comprising the four elements of dialectical management of strategy, power, time and space. The following section expands on these points.

9.1 VALUE-BASED LEADERSHIP

One element of value-based leadership is the ability of the community of leaders to build resonance of value. This arises from a uniform coherence regarding individual interpretation of strategic visions and purpose; it results from the assimilation of actors' subjectivity and values through the process of dialog. In other words, in-depth dialog enables sharing of strategic vision and aims among actors. Realistically, however, interpretations of visions and aims differ greatly from actor to actor. It is especially difficult to transform conservative actors in traditional organizations driving mainstream businesses. In these cases, community leaders need to conduct in-depth dialog, repeatedly returning to the starting points of 'Why?' and 'What are we doing this for?' Then by reaching mutual understanding of different individual interpretations and sharing and resonating values, the actors create a sense of unity on strategy formulation and implementation. It follows that community leaders must possess the leadership that drives resonance of value (Kodama, 2001) among actors. I call this the community leaders' 'resonating leadership'.

The second element of value-based leadership is the community leaders' and members' application of 'What' and 'How' to provide new value to customers through the 'resonance of value' among community leaders. Here, the process of sharing and applying high-quality practical knowledge among actors is key (Lave, 1998; Hutchins, 1991, 1995; Suchman, 1987; Brown and Duguid, 1991, 1998; Cook and Brown, 1999; Boland and Tenkasi, 1995; Tsoukas, 1997; Spender, 1992; Orr, 1996; Schon, 1983, 1987; Weick and Browning, 1986; Wenger, 1998; Wenger *et al.*, 2002). This is practical leadership that mobilizes the strategic activity cycle and community knowledge creating cycle spirally (see Figures 2.2 and 2.3). I will call this the community leaders' 'practical knowledge leadership'.

Resonating leadership and practical knowledge leadership creating new value are given the umbrella term 'value-based leadership.' Defining this term a little more specifically, elements of value-based leadership include the community leaders' ability to implement the appropriate decision-making process and derive optimum action through the creation of resonance of value and practical knowledge with the aim of creating new knowledge and providing new value to the customer by activating the function of the 'individual, specific, strategic activity cycle'. Next, I will describe the elements of resonating leadership and practical knowledge leadership separately.

9.1.1 The Resonating Leadership of the Community Leader

Community leaders who are members of, or are otherwise connected to an organization (as top or middle managers, or as independent entrepreneurs) must have the ability to ascertain swiftly and interactively their organization's external environment, technological speed, market structure and customer needs, and always clarify the vision concept of what they should and want to do to establish its competitive edge. Then community leaders must possess the power of leadership to create human networking within and outside the company, including customers, based on a clarified concept of strategy formulation regarding the vision and strategic aims (perhaps imbued with their own thinking and belief). As mentioned in Chapter 2, human networking power through specific, changing connections and networks drives dialog and collaboration with the community leaders that make up a company's core leaders (internal and external) and creates new knowledge.

To create new knowledge, it is important to build a shared sense of values and resonance regarding visions, concepts and strategic aims through constructive and creative dialog (Kodama, 2001) with internal and external community leaders. As a result, a resonance of value platform is formed among multiple community leaders, and strategic partnerships established between them. I will call the community leaders' set of strategic thoughts and behavior 'resonating leadership' (see Figure 9.1). But it is no simple matter to build a platform of resonance of value whose vision, aims and concepts aimed at new business are comprehensible to other companies. Because of this, it is necessary to conceptualize the complex business model and the issues and processes faced, and to specify and simplify to encourage other people's interest and motivation. It also becomes important to create a win–win structure for all community leaders concerning the gaining of future business. In other words, through forming SCs and NSCs, it is essential to generate core competence synergies while creating a relationship where each party reinforces the other's strengths. In order to achieve this, what becomes important is not the connection to support the partner's value chain (Porter, 1985) and the power of its value networks (Christensen, 1997), but to discover a business model that has an impact on both businesses.

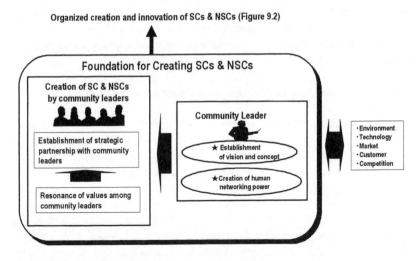

Figure 9.1 Foundation for creating SCs and NSCs

'Resonating leadership' becomes the engine behind the formation of SCs and NSCs to generate sustained innovation. In reality, community leaders must build a platform of resonance (values) at an organizational level including large numbers of community members within SCs and NSCs from several different companies. This secure platform of resonance acts as a base on which community leaders can initiate spirals of community knowledge creating cycles. Through the spiral process of this community knowledge, actors develop and sell products and services meeting customer needs, repeatedly improve quality, and repeat the improvement and new product development in a spiral pattern. The sequenced innovation process of this community knowledge results in the provision of sustained value creation and the achievement of the community leaders' business aims (see Figure 9.2)

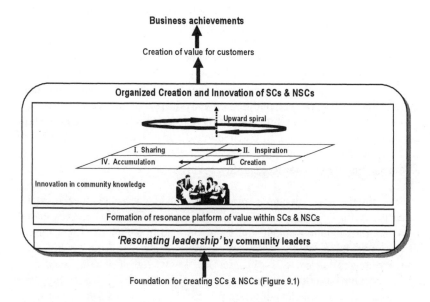

Figure 9.2   Organized creation and innovation of SCs and NSCs

9.1.2   The Practical Knowledge Leadership of the Community Leader

In a business context, 'knowledge' springs from competitiveness (Kogut and Zander, 1992; Starbuck, 1992; Nonaka and Takeuchi, 1995; Grant, 1996a, 1996b; Teece, 1998). When carrying out real business activities, however, dynamic knowledge (the knowing process), or knowing the actual implementation process, is more important than knowledge (knowing that) itself, which is static. The dynamic acquisition and application of actors' knowledge is an especially important element from the perspective of the practice-based view of strategic management described in Chapter 2.

Many scholars perceive 'knowledge' from the following perspective. Knowledge is acquired through deliberate activity as actors' past experience in a variety of contexts (Schutz, 1932). As with Ryle's (1949) articulation of 'knowing that' and 'knowing how', 'know-how' differs from 'know-what',

and is defined as the 'particular ability to put know-what into practice'
(Brown and Duguid, 1998, p.91). Ryle (1949) also mentions that someone
with very little medical knowledge cannot become an excellent surgeon, but
carrying out excellent surgery is not the same as possessing medical
knowledge. Schon (1983), moreover, said that 'Our knowing is in our
action'. What is highlighted here in Schon's important observation is the
essential role of human agency in knowledgeable performance. In the same
way, Maturana and Varela (1998) mention 'Knowing as effective action',
'All doing is knowing', and 'Knowing is doing'.

Furthermore, from the perspective of both corporate structure and
individuals, actors are understood to act knowledgeably as a routine part of
their everyday activity. Actors are always purposeful and reflexive, and
routinely monitor and coordinate their own thoughts and actions and those
of relevant parties (actors within and outside the organization, including
customers and partners) while constantly acting practically to create human
networks. The social and physical contexts in which their activities are
constituted are also important. Giddens and Pierson (1998) define actors'
action as 'immense knowledgeability involved in the conduct of everyday
life'.

For practitioners, dynamic practical knowledge as applied in daily
activities is the most important. From the perspective of a 'practice-based
view of strategic management' too, as mentioned in Chapter 2, the origin of
the driving force of the 'strategy activity cycle' and the 'community
knowledge creating cycle' is the practical knowledge leadership possessed
by actors. So what is the nature of the 'practical knowledge leadership' that
demonstrates this 'practical knowledge?'

The origin of the notion of practical knowledge can be traced to the
ancient Greek philosopher Aristotle's *Nichomachean Ethics* (Aristotle,
1980). The notion of the human activity of practice also originated in
ancient Greece. Aristotle's practical knowledge affords a valuable insight
regarding leadership among practitioners in the current business
community. So why Aristotle? I have pondered this during more than 20
years in the workplace, and have ascertained that business activities are the
practical application of study and innovation. Are the theoretically analytical
and positivist strategies and organizational theories that rigorously exclude
thoughts and action based on actors' subjectivity and sense of values
appropriate for today's businessperson? Of course, this is not to doubt the
importance of natural science based on positivist-derived universal laws
which themselves draw on theoretical description and analysis of facts
arising from objective observation, nor the logical positivism in the
engineering field (I am also a specialist in electronics and ICT). From the
nineteenth century onward, however, a great deal of modern scholarship has

emphasized the scientific and positivist approach, and this has come to overshadow the philosophical, ideological, interpretive, and especially the practical Aristotelian approaches of a large number of informed thinkers.

Recently, however, well-informed philosophers and historians have been suggesting the importance of Aristotelian thinking for its potential to provide actors with the creativity and innovative thinking that does not exist in scientific rationalism, and to impart the insights of practical knowledge that differ from the mechanistic orthodoxy that has dominated the social sciences (Toulmin, 1990; MacIntye, 1985). The field of political science (Beiner, 1983; Flyvbjerg, 2001), moreover, acknowledges the importance of executing political judgment on the basis of practical wisdom. The field of education (Halverson, 2004) also suggests the importance of benefiting from the application of practical wisdom, and cultivating actors possessing practical knowledge leadership. This practical wisdom is Aristotle's concept of '*phronesis*', described below.

Recent developments in management theory have suggested a shift from the scientific to the professional model (Bennis and O'Toole, 2005) that emphasizes a balance between science and application. One of the cornerstones of their focus on application is practical knowledge, and I believe that *phronesis* is one of the important elements of this.

According to Aristotle, there are three intellectual virtues, the possession of which, along with the possession of moral virtues, will enable an individual to achieve *eudaimonia* (well-being). As a first virtue, there is scientific knowledge (*episteme*), which consists of deduction from basic principles. Scientific knowledge corresponds to universal, objective knowledge through theoretical analysis. As a second virtue, there is craft knowledge (*techne*), which is about how to make things. In other words, craft knowledge is the skill and expertise needed to make things, applying technology and other forms of practical knowledge and skill. As a third virtue, there is practical wisdom (*phronesis*), which deals with both universals and particulars. *Phronesis* is knowing what is good for human beings in general as well as having the ability to apply such knowledge to particular situations. Practical wisdom (*phronesis*) can be thought of as practical knowledge that an actor can use to optimize the decision-making process and behavior in response to intermittently situations.

Phronesis includes the virtue of theoretical excellence aiming at the correct strategic targets, and is also a methodology that expediently accomplishes strategic aims on this basis. This means that people possessing practical wisdom excel in thought, either in whole or in part. According to Aristotle, *phronesis* is neither learning nor technology. In other words, regarding the good and bad of people's circumstances, it is knowledgeable attitudes and behavior in practical circumstances that do not lose sight of the truth. This means that *phronesis* is people seeing through to the true nature of things and accomplishing practical actions correctly, skillfully and adaptably. For current business activities, within the various contexts that change over time, when executing individual, specific problem points, issues and strategic aims, actors place emphasis not only on rigorous theoretical thinking and action through logical analysis, but also on optimally and accurately judging those intermittently occurring circumstances and correctly achieving the strategic aims. This is surely the meaning of the concept of *phronesis*. With this process, even if an unpredictable range of issues and problems between organizations occur, actors improvise (Weick, 1995) to find the best method and deal with it appropriately.

Again, *techne* can be thought of as both 'craft knowledge' and 'practical knowledge', but there is a crucial difference between craft knowledge as production and practical wisdom as action. *Techne* refers strictly to activities with limits that skillfully draw out and exploit the potential of nature and materials. In other words, *techne* at that time was not transforming nature and manufacturing through high-grade, high-performance engineering, as in today's modern technology, but knowledge that harmonized and adapted to nature, and displayed the utmost use of those products. For Aristotle, craft knowledge was ultimately subordinate to *phronesis*, because in human affairs the moral virtues and practical knowledge go together (Tsoukas and Cummings, 1997). In Aristotle's words (1144a 18), 'It is impossible to be practically wise without being good'. Therefore practical wisdom involves knowing the right values and being able to put them into practice in concrete situations.

Tsoukas and Cummings (1997) seek to return to Aristotle, in particular his views on practical knowledge and narrative rationality (Brown and Duguid, 1991; Orr, 1996; Suchman, 1987; Hutchins, 1991; Schon, 1983; Tsoukas, 1997), reconnecting means and ends, facts and values, and his teleological understanding of the world relevant for practitioners today (Ackoff, 1981a; Mangham, 1995; Mulligan, 1987; Van de Ven and Poole, 1995), in an attempt both to inform current developments in management theory and to provide impetus and inspiration for further thinking in these areas. Nonaka and Toyama (2005) incorporate the concept of *phronesis* in their knowledge-creating theory, and propose that *phronetic* leadership is important for leaders who drive knowledge creating activities as strategy.

Realistically, a company's strategic activity is not determined entirely by strategy formulation and implementation from objective and logical analysis but, as explained in Chapter 2, actors repeat strategy formulation and implementation through the trial and error of daily practical activity. Analytical strategy theories based on positivism have come to exclude the practical processes of people acting on a micro scale. As mentioned in

Chapter 1, however, in the modern business community, where the rapid technological change of industry crossover and new e-business is accelerating, actors must optimize and skillfully take on a range of issues (including complex power and political issues within and outside the organization, complex relationships with customers, and diverse and constantly changing business models) that logical analytical methods alone cannot solve. The actor's practical activities to realize Chapter 6's complex joint venture business and customer value creation business described in Chapters 7 and 8 were none other than this 'practical knowledge leadership'. Practical knowledge, the source of behavior and application of actors both physically and mentally equipped becomes the motive power to drive the strategy activity cycle and the community knowledge creating cycle correctly and appropriately (see Figure 9.3). Acquisition of high-quality practical knowledge and the superior practical knowledge leadership it is based on are essential for the top and middle management that make up the community leaders of the twenty-first century company.

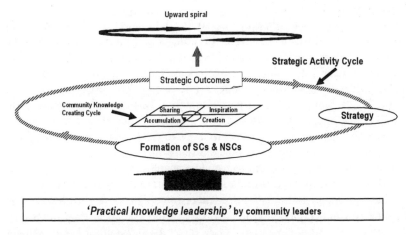

Figure 9.3   Practical knowledge leadership

9.2   THE DIALECTICAL LEADERSHIP OF THE COMMUNITY LEADER

Superior practitioners have clearly achieved a rich sense of balance. Many people such as this can be described as 'people with a range of abilities', 'people with the ability to integrate', or 'people with the ability to see the whole picture'. That master of American literature, F. Scott Fitzgerald, wrote the following in his 1945 novel *The Crack-Up*: 'Before I go on with this short history, let me make a general observation – the test of a first-rate intelligence is the ability to hold two opposed ideas in the mind at the same time, and still retain the ability to function (p. 69)'. This is certainly dialectical thinking. Moreover, Kanter (2001, p.288) says that leaders successful in net business possess in common the dual elements of intellectual or analytic skills (cognitive intelligence) plus intuitive or empathic skills (emotional intelligence). Gardner (1999) is thinking along similar lines with 'multiple human intelligences', and Amabile (1992, 1996) mentions that actors and organizations need both intrinsic and extrinsic motivation to achieve creativity and innovation. So what kind of thoughts and behavior should community leaders equipped with these contrasting elements and abilities display? I will give the name 'dialectical leadership' to the following four elements used by community leaders to drive dialectical management.

9.2.1 Dialectical Management of Strategy: The Synthesis of Efficiency and Creativity

As a first important element regarding the dialectical leadership that synthesizes the different behaviors of leadership's dominant dualities, the community leaders in the SCs and NSCs use integrative competences. They exhibit strategic leadership as directors based on integrated, centralized leadership, which can produce both long-term and short-term strategy, focus on the big picture as well as urgent issues, and perform efficiently and with certainty. However, they also exhibit 'creative leadership' based on the autonomous, decentralized leadership that can produce creative thinking and behavior among community members (Figure 9.4).

Community leaders in top and middle management must achieve long- and short-term strategic aims related to the operation of current mainstream business by demonstrating strategic leadership efficiently and with certainty. To do this requires the essential leadership elements to drive the exploitation activities of the strategic activity cycle (cycle B) in Figure 3.1. Community leaders do not aim to manage employees and work, but rather to strengthen strategy formulation and implementation through learning as a result of daily improvement and reform activities (by, for example, upgrading product versions and quality control) using strategic leadership.

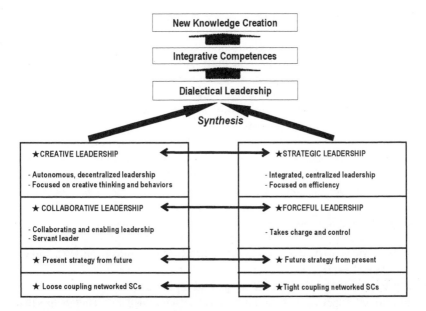

Figure 9.4   Dialectical leadership

Moreover, in deliberate strategy as well as long- and short-term strategic aims, community leaders in each department demonstrate strategic leadership, and challenge breakdowns in the current situation. Another important duty for community leaders is to transform the organization incrementally (or radically) (Popper and Lipshitz, 2000; Politis, 2001; Sadler, 2001; Paul et al, 2002; Conger and Kanungo, 1998). Moreover, community leaders must create new meaning for subordinates regarding current and future work, and transform their values, conditions and behavior.

Further, the top management team community leaders must possess and demonstrate opposing leadership elements simultaneously, as mentioned above. This is 'creative leadership'. To demonstrate creative leadership, the long- and short-term strategic aims regarding future business development must be implemented creatively and flexibly. These are the leadership elements necessary to drive the exploration activity of strategic activity cycle A (see Figure 3.1). It is not necessary, however, for the top management teams of community leaders to implement exploration activity themselves (part of this, however, also exists in a top management with entrepreneurial vitality that is full of new ideas and imagination), but rather it is important to support this kind of creative business development environment among middle and lower-level management community leaders. Top management must build firm trust with the middle management team to help the latter demonstrate emergent or entrepreneurial strategy (Kodama, 2003a, 2003b) based on creativity and imagination aimed at new business development. Top management must also constantly monitor exploration activity and manage resource distribution and decision-making processes, and the middle management community leaders themselves must display autonomous, decentralized leadership to their subordinates, and enhance their new concepts and creativity.

Thus community leaders require leadership that simultaneously displays the conflicting elements of efficiency and creativity in corporate activities. The pursuit of efficiency requires the ability to solve problems or find optimal solutions through the analytical or structural approach. The pursuit of creativity, on the other hand, requires actors to cultivate the ability to grasp unseen elements, imagine and predict, and temporarily investigate using an interpretative or process approach. Lester and Piore (2004) suggest that both the analytical and interpretive processes are important for actors in the product development workplace. Drucker (2003) says that innovation is at once a numerical analytical activity and a perceptual observation activity. Nonaka and Takeuchi (1995) cite product development case studies to show that subjective tacit knowledge and objective explicit knowledge are both important for incremented activities. Meanwhile, Lewis *et al.* (2002) report that a balance of a number of paradoxes is required for successful product development. They clarify the frequent but ambiguous calls for subtle control: effective managers provide strong leadership to keep teams focused and on schedule, while empowering team members to foster motivation and creativity. Moreover, Kodama (2005b, 2005c) suggests the importance of improvisation and dialectical thought as the ideal means of project manager leadership in industries subject to rapid market changes. O'Reilly and Tushman (2004) emphasize that general managers manage ambidextrous organizations and simultaneously display ambidextrous leadership oriented to both established business and innovation. In any case, opposing modes exist within corporate strategy formulation and implementation, and community leaders require the ability to manage them simultaneously.

9.2.2 The Dialectical Management of Power: Push-and-Pull Power Balance and Synthesis

What leadership should top and middle management and community leaders display within and outside the organization in order to sustain competitive superiority? Needless to say, community leaders must have the power to consolidate people and the entire organization. The top-down, leadership-only, bureaucratically organized structure that dominated in the days of the mass-production business model has fallen out of favor in the current knowledge-based society. In the twenty-first century company, it has become important to pursue operational efficiency systematically while generating knowledge innovation from uncertainty and diversity. In other words, knowledge possessed by people and corporations is the source of competitiveness, and this knowledge disperses among actors or across the boundaries between actors within and outside the organization, including customers. So how to integrate this value-laden knowledge? And in order to do this, how to activate the people and organizations possessing diverse knowledge? And what should the leadership be like in order to effect this? These are all important issues.

As Kotter (1999) suggests, leadership formulates vision and strategy, and concentrates actors' knowledge with the aim of implementing this strategy. Moreover, leadership empowers actors to achieve vision, and having the power to overcome difficulties in order to achieve this is essential. Kotter (1982, 1988, 1990) emphasizes the importance of the two axes of vision and network. To achieve new business as a vision, it is important to build a human network of SCs and NSCs within and outside the company, including customers. This formation of vision from transformational leadership (Kotter, 1988; Tichy and Devanna, 1986; Bennis and Nanus, 1985) is especially important at top management level, and both top and middle management have a large role to play in network formation.

Moreover, transformational leadership affords different insights from the top-down elements for implementing leadership and duties (requiring pull-type leadership that draws subordinates upward) as a traditional leadership style. Transformational leadership empowers actors and motivates them to achieve visions. The subordinate actors display their own leadership and can implement their own business while collaborating with others. The community leaders inspire new power in the subordinates (this requires push leadership, encouraging the subordinates and creating a sense of purpose).

Transformational leaders are constantly questioning the present solutions, thinking differently, and encouraging creativity and innovation. They relate to each actor personally, treating each as an individual with distinct needs and abilities. This type of leadership inspires followers to overcome their own self-interest for the good of the organization (Burns, 1978; Popper and Lipshitz, 2000; Politis, 2001; Sadler, 2001; Paul *et al.*, 2002).

Although there is a great deal of established research regarding leadership theory, I have gained the following insights through field research into significant leadership behavior of top and middle management community leaders (see, for example, Kodama, 2005b). This is the element relating to the push and pull power balance and synthesis of community leaders' leadership. Specifically, community leaders not only exhibit their 'forceful leadership' as directors who can take charge and control community members, but also become listeners, recipients and collaborators based on 'collaborative leadership' (Chrislip and Larson, 1994; Bryson and Crosby, 1992), empowering community members through enabling leadership and enhancing intrinsic motivation (Osterlof and Frey, 2000) among community members in their knowledge creation activities.

So the contradictory elements of leadership have two compatible aspects. 'Forceful leadership' as a top-down leadership style is necessary not just for community leaders, but also as an element of transformational leadership that simultaneously empowers actors as knowledge workers. Their role as supporters and followers providing ongoing collaboration and support for the community so that it can pursue dreams and a sense of accomplishment for the business and its vision requires the element of 'servant leadership' (Greenleaf, 1979; Spears, 1995). Collaborative leadership is a 'leaderless orchestra' (Seifter and Economy, 2001), where each actor displays individual leadership and undertakes duties within the range of his or her competence, while also implementing overall strategy through collaboration with others. At this time, community leaders have to exploit the abilities of subordinates to the maximum as either followers or servants (see Figure 9.4).

9.2.3 Dialectical Management of Time

I discussed the element of timing synthesis in Chapter 3, section 3.1. Timing synthesis comprises the thought processes of community leaders for making decisions on timing-specific elements as they formulate and implement strategy. Specifically, this is timing strategy that thinks from the future to the present and the present to the future. Community leaders need the kind of leadership where two types of strategic activity cycle co-exist in the corporate strategy process (see Figure 3.1). Realistically, this kind of leadership is required of top management in each division, from general supervisor to senior executive management and above. The CEO, for example must consider timing strategies from the two perspectives of optimizing each business domains focusing on the company overall and optimizing the business domains as an integrated whole to create synergy. Meanwhile, top management community leaders entrusted with empowerment have to formulate timing strategies within their own well-prepared business domain to optimize the department, and also optimize the company as a whole. An important point of focus here is how best to create the organization and management needed to formulate and implement future strategies.

As I discussed in Chapters 3 and 4, organizations that promote future strategies (exploration activity: Cycle A) must be either completely different from mainstream businesses that implement current strategies (exploitative activity: Cycle B), or else form cross-functional teams (CFTs) to execute established business while promoting new future strategies. According to O'Reilly III and Tushman (2004), to succeed with innovation that fully coexists with exploratory and exploitative business, it is desirable to build new organizations distinct from existing organizations, and to place these organizations under a traditional management structure. O'Reilly III and Tushman name these 'ambidextrous organizations'. New organizations with new corporate features have the same functions (including R&D, financial affairs, marketing and sales) as established organizations, and are subject to conflict and discord with established organizations. In order for existing and new organizations to share management resources and specialist knowledge, however, the general manager of the ambidextrous organizations displays ambidextrous leadership to manage both organizations (see pattern A in Figure 9.5). Some American and European companies have successfully set up functions in this way to generate innovation.

With some exceptions, companies tend to create new organizations with the same set of functions as the existing organizations, and few companies have free use of resources. Specifically, as seen in Chapters 3 and 4, methods exist for building new project or informal task teams possessing development functions and activating the established organization's resources for other functions, such as sales, finance and marketing. These methods naturally give rise to discord and conflict with the established organization. The ability of top management to build a vision and gain the empathy of actors in the established organization for future strategy through 'story telling' is the key to successful innovation. Thus community leaders must display resonating leadership and build resonance of value as well as create SCs and NSCs that cross established and new organization boundaries (see Pattern B in Figure 9.5). This building of SCs and NSCs compares with the building of ambidextrous organizations mentioned above, and enables a strong linkage (Cycle A to Cycle B) between future and current strategy. The reason is that both new and former organizations have the potential to turn discord and conflict to collaboration through resonance of value as a result of building SCs and NSCs (Kodama, 2003b).

I have described above how implementing dialectical timing strategies requires the construction of new organizations and the fusion of new and established organizations through strong linkage of vision, strategy and organizational culture. The leadership of the community leaders who drive this dialectical management of time is an important element of dialectical leadership (see Figure 9.4).

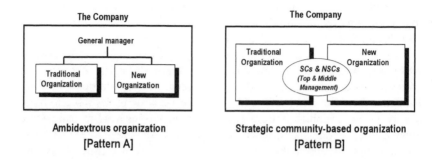

Figure 9.5   Organizational structure to achieve strategy of timing

9.2.4   Dialectical Management of Space

In Chapter 3, section 3.1, I discussed the element of synthesizing strategies of space. These include the thought process of the community leaders in making decisions on connection and network-specific elements when formulating and implementing strategy. Aiming to create new knowledge, community leaders somehow build constantly-changing specific connections and networks. An important focus here regarding the community leaders' construction of NSCs is the leadership to achieve the creation of tightly and loosely coupled NSCs.

The creation of tightly coupled networked SCs builds a strong value chain through a vertically integrated business model. In the auto industry, for example, sharing of in-depth knowledge and integration was implemented among automakers and component makers through the building of tightly coupled NSCs with the component manufacturers' *keiretsu* network (see, for example, Amasaka, 2004). Chapters 1 and 5 described the creation of tightly coupled NSCs constructed between Japan's NTT DoCoMo and other mobile phone companies, and NEC, Fujitsu, and other mobile handset manufacturers. In order to integrate SC knowledge distributed within and outside the company, actors closely integrate individual SCs through strong network ties, and embed diverse knowledge in NSCs. These kinds of tightly coupled NSCs function well under fixed conditions, such as cases of strong mutual dependency on inherent technology or expertise, or of strong interdependency relating to actors' mutual adjustments and creation of meaning during technology development. When it becomes necessary to develop technological maturity and standardization, integrate new technology or different technology that has transcended its specialist field, or reduce costs, however, established, tightly coupled NSCs can be a burden.

Accordingly, community leaders must rebuild NSCs that have strong ties to the rigid value chain (Porter, 1985) and value network (Christensen, 1997) according to environment, market or technology changes. Community leaders must act as needed to change strongly tied NSCs to loosely coupled NSCs, or else to break up the SC itself (Kodama, 2006). Otherwise, the company will face such problems as path-dependency (Rosenberg, 1982; Hargadon and Sutton, 1997), competency traps (Levitt and March, 1988; Martines and Kambil, 1999), and core rigidities (Leonard-Barton, 1992, 1995).

Among the loosely coupled NSCs, community leaders must try to form multiple SCs within and outside the company, and undertake peripheral domain and inter-industry boundary scanning. The reason, as indicated in Chapter 1, is the increasing necessity for the ICT community and knowledge-based society to fuse and integrate different technologies that cross industry boundaries, and to construct diverse business models. It follows that community leaders must positively promote such joint trials as incubation and consortiums with customers and potential partners from outside the company that have crossed over from other industries. At this time, however, in-house SCs (those that influence their own company's decision making) are coupled with weak network ties, and the search for and monitoring of future business opportunities comes from these weakly integrated SCs. So community leaders will accurately ascertain the timing of business opportunities and convert weak ties to strong in order to achieve knowledge integration and realize new products and business models.

The development of new business models for mobile phone services, as described in Chapters 1 and 5, involves the implementation of 'strategies of space'. These are the dynamic creation of new business models with temporal changes drawn from different industries and fields as a result of actors' skillful management of tightly and loosely coupled NSCs. NTT DoCoMo is an example of a pioneering business model appearing first in Japan that incorporated other industries as a result of developing a new technology platform for its mobile e-commerce service that initiated the i-mode service, credit-card loaded mobile handsets, and accounts settlement and authentication.

In this way, community leaders are building constantly changing specific connections and networks and maintaining the existence of network ties with the opposing features of tightly and loosely coupled NSCs (see Figure 9.6) in order to respond to environmental change or else create their own new environment. To achieve this, community leaders must be equipped with the elements of practical knowledge leadership based on diverse experience and practical ability. The leadership of the community leaders

driving dialectical management of space is an important element of
dialectical leadership (see Figure 9.4).

I have described above the dialectical leadership elements of community
leaders, where community members, including community leaders, are able
to participate in decision-making in the SCs and NSCs and to enhance
mutual understanding and strengthen links within the SCs and NSCs. As a
result of integrative competences through dialectical leadership (dialectical
management of strategy, power, time and space), community leaders and
other members can create knowledge of strategic, creative new product and
service developments, business concepts and reforms in business processes
(see Figure 9.4). This image of leadership is not the old type that was
buttressed by a rigid hierarchy but a new model of leadership aimed at
achieving innovation. This new type of leadership – dialectical leadership –
is oriented simultaneously toward the growth of individuals and of groups or
organizations in the form of SCs and NSCs.

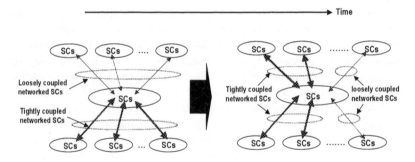

Figure 9.6   SCs and NSCs to achieve strategy of space

9.2.5   Dialectical Thinking and Action

In this section, I will suggest a number of implications regarding community
leaders' dialectical thinking and action. Community leaders promote
dialectical dialog and discussion among leaders in order to cultivate a
thorough understanding of problems and issues. By communicating and
collaborating with each other, leaders become aware of the roles and values
of each other's work. As a result, community leaders are able to transform
the various conflicts that have arisen among them into constructive conflicts
(Robbins, 1974). This process requires leaders to follow a pattern of
dialectical thought and action in which they ask themselves what sorts of
actions they themselves would take, what sorts of strategies or tactics they
would adopt, and what they could contribute toward achieving the
businesses and the innovation of new knowledge creation. And in achieving

new knowledge creation and innovation, the community leaders promote the sympathy and resonance of the leaders' values, and the combined synergy among the leaders results in the high levels of integrative competences that enable actors to realize this new product and service development and form new business models. In another sense, it can be seen that community leaders have used the resonance of values among leaders in their SCs and NSCs and their leadership synergy based on dialectical management to form high levels of integrative competences, which in turn have generated a solid network of SCs.

Dialectical management is based on the Hegelian approach, which is a practical method of resolving conflict within an organization (Benson, 1977; Peng and Nisbett, 1999; Seo and Creed, 2002; Nisbett, 2003). Dialectic first appeared in the question and answer technique of Socrates in Plato's theory of ideas, and it became an approach to thinking about things that was discussed and developed throughout the history of philosophy. Hegel, in particular, considered dialectic to be a law of dynamic development in cognition and existence (1967), and proposed the thesis, antithesis and synthesis scheme of logic and the concept of '*Aufheben*' (to sublate). Through Marx (1930, 1967), Engels (1952) and others, Hegel's ideological dialectic developed into a practical methodology. They applied dialectic approaches to civilization and culture, produced thesis and antithesis with respect to propositions and historical fact, and proposed a methodology by which problem areas and conflicts were resolved through the synthesis of the two sides. The synthesis then became a new thesis, both of these were denied by antithesis, and this produced another new thesis in a never-ending process; the process of historical development was proposed to be an eternal process.

To explain dialectics in a somewhat simpler way produces the following image. There are cases, for example, in which new ideas emerge from dialogs with community members who have opposing ideas. This is the basis of dialectical dialog. Debate is based on binominal opposition between black and white or good and bad, and one side tries to win out over the other. However, this is fundamentally different from dialectical dialog. While allowing one person to think one way and another person to disagree and think another way, people attempt, as far as possible, while engaged in this face-to-face opposition, to produce a new viewpoint built on the strengths of each other's ideas and to search for a truth that results in propositions on a higher dimension. This sort of constructive, productive, creative dialog is called dialectical dialog. The process of sublating and integrating ideas at this time in order to reach a higher dimension of conflict resolution is the process of dialectical dialog. It is the process of synthesizing a certain thesis and the antithesis that negates this thesis to give birth to a new proposition approaching a higher truth. In this way, diverse and contradicting knowledge (equivalent to the various SCs in the case studies presented in this book) is synthesized, and the effect of synthesis is the integrative competences of dynamically generating new knowledge.

Dialectic, on the other hand, was also applied to organization theory, stimulating discussion based on absolute truths or morality in devotion to the community (Benson, 1977) or in the process of corporate reform (Van de Ven and Pool, 1995). In addition, Peng and Nisbett (1999) and Peng and Akutsu (2001) analyzed the psychological reactions that could easily result from two apparently contradictory propositions and, while risking crises that allow contradictions, proposed 'dialectical thinking in a broad sense' that judged parts of both propositions to be correct.

This sort of dialectical thought has also been reported in literature on institutional theory or strategic alliances. For example, Seo and Douglas Creed (2002) used a dialectical perspective to provide a unique framework for understanding institutional change that more fully captures its totalistic, historical and dynamic nature, as well as fundamentally resolves a theoretical dilemma of institutional theory. Furthermore, Das and Teng (2000) draw on dialectics to provide an explanation for the instability and failure of strategic alliances, and Rond and Bouchikhi (2004) also explore the characteristics and contributions of a dialectical lens in understanding inter-organizational collaborations in strategic alliances.

Nisbett (2003) points out that Orientals in their thinking tend to look out over the forest as a whole while Westerners stare at the large trees, and he maintains that, in contrast to the analytical thought of Westerners, Orientals exercise a dialectical thinking that is all-inclusive or holistic. Though the actors that appear in the various pragmatic boundaries (Carlile, 2004) in these cases are Japanese, with some from the U.S. and Asia, they strive to promote dialectical dialog and thinking among themselves concerning such issues as technology, business models, tasks, and cross-cultural matters. In order to address issues concerning the sort of complex business models, technology integrations and customer value creation involved in these cases and to tackle the conflicts produced by numerous contradictions among various organizational cultures in multiple corporations and organizations, the holistic thinking of the actors, in a practical sense, provides us with valid understanding.

NOTES

1. Over the past ten years, I have researched the development of 89 new products, services and businesses. Among these, 25 have derived from the participant observation technique (McCall and Simmons, 1969), 42 from the ethnography technique (Hammersley and Atkinson, 1995;

Spradley, 1979), and the remaining 27 from collected law data from detailed interviews. To begin with, I collected detailed law data relating to management generally in the workplace from in-depth interviews and informal dialogs regarding daily discussions, meeting patterns, and the daily work situation for top management, middle management and staff. I have also gathered a large amount of data from both formal and informal meetings and dialogs with customers and external partners. Among these, I have classified data concerning directly and indirectly related elements of actors' leadership, such as the thoughts and behavior of actors as a result of shared visions and strategic aims, shared values, teamwork, collaboration, motivation trust, discord and conflict. I then categorized that data according to a grounded theory (Glaser and Strauss, 1967) and assigned it to established theory. Finally, I derived this book's core framework of community leaders' best means of leadership.

10. Managerial implications and conclusion

In this book, I have discussed a framework for companies creating new knowledge from a perspective of knowledge creation, strategy, organization, corporate culture and leadership through in-depth case studies. The starting point of a company's strategic management is dynamic practical activity on the basis of knowledge creation. Actors apply strategy through trial and error on the basis of high-quality practical knowledge. Knowledge, moreover, is a dynamic process that is deeply embedded in experience through actors' thoughts and behavior, and is accumulated in individual actors and groups through reflective and sustained practice. The strategic activity and community knowledge creating cycle models have been presented as a theoretical framework creating a company's knowledge innovation.

The infrastructure (or concept platform) of these two models comprises the formation of SCs and NSCs. A large number of actors pursue discrete, specific business (individual strategic activity cycles) within and outside the company, and build dynamic human networks, including customers and external partners, in a constantly changing dynamic context on a micro-level involving the questions 'Who', 'Why', 'What', 'When', 'To whom' and 'How'. Then the actors formulate and implement strategy while creating specific, constantly changing SCs and NSCs.

SC and NSC formation refers to the strategy and process of creating, sharing and utilizing knowledge required by the corporation to acquire ongoing competitiveness. Knowledge creation occurs (or is facilitated) through SCs and NSCs comprising actors who exchange knowledge from their different specialties. In other words, I believe that actors of various management layers from a company and its partners (including customers) are the primary players involved in knowledge creation activities leading to innovation through strategic and conscious community networking. Specifically, as shown in these case studies, it is possible to enhance business efficiency by consolidating in an organization and sharing individual and corporate knowledge assets through the formation of SCs and NSCs, while also creating value or innovation in the form of creative new products, new services and new business models embodying the new knowledge.

Throughout this book, I have mentioned important elements of management for corporate leaders and managers as the formation of SCs and NSCs gives rise to innovation. The conditions required for top and middle management to achieve their aim of innovation is an issue for managers and executives in companies (including multinationals) both in Japan and elsewhere.

One element that is important for middle management is the need to understand and share context in the various SCs and NSCs. The presence of a common vision, common interests, common merits, common knowledge (Carlile, 2004) and common ground (Bechky, 2003) among the actors is essential. A range of friction and conflicts occurs especially at the boundaries of knowledge differences among actors with disparate job functions and technical expertise or skills (Brown and Duguid, 2001).

People generally have fixed thought worlds (Dougherty, 1992). As well as a fixed world view formed from past social and life experience, their job function as a businessperson, practical knowledge as a professional with business experience, and world view as tacit knowledge are deeply embedded in the actors' bodies and psyche. As the degree of novelty and uncertainty of the targeted strategy content rises, the differences arising in the actors' thought worlds provide fertile ground for mutual friction and conflict (Carlile, 2002, 2004). The transformation of actors' established knowledge becomes necessary, especially with innovation involving new product development from completely non-traditional concepts; conversely, the path-dependent, established knowledge deeply embedded in individual actors is hindered by the novelty of challenge. Because of this, mutual understanding is first necessary for actors to create new meaning from in-depth dialog. In the context of Japanese trends, the existence of '*Ba*' (Nonaka and Konno, 1998) becomes necessary.

Ba (translating literally as 'place') is a place, space or facility where individuals interact to exchange ideas, share knowledge, conceptualize and create new knowledge in tacit as well as explicit forms. Bennett reported as follows after examining the Japanese character that represents *Ba* (Bennett, 2001): 'The top right character represents the sun; the character on the left the earth; and the bottom right (loosely) rays of light falling to the ground'. Thus to the Western (though not the Japanese) eye, *Ba* is interpretable as a 'place of illumination', where sun and earth unite and enlightenment happens'.

Therefore, *Ba* is a place offering a shared context. Knowledge needs a context to be created, as it is context-specific. The context defines the participants and the nature of the participation. It is social, cultural and even historical, providing a basis for one to interpret information, thus creating meaning and becoming knowledge. *Ba* is not necessarily just a physical space, or even a geographical location or virtual space through ICT (Information and Communication Technology), but a time–space nexus as much as a shared mental space. Any form of new knowledge can be created regardless of the business structure, as *Ba* transcends formal business structures. Participating in a *Ba* means transcending one's own limited perspective or boundary and contributing to a dynamic process of knowledge creation. In an SC, members (including customers) who possess different values and knowledge consciously and strategically create a *Ba* in a shared context that is always changing. They continually create new knowledge and competencies as a new *Ba* by merging and integrating a single *Ba* or multiple numbers of *Ba* both organically and from multiple points of view.

It is important for actors to form *Ba* and closely share and understand the new meaning created from the novelty of new challenge. Expressions such as 'I agree with the general remarks', 'There are problems with the details' and 'I am against it!' are frequently heard among actor dialogs at the business workplace. Individual, specific discussions such as these arise: 'I understand now what we have to do. But specifically, who will do it, and in what way?' This kind of discussion cannot avoid creating inter-organizational friction and conflict, but it provides the opportunity to face the challenge of new issues and channel the friction and conflict over current problem areas into innovation. Community leaders at each management layer, including top management, must positively and earnestly deal with issues such as 'Where and why do we have friction and conflict?' and 'What are the problem points and solution methods for this?' through in-depth dialog among actors. Easy compromise over friction and conflict, including relations with external partners, is taboo, since it could nip a company's new growth in the bud.

Since friction and conflict are the motive power of corporate growth, actors need to find common viewpoints by establishing common interests (such as the common advantages to each organization) among actors, building win-win relationships with and motivating partners, and clarifying common strategic aims and specific action plans. Moreover, boundary objects such as creating images of target objects (including prototypes), computer simulation tools and process maps (see, for example, Star, 1989), can become tools for promoting creative and productive dialog among actors. It also becomes important to clarify in-house decision-making processes and rules relating to significant subjects in the company, such as present and future priorities, what kind of action should be taken now, and what investments must be made for the future, and these must be shown to the employees to be fair. If this does not happen, the actors collaborating in-house cannot create trust and a sense of unity with each other. By establishing common ground among actors (Bechky, 2003) and transforming mutual friction and conflict to 'creative abrasion' (Leonard-Barton, 1995) and 'productive friction' (Hagel III and Brown, 2005), it becomes possible to establish trust among actors and promote collaboration. Kanter (2001, p.231) says that 'Conflict is seen as creative and something to be encouraged (instead of disruptive and something to be avoided)'.

The second important element is that of value shared among actors as resonance value (Kodama, 2001). This includes the element of community practice (Wenger et al, 2002) as one element of the strategic community. This aspect promotes mutual learning within the community by gaining an understanding of mutual contexts among members and resonating value, and continually generates new knowledge. In the strategic community, the community membership and the community leader who becomes the center of activities are gradually established, and these people dynamically produce the context in which they work toward fulfilling the community's mission, which involves the development of new products, services and business models. Community members create new knowledge by learning from one another and sharing.

The first point of *Ba* and the second of community of practice are complementary. *Ba* is space–time in which actors dynamically create new meaning amidst changing contexts, and philosophical thinking that promotes knowledge innovation. Community of practice, meanwhile, is the space–time of shared context with the purpose of taking the time to learn gradually from each other in a stable relationship. These two common points have as their origin the 'knowledge possessed by people', and in *Ba* and the community of practice, the trust among actors rests on these platforms. Of course, innovation could not take place without the process of actors' daily learning and the shared dynamic context. It follows that the elements of *Ba* and community of practice are also important elements of the strategic community's thinking.

The third important element is that of improvisation when forming SCs and NSCs. Like musicians playing jazz or surfers riding waves, middle managers must make practical decisions spontaneously so that they do not miss out on business opportunities (Weick, 1987; Kanter, 2001; Brown and Eisenhardt, 1998). In competitive environments characterized by rapid change, especially, actors must respond to the environment while simultaneously creating a new environment themselves. In order to do this, the actors must deliberately improvise.

The fourth important element is the need for middle managers in SCs and NSCs to embrace a deep commitment as they aim to realize their vision. The fifth important element concerns innovative leadership mentioned in

Chapter 9. Of course, these prerequisites are not easy for middle management as community leaders to bring about. However, as middle managers engage in repeated practice and self-examination, including organizational learning from failures, the required skills and know-how become deeply embedded in the actors themselves as tacit knowledge and experience.

Next, I would like to talk about elements that are important for top management. The first of these elements is the provision of support for the activities of middle managers in SCs and NSCs. To this end, appropriate executives in the top layer need to promote opportunities for dialog with middle managers while also gaining a deep understanding of middle managers' business activities and providing constructive support. The second important element is to build a leadership team as a top management team involving the layers of managers and to perform in a proactive manner. In their endeavors to develop new products, services and business models, they need to put their heads together with middle management to share their knowledge closely, and to consider such matters as decision-making on the distribution of resources and important issues concerning the development process.

The third important element is the creation of a heterogeneous organization that creates innovation. This involves creating a new organizational culture that does not exist for actors from established, traditional organizations by forming a mixed team of actors with heterogeneous, diverse abilities and actors with backgrounds in different specialist fields. The ideal way is to gather talented people possessing different ideas from inside and outside the company. Then the different teams and organizations breathe new life into the established, traditional organizations, and bring fresh stimulation and inspiration (and, of course, friction) to large numbers of actors directed towards breaking the mold, reform, creation and innovation.

Innovation arises from SCs and NSCs where actors from heterogeneous cultures and specialist fields mingle. At these SCs and NSCs as 'junctions of ideas' (Johansson, 2004), actors must courageously transcend knowledge boundaries among themselves. It follows that top management should create and sustainably support the kind of organizational environment that is promoted by creative and productive dialog with established, traditional organizations.

The fourth important element concerns the provision of a knowledge creation environment (Prahalad and Ramaswamy, 2004). The provision of an ICT environment, especially in global business, is essential for supporting the formation of SCs and NSCs and for efficiently promoting business activities (Kodama, 1999a). In addition, top management should review personnel and remuneration systems and actively adopt reward systems as ways to maintain continuously the positive results of middle managers engaged in knowledge sharing, integration and creation within corporations spanning formal organizations.

To sum up, through in-depth case studies and theoretical discussion, I have presented one view of the capabilities of leading companies in the knowledge-based society for strategic community-based organizations that form dynamic innovative processes in SCs and NSCs. One of the keys to producing innovation in a knowledge-based society is for companies organically and innovatively to network different knowledge created from the formation of a variety of SCs within and outside the company, and acquire integrative competences through innovative leadership by community leaders in an organization's management layers, including top and middle management.

In a business environment fraught with uncertainty and turbulent change, it is becoming increasingly important for corporations to create new knowledge for their goals (through knowledge integration and transformation) by dynamically forming or rebuilding SCs and then networking them. I will use the term 'strategic community-based organization' to refer to a corporate entity that employs a dynamic process promoting the continual, conscious formation of SCs among internal corporate organizations and partners (including customers), and which becomes a driving force that generates incremental, discontinuous or radical innovation. Finally, I will present the following three issues for study as elements leading to successful knowledge innovation.

The first element concerns the leadership behavior of managers in all layers of the corporation, including top management, as it relates to SC and NSC formation. Leadership behavior is defined as the pattern or style of leadership, or the philosophy or actions, adopted by the managers as community leaders. As discussed in Chapter 9, this indicates the importance of value-based leadership as an element of resonating leadership and practical knowledge leadership, and of dialectical leadership as a driver of dialectical management, with its elements of strategy, power, strategy of time and strategy of space. Community leaders must balance the two elements of value-based and dialectical leadership simultaneously. This is the thinking of community leaders' innovative leadership.

The second element concerns the strategy-making process, the timing of SC formation, and the resource distribution process that the corporation should adopt (details analyzed at individual business or project levels) (Mintzberg, 1978; Christensen and Raynor, 2003). The balancing of deliberate and emergent strategies is an important issue for avoiding such areas as path-dependency (Rosenberg, 1982; Hargadon and Sutton, 1997), competency traps (Levitt and March, 1988; Martines and Kambil, 1999), and core rigidities (Leonard-Barton, 1992, 1995).

The third element is an issue that concerns knowledge integration itself: how to integrate SCs possessing diverse knowledge of value dispersed both within and outside the company. Here, dialectical management may offer a practical solution (Kodama, 2005b). In the future, it is probably necessary to establish and verify a theoretical framework through dynamic process studies into more examples of product, service or business development.

Superior core technologies continue to disperse and reform throughout the world in such advanced business fields as IT, e-business, content provision, electronics and biotechnology. Under the conditions of existing hierarchical organizations and closed autonomous systems developed in the age of mass production, many companies are having an increasingly hard time controlling innovation on their own. With a style of management that uses NSCs to integrate diverse aspects of advanced knowledge, however, knowledge dispersed both within and outside organizations (including customers) in an open environment is likely to become increasingly important for corporations aiming to generate competitive advantage in a networked economy. It remains essential, however, for corporations to maintain and continue to nurture the original core competences that are difficult for other parties to imitate (see for example Hamel and Prahalad, 1994).

In the knowledge-based society of the twenty-first century, the diverse knowledge that people possess (not only knowledge related to technology) will become a source of valuable products, services and new business models that turn into new competitive advantages. I believe that strategic, community-based organizations will provide valuable fresh insights to many practitioners aiming to realize innovation (Proctor, Tan and Fuse, 2004).

Bibliography

AERA (1999), *Gendai no Shozo* (in Japanese), 31, 62–6.

Ackoff, R.L. (1981a), *Creating the Corporate Future*, New York: Wiley.

Ackoff, R.L. (1981b), 'The Art and Science of Mess Management', *Interface*, 11(1), 20–26.

Adams, J.S. (1980), 'Interorganizational Processes and Organization Boundary Activities', in Staw, M.M. and Cummings, L.L. (eds) *Research in Organizational Behavior*, 2, Greenwich: JAI Press, 321–55.

Akita Sakigake Shimbun (1999) 'Decision Taken to Select Yajimamachi, Akita Prefecture, as Leading-Edge Model Region', 25 December, p.8.

Albrinck, J., Horney, J., Kletter, D. and Neilson, G. (2001), 'Adventures in corporate venturing', *Strategy and Business*, 22:119–29.

Allen, T.J. (1977), *Managing the Flow of Technology*, Cambridge, MA: MIT Press.

Amabile, M.T. (1992), 'Motivational Synergy: Toward New Conceptualization of Intrinsic and Extrinsic Motivation in the Workplace', *Human Resource Management Review*, 3, November, 185–201.

Amabile, M.T. (1996), *The Motivation for Creativity in Organizations*, Cambridge, MA: Harvard Business School Press.

Amasaka, K. (2004), 'Development of "Science TQM", a New Principle of Quality Management: Effectiveness of Strategic Stratified Task Team at Toyota', *International Journal of Production Research*, 42(17), 3691–706.

Anand, B. and Khanna, T. (2000), 'Do Firms Learn to Create Value? The Case of Alliances', *Strategic Management Journal*, 21(3), 295–315.

Ansoff, H. I. (1965) *Corporate Strategy*, New York: McGraw Hill.

Aristotle (1980), *The Nicomachean Ethics*, translated with an introduction by David Ross, Oxford: Oxford University Press.

Asahi Shimbun (1999), 'Your Home to Double as Clinic: Diagnosis by Videophone, Drugs Delivered to Your Door', 25 December, 19.

Atkinson, P. and Hammersley, M. (1994), 'Ethnography and Participant Observation', in Denzin, N.K. and Lincoln, Y.S. (eds), *Handbook of Qualitative Research*, Thousand Oaks, CA: Sage Publications, 105–17.

Baldwin, C.Y. and Clark, K.B. (2000), *Design Rules, Vol. 1: The Power of Modularity*, Cambridge, MA: MIT Press.

Barabasi, A. (2002), *Linked: The New Science of Networks*, Cambridge, MA: Perseus Books Group.

Barber, B. (1983), *The Logic and Limits of Trust*. New Brunswick, NJ: Rutgers University Press.

Barley, S.J. and Tolbert, P.S. (1997), 'Institutionalization and Structuration: Studying the Links Between Action and Organization', *Organization Studies*, 18(1), 93–117.

Barnard, C.I. (1938), *The Function of the Executive*, Cambridge, MA: Harvard University Press.

Barnard, C.I. (1948), *Organization and Management*, Cambridge, MA: Harvard University Press.

Barney, J.B. (1986), 'Organizational culture: can it be a source of sustained competitive advantage?', Academy of Management Review, 11(3), 656–65.

Barney, J. (1991), 'Firm Resources and Sustained Competitive Advantage', *Journal of Management*, 17(3), 99–120.

Bartlett, C. and Ghoshal, S. (2000), *Transnational Management*, Boston, MA: McGraw Hill.

Bazerman, M.H. and Neale, M.A. (1992), *Negotiating Rationally*, New York: Free Press.

Bechard, R., Goldsmith, M. and Fesselbein, F. (1996), *The Leader of the Future*, San Francisco: Jossey-Bass Inc.

Bechky, B.A. (2003) 'Shared meaning across occupational communities: The transformation of understanding on a production floor', *Organization Science*, 14(1), 312–30.

Beiner, R. (1983), *Political Judgement*, London: Methuen and Co.

Bennett, R. (2001), '"Ba" as a determinant of Salesforce Effectiveness: An Empirical Assessment of the Applicability of the Nonaka–Takeuchi model to the Management of the Selling Function', *Marketing Intelligence and Planning*, 19(3), 188–99.

Bennis, W.G. and Nanus, B. (1985), *Leaders: The Strategies for Taking Charge*, London: HarperCollins.

Bennis, W.G. and O'Toole, J. (2005), 'How Business Schools Lost Their Way', *Harvard Business Review*, May, 96–104.

Benson, J. (1977), 'Organization: A Dialectical View', *Administrative Science Quarterly*, 22, 221–42.

Black, A., Wright, O. and Bachman, J.E. (1998), *In Search of Shareholder Value*, London: Pitman.

Block, Z. (1982), 'Can Corporate Venturing Succeed?', *Journal of Business Strategy*, 3(2), 21–34.

Block, Z. and MacMillan, I.C. (1993), *Corporate Venturing: Creating New Business within the Firm*, Cambridge, MA: Harvard Business School Press.

Bogner, W.C. and Bar, P.S. (2000), 'Making Sense of Hypercompetitive Environments: A Cognitive Explanation for the Persistence of High Velocity Competition', *Organization Science*, 11(2), 212–26.

Boland, J. and Tenkasi, R. (1995), 'Perspective Making and Perspective Taking: Implications for Organizational Learning', *Organization Science*, 9(3), 605–22.

Boyett, I. and Currie, G. (2004), 'Middle Managers Moulding International Strategy: An Irish Start-Up in Jamaican Telecoms', *Long Range Planning*, 37(1), 51–66.

Bradach, J. and Eccles, R. (1989), 'Price, Authority, and Trust: From Ideal Types to Plural Forms', in Sewell, W. (ed.) *Annual Review of Sociology*, 15, Palo Alto, CA: Annual Reviews, 97–118.

Brown, J.S. and Duguid, P. (1991), 'Organizational Learning and Communities-of-Practice', *Organization Science*, 2(3), 40–57.

Brown, J.S. and Duguid, P. (1998), 'Organizing knowledge', *California Management Review*, 40(3), 90–111.

Brown, J.S. and Duguid, P. (2001), 'Knowledge and Organization: A Social–Practice Perspective', *Organization Science*, 12(6), 198–213.

Brown, S.L. and Eisenhardt, K.M. (1979), 'The Art of Continuous Change: Linking Complexity Theory and Time-Paced Evolution in Relentless Shifting Organizations', *Administrative Science Quarterly*, 42, 1–34.

Brown, S.L. and Eisenhardt, K.M. (1995), 'Product Development: Past Research, Present Findings, and Future Directions', *Academy of Management Review*, 20(2), 343–78.

Brown, S.L. and Eisenhardt, K.M. (1998), *Competing on the Edge*, Boston, MA: Harvard Business School.

Bryson, J. and Crosby, B.C. (1992), *Leadership for the Common Good: Tackling Public Problems in a Shared-Power World*, San Francisco: Jossey-Bass.

Buckley, W. (1967), *Sociology and Modern Systems Theory*, New Jersey : Prentice-Hall.

Buckman, R. (2003), *Building a Knowledge-Driven Organization*, New York: McGraw Hill.

Burgelman, R.A. (1983a), 'A Model of the Interaction of Strategic Behavior, Corporate Context, and the Concept of Strategy', *Academy of Management Review*, 8(6): 61–70.

Burgelman, R.A. (1983b), 'A process model of internal corporate venturing in the diversified major firm', *Administrative Science Quarterly*, 28: 223–4.

Burgelman, R.A. and Välikangas, L. (2004), 'Managing Internal Corporate Venturing Cycles', *Sloan Management Review*, 46(4), 26–34.

Burns, M. (1978), *Leadership*, London: Harper and Row.

Burt, R. (1997), 'The Contingent Value of Social Capital', *Administrative Science Quarterly*, 42(2), 339–65.

Burt, S. (1992), *Structural Holes: The Social Structure of Competition*, Cambridge, MA and London: Harvard University Press.

Burtha, M. (2001), 'Working with leaders', *Knowledge Management Review*, 4(5), 7–8.

Business Week (2000), 'Feature Article on i-mode', 17 January, www.businessweek.com/2000/00_03/b3664016.htm, 27 July 2006.

Busoni, S. and Prencipe, A. (2001), 'Exploring the Links between Products and Knowledge Dynamics', *Journal of Management Studies*, 38, 1019–35.

Busoni, S. Prencipe, A. and Pvatt, K. (2001), 'Knowledge Specialization, Organizational Coupling, and the Boundaries of the Firm: Why do Firms Know More Than They Make?' *Administrative Science Quarterly*, 46, 1185–200.

Carlile, P. (2002), 'A Pragmatic View of Knowledge and Boundaries: Boundary Objects in New Product Development', *Organization Science*, 13(4), 442–55.

Carlile, P. (2004), 'Transferring, Translating, and Transforming: An Integrative Framework for Managing Knowledge Across Boundaries', *Organization Science,* 15(5), 555–68.

Chakravarthy, B. (1997), 'A New Strategy Framework for Coping with Turbulence', *Sloan Management Review*, 38, 69–82.

Chandler, A.D. (1962), *Strategy and Structure: Chapters in the History of American Enterprise*, Boston, MA: MIT Press.

Chesbrough, H. (2003), *Open Innovation*, Boston, MA: Harvard Business School Press.

Chia, R. (2004), 'Strategy as Practice: Reflection on the Research Agenda', *European Management Review*, 1(1), 29–34.

Chrislip, D. and Larson, C. (1994), *Collaborating Leadership: How Citizens and Civic Leaders Can Make a Difference*. San Francisco: Jossey-Bass.

Christensen, C.M. (1997), *The Innovator's Dilemma: When New Technologies Cause Great Firms to Fail*, Boston, MA: Harvard Business School Press.

Christensen, C.M. and Raynor, M. (2003), *The Innovator's Solution*, Boston, MA: Harvard Business School Press.

Clark, K.B. (1985), 'The Interaction of Design Hierarchies and Market Concepts in Technological Evolution', *Research Policy*, 14(2), 235–51.

Clark, K.B. and Fujimoto, T. (1991), *Product Development Performance*, Boston, MA: Harvard Business School Press.

Cohen, D. and Prusak, L. (2000), *In Good Company: How Social Capital Makes Organizations Work*, Boston, MA: Harvard Business School Press.

Coleman, J. (1988), 'Social Capital in the Creation of Human Capital', *American Journal of Sociology*, 94, 95–120.

Conger, A. and Kanungo, R. (1998), *Charismatic Leadership: The Elusive Factor in Organizational Effectiveness*, San Francisco: Jossey-Bass.

Cook, S. and Brown. J. (1999), 'Bridging Epistemologies: The Generative Dance between Organizational Knowledge and Organizational Knowing', *Organization Science*, 10(2), 381–400.

Cramton, C. (2001), 'The Mutual Knowledge Problem', *Organization Science*, 12, 346–71.

Dacin, M.T., Ventresca, M.J. and Beal, B.D. (1999), 'The Embeddedness of Organizations: Dialogue and Directions', *Journal of Management*, 25, 317–56.

Daft, R.L. and Weick, K.E. (1984), 'Toward a Model of Organizations as Interpretation Systems', *Academy of Management Review*, 9(2), 284–95.

Das, T.K. and Teng, B. (2000), 'Instabilities of Strategic Alliances: An Internal Tensions Perspective', *Organization Science*, 11(1), 77–101.

Dasgupta, P. (1988), Trust as a Commodity, in Gambetta, D. (ed.), *Trust: Making and Breaking Cooperative Relations*, New York: Basil Blackwell, 49–72.

Dataquest (1997), *Multimedia Forecast – 1997 Market Statistics*, 49.

D'Aveni, R. (1994), *Hypercompetition: Managing the Dynamics of Strategic Maneuvering*, New York: Free Press.

D'Aveni, R. (1995), 'Coping with Hypercompetition: Utilizing the New 7S's Framework', *Academy of Management Executive*, 9(3), 45–60.

Davenport, T.H., de Long, D.W. and Beers, M.C. (1998), 'Successful Knowledge Management Project', *Sloan Management Review*, Winter, 43–57.

Davenport, T.H. and Prusak, L. (1998), *Working Knowledge*, Boston, MA: Harvard Business School Press.

Day, G. and Schoemaker, P.J. (2005), 'Scanning the Periphery', *Harvard Business Review*, November, 135–48.

DiMaggio, P. and Powell, W. (1983), 'The Iron Cage Revisited: Institutional Isomorphism and Collective Rationality in Institutional Fields', *American Sociological Review*, 48, 147–60.

Dougherty, D. (1992), 'Interpretive Barriers to Successful Product Innovation in Large Firms', *Organization Science*, 3(2), 179–202.

Doz, Y. and Hamel, G. (1998), *Alliance Advantage: The Art of Creating Value through Partnering*, Boston MA: Harvard Business School Press.

Drucker, P.F. (1954), *The Practice of Management*, New York: Harper and Row.

Drucker, P.F. (1985), *Innovation and Entrepreneurship*, New York: Harper and Row.

Drucker, P.F. (2003), *The Essential Drucker: The Best of Sixty Years of Peter Drucker's Essential Writings on Management*, New York: Harper Business.

Duncan, R.B. (1972), 'Characteristics of Organizational Environmental and Perceived Environmental Uncertainty', *Administrative Science Quarterly*, 17(2), 313–27.

Duncan, R.B. (1973), 'Multiple Decision-Making Structures in Adapting to Environmental Uncertainty', *Human Relations*, 26, 110–23.

Dutton, J.E., Walton, E. and Abrahamson, R. (1989), 'Important Dimension of Strategic Issues', *Journal of Management Studies*, 26(4), 379–386.

The Economist (2002), 'Struggling with a Supertanker', 7 February.

Eden, V. and Ackevmen, E. (1998), *Making Strategy: the Journey of Strategic Management*, London: Sage.

Eisenhardt, K.M. (1989), 'Building Theories from Case Study Research', *Academy of Management Review*, 14, 532–50.

Eisenhardt, K.M. and Bingham, M. (2005), 'Disentangling Resources from the Resource Based View: A Typology of Strategic Logics and Competitive Advantage', *Managerial Decision Economics*, forthcoming.

Eisenhardt, K.M. and Brown, S.L. (1998), 'Time Pacing: Competing in Markets that Won't Stand Still', *Harvard Business Review*, March–April, 59–69.

Eisenhardt, K.M. and Martine, J. (2000), 'Dynamic Capabilities: What Are They?' *Strategic Management Journal*, 21(10–11), 1105–21.

Eisenhardt, K.M. and Santos, F.M. (2002), 'Knowledge-Based View: A New Theory of Strategy', in Pettigrew, A., Thomas, H. and Whittington, R. (eds), *Handbook of Strategy and Management*, London: Sage.

Eisenhardt, K.M. and Sull, D.N. (2001), 'Strategy as Simple Rules', *Harvard Business Review*, 79, 106–16.

Engels, F. (1952) Dialektik der Natur, Berlin, Dietz.

Fitzgerald, F.S. (1945), *The Crack–Up,* edited by Edmund Wilson, New York: J Laughlin.

Floyd, S.W. and Lane, P. (2000), 'Strategizing Throughout the Organization: Management Role Conflict and Strategic Renewal', *Academy of Management Review*, 25(1), 154–77.

Flyvbjerg, B. (2001), *Making Social Science Matter: Why Social Inquiry Fails and How it Can Succeed Again*, Cambridge: Cambridge University Press.

Ford, F.D. and Backoff, R.W. (1988), 'Organization Change In and Out of Dualities and Paradox', in Quinn, R.E. and Cameron, K.S. (eds), *Paradox and Transformation: Toward a Theory of Change in Organization and* Management, Cambridge, MA: Ballinger, 19–63.

Freeland, R.E. (2000), *The Struggle for Control of the Modern Corporation: Organizational Change at General Motors, 1924–1970*, Cambridge: Cambridge University Press.

Fuji Chimera Research Institute, Inc. (1998), *Communications and Broadcast Network Multimedia Marketing Survey Overview-98*, Tokyo: The Institute.

Fukushima Minpo Shimbun (1997), 'Kooriyama Women's University Offers Distance/Lifelong Learning Courses Featuring University Lectures over Television Monitors', 11 June, 3.

Fuller, S. (2001), *Knowledge Management Foundations*, London: Butterworth-Heinemann.

Galbraith, J.R. (1973), *Designing Complex Organizations*, Reading, MA: Addison-Wesley.

Galbraith, J.R. and Nathanson, D.A. (1978), *Strategy Implementation: The Role of Structure and Process*, St Paul, MN: West Publishing.

Gardner, H. (1999), *Intelligence Reframed: Multiple Intelligences for the 21st Century*, New York: Basic Books.

Gawer, A. and Cusmano, M.A. (2004), *Platform Leadership*, Boston, MA: Harvard Business School Publishing.

Gersick, C.J. (1994), 'Pacing Strategic Change: The Case of a New Venture', *Academy of Management Journal*, 37, 9–45.

Ghemawat, P. and Costa, J. (1993), 'The Organizational Tension between Static and Dynamic Efficiency', *Strategic Management Journal*, 14(1), 59–73.

Giddens, A. (1984), *The Constitution of Society*, Berkeley, CA: University of California Press.

Giddens, A. and Pierson, C. (1998), *Conversation with Anthony Giddens: Making Sense of Modernity*, Oxford: Blackwell Publishers Ltd.

Gladwell, M. (2000), *The Tipping Point: How Little Things Can Make a Big Difference*, New York: Little Brown and Company.

Glaser, B. and Strauss, A. (1967), *The Discovery of Grounded Theory: Strategies for Qualitative Research*, Chicago: Aldine.

Gomes-Casseres, B. (1993), *Managing International Alliances: Conceptual Framework*, Boston, MA: Harvard Business School, Note 9-793-133.

Gompers, P.A. and Lerner, J. (1999), *The Venture Capital Cycle*, Cambridge, MA: MIT Press.

Gopinath, C. and Hoffman, R.C. (1995), 'The Relevance of Strategy Research: Academic and Practitioner Viewpoints', *Journal of Management Studies*, 32(5), 575–94.

Graebner, M. (2004), 'Momentum and Serendipity: How Acquired Leaders Create Value in the Integration of High-Tech Firms', *Strategic Management Journal*, 25(8/9), 751–77.

Granovetter, M. (1973), 'The Strength of Weak Ties', *American Journal of Sociology*, 78(6), 1360–80.

Granovetter, M. (1985), 'Economic Action and Social Structure: The Problem of Embeddedness', *American Journal of Sociology*, 91, 481–510.

Grant, R. (1991), 'Resource-Based Theory of Competitive Advantage: Implications for Strategy Formulation', *California Management Review*, Spring, 114–35.

Grant, R. (1996a), 'Toward a Knowledge-Based Theory of the Firm', *Strategic Management Journal*, 17(Winter Special Issue), 109–22.

Grant, R. (1996b), 'Prospering in Dynamically-Competitive Environments: Organizational Capability as Knowledge Integration', *Organization Science*, 7(4), 375–87.

Grant, R. (1997), 'The Knowledge-Based View of the Firm: Implications for Management Practice', *Long Range Planning*, 30, 450–54.

Grant, R. and Baden-Fuller, C. (1995), 'A Knowledge-Based Theory of Inter-Firm Collaboration', *Academy of Management Best Paper Proceedings*, 38, 17–21.

Gray, B. (1989), *Collaborating: Finding Common Ground for Multiparty Problems*, San Francisco, CA: Jossey-Bass.

Gray, B. and Wood, D.J. (1991), 'Collaborative Alliances: Moving from Practice to Theory', *Journal of Applied Behavioral Science*, 27(1), 3–23.

Greenlea, R. (1979), *Servant Leadership*, New York: Paulist Press.

Grinyer, P. and McKiernan, P. (1994), 'Triggering Major and Sustained Changes in Stagnating Companies', in Daems, H. and Thomas, H. (eds), *Strategic Groups, Strategic Moves and Performance*, New York: Pergamon, 173–95.

Gulati, R. (1995), 'Does Familiarity Breed Trust? The Implications of Repeated Ties for Contractual Choice in Alliances', *Academy of Management Journal*, 38(1), 85–112.

Gulati, R. (1999) 'Network Location and Learning: The Influence of Network Resources and Firm Capabilities on Alliance Formation', *Strategic Management Journal*, 20(5), 397–420.

Guth, W.D. (1976), 'Toward a Social System Theory of Corporate Strategy', *Journal of Business*, 49(3), 374–88.

Hagel III, J. and Brown, J.S. (2005), 'Productive Friction', *Harvard Business Review*, 83(2), 139–45.

Håkansson, H. (1982), *International Marketing and Purchasing of Industrial Goods: An International Approach*, Chichester: John Wiley.

Halverson, R. (2004), 'Accessing, Documenting, and Communicating Practical Wisdom: The Phronesis of School Leadership Practice', *American Journal of Education*, 111(1), 90–121.

Hamel, G. (1996), Strategy as Revolution, *Harvard Business Review*, July–August, 69–82.

Hamel, G. (2000), *Leading the Revolution*, Boston, MA: Harvard Business School Press.

Hamel, G., Doz, Y. and Prahalad C.K. (1989), 'Collaborate with Your Competitors and Win', *Harvard Business Review*, January–February, 133–9.

Hamel, G. and Getz, G. (2004), 'Funding Growth in an Age of Austerity', *Harvard Business Review*, July–August, 76–84.

Hamel, G. and Prahalad, C.K. (1989), 'Strategic Intent', *Harvard Business Review*, 67(3), 139–48.

Hamel, G. and Prahalad, C.K. (1994), *Competing for the Future*, Boston, MA: Harvard Business School Press.

Hammersley, M. and Atkinson, P. (1995) Ethnography: Principles in practice 2nd edn, London: Routledge.

Haour, G. (2004), *Resolving the Innovation Paradox*, London, UK: Palgrave Macmillan.

Hardy, C. and Phillips, N. (1998), 'Distinguishing Trust and Power in Interorganizational Relations: Forums and Facades of Trust', in Lane, C. and Bachmann, R. (eds) *Trust Within and Between Organizations*, Oxford, UK: Oxford University Press, 64–87.

Hargadon, A. and Sutton, R. (1997), 'Technology Brokering and Innovation in a Product Development Firm', *Administration Science Quarterly*, 42, 716–49.

Hart, L.S. (1992), 'An Integrative Framework for Strategy-Making Process', *Academy of Management Review*, 17(5), 327–51.

Hayes, M.J. and Abernathy, W.J. (1980), Managing Our Way to Economic Decline, in Tushman, M. and Moore, W.L. (eds), *Readings in the Management of Innovation*, Marshfield, MA: Pitman, 11–25.

Hedlund, G. (1986), 'The Hypermodern MNC: A Heterarchy?' *Human Resource Management*, 25, 9–35.

Hegel, G.W.F. (1967), *The Phenomenology of Mind*, New York: Harper & Row.

Heide, J. (1994), 'Inter-Organizational Governance in Marketing Channels', *Journal of Marketing*, 50(5), 40–51.

Henderson, R.M. and Clark, K.B. (1990), 'Architectural Innovation: The Reconfiguration of Existing Product Technologies and the Failure of Established Firms', *Administrative Science Quarterly*, 35(1), 9–30.

Heskett, J.L., Jones, T.O., Loveman, G.W., Sasser, E.R. and Schlesinger, L.A. (1994), 'Putting the Service–Profit Chain to Work', *Harvard Business Review*, March/April, 164–74.

Hesselbein, F., Goldsmith, M., Beckhard, R. and Schubert, R.F. (1998), *The Community of the Future*, San Francisco: Jossey-Bass Inc.

Hodo, C. and Nakazono, G. (1998), 'A Behavioral Revolution Through NTT and Application of the Intranet', *Diamond Harvard Business Review*, 28 December/January.

Hofer, C.W. and Schendel, D. (1978), *Strategy Formulation*, St. Paul, Minnesota: West.

Hooper, A. and Potter, J. (2000), *Intelligent Leadership*, London: Random House Business Books.

Huff, A.S. (1990), 'Presidential Address: Change in Organizational Knowledge Production', *Academy of Management Review*, 25(1), 45–74.

Hutchins, E. (1991), 'Organizing Work by Adaptation', *Organization Science*, 2(1), 14–39.

Hutchins, E. (1995), *Cognition in the Wild*, Cambridge, MA: MIT Press.

Janis, I.L. (1982), *Groupthink*, 2nd edn, Boston: Houghton Mifflin.

Jantsch, E. (1980), *The Self-Organizing Universe*, Oxford, UK: Pergamon Press.

Jarzabkowski, P. (2004), 'Strategy as Practice: Recursiveness, Adaption, and Practice-in-Use', *Organization Studies*, 25(4), 529–60.

Jarzabkowski, P. and Searle, R. (2004), 'Harnessing Diversity and Collective Action in the Top Management Team', *Long Range Planning*, 37(5), 399–419.

Johansson, F. (2004), *The Medici Effect*, Boston, MA: Harvard Business School Press.

Johnson, G. (1987), *Strategic Change and the Management Process*, Oxford: Blackwell.

Johnson, G. Melin, L. and Whittington, R. (2003), 'Micro Strategy and Strategizing: Toward an Activity-Based View', *Journal of Management Studies*, 40(1), 3–22.

Johnson, G., Smith, S. and Codling, B. (2000), 'Micro Process of Institutional Change in the Context of Privatization', *Academy of Management Review*, Special Topic Forum, 25(3), 575–80.

Kale, P., Singh, H. and Perlmutter, H. (2000), 'Learning and Protection of Proprietary Assets in Strategic Alliances: Building Relational Capital', *Strategic Management Journal*, 21(3), 217–37.

Kanter, R.M. (1983), *The Change Masters*, New York: Simon and Schuster.

Kanter, R.M. (2001), *Evolve! Succeeding in the Digital Culture of Tomorrow*, Boston, MA: Harvard Business School Press.

Kanter, R.M., Kao, J. and Wiersema, F. (1997), *Breakthrough Thinking at 3M, Dupont, GE, Pfizer, and Rubbermaid*, London: HarperCollins Publishers, Inc.

Karmin, S. and Mitchell, W. (2000), 'Path-Dependent and Path-Breaking Change: Reconfiguring Business Resources Following Acquisitions in the U.S. Medical Sector, 1978–1995', *Strategic Management Journal*, 21(11), 1061–81.

Kim, W.C. and Mauborgne, R. (2005), *Blue Ocean Strategy*, Boston, MA: Harvard Business School Publishing.

Knight, J.A. (1998), *Value-Based Management*, New York: McGraw Hill.

Kodama, M. (1999a), 'Strategic Innovation at Large Companies Through Strategic Community Management: An NTT Multimedia Revolution Case Study', *European Journal of Innovation Management*, 2(3), 95–108.

Kodama, M. (1999b), 'Customer Value Creation through Community-Based Information Networks', *International Journal of Information Management*, 19(6), 495-508.

Kodama, M. (2001), 'Creating New Business Through Strategic Community Management', *International Journal of Human Resource Management*, 11(6), 1062–84.

Kodama, M. (2002a), 'Strategic Partnership with Innovative Customers: A Japanese Case Study', *Information Systems Management*, 19(2), 31–52.

Kodama, M. (2002b), 'Transforming an Old Economy Company through Strategic Communities', *Long Range Planning*, 35(4), 349–65.

Kodama, M. (2003a), 'Strategic Community-Based Theory of the Firms: Case Study of NTT DoCoMo', *The Journal of High Technology Management Research*, 14(2), 307–30.

Kodama, M. (2003b), 'Strategic Innovation in Traditional Big Business', *Organization Studies*, 24(2), 235–68.

Kodama, M. (2004), 'Strategic Community-Based Theory of Firms: Case Study of Dialectical Management at NTT DoCoMo', *Systems Research and Behavioral Science,* 21(6), 603–34.

Kodama, M. (2005a), 'How Two Japanese High-Tech Companies Achieved Rapid Innovation via Strategic Community Networks', *Strategy and Leadership*, 33(6), 39–47.

Kodama, M. (2005b), 'Knowledge Creation through Networked Strategic Communities: Case Studies in New Product Development', *Long Range Planning*, 38(1), 27–49.

Kodama, M. (2005c), 'New Knowledge Creation through Dialectical Leadership: A Case of IT and Multimedia Business in Japan', *European Journal of Innovation Management*, 8(1), 31–55.

Kodama, M. (2006), 'Knowledge-Based View of Corporate Strategy', *Technovation*, 26(12), 1390-406.

Kodama, M. (2007), 'Innovation through Boundary Management: Case Study in Reforms at Matsushita Electric', *Technovation*, 27(1), forthcoming.

Kodama, M., Tsunoji, T. and Motegi, N. (2002), 'FOMA Videophone Multipoint Platform', *NTT DoCoMo Technical Journal*, 4(3), 6–11.

Kogut, B. and Zander, U. (1992), 'Knowledge of the Firm, Combinative Capabilities and the Replication of Technology', *Organization Science*, 5(2), 383–97.

Kotter, J. (1982), *The General Manager*, New York, NY: Free Press.

Kotter, J. (1988), *The Leadership Factor*, New York, NY: Free Press.

Kotter, J. (1990), *A Force for Change: How Leadership Differs from Management*, NY: Free Press.

Kotter, J. (1999), *Kotter on What Leaders Really Do*, Boston, MA: Harvard Business School Press.

Lalle, B. (2003), 'The Management Science Researcher Between Theory and Practice', *Organization Studies*, 24(7), 1097–114.

Lane, C. and Backmann, R. (1998), *Trust Within and Between Organizations: Conceptual Issues and Empirical Applications*, Oxford, UK: Oxford University Press.

Larsson, R., Bengtsson, L., Henriksson, K. and Sparks, J. (1998) 'The Interorganizational Learning Dilemma: Collective Knowledge Development in Strategic Alliances', *Organization Science*, 9(3), 285–305.

Lave, J. (1998), *Cognition in Practice*, Cambridge, UK: Cambridge University Press.

Lave, J. and Wenger, E. (1990), *Situated Learning: Legitimate Peripheral Participation*, Cambridge, UK: Cambridge University Press.

Lawrence, P. and Lorsch, J. (1967), *Organization and Environments: Managing Differentiation and Integration*, Cambridge, MA: Harvard Business School Press.

Lawrence, T.B., Phillips, N. and Hardy, N. (1999), 'Watching Whale-Watching: A Relational Theory of Organizational Collaboration', *Journal of Applied Behavioral Science*, 35, 479–502.

Leifer, R. and Mills, P. (1996), 'An Information Processing Approach for Deciding upon Control Strategies and Reducing Control Loss in Emerging Organizations', *Journal of Management*, 22, 113–37.

Leonard-Barton, D. (1992), 'Core Capabilities and Core Rigidities: A Paradox in Managing New Product Development', *Strategic Management Journal*, 13, 111–25.

Leonard-Barton, D. (1995), *Wellsprings of Knowledge: Building and Sustaining the Sources of Innovation*, Boston, MA: Harvard Business School Press.

Lester, R. and Piore, M. (2004), *Innovation*, Boston, MA: Harvard University Press.

Levitt, B. and March, J.B. (1988), 'Organization learning', in Scott, W.R. and Blake, J. (eds), *Annual Review of Sociology*, 14, Palo Alto, CA: Annual Reviews, 319–40.

Lewis, M., Dehler, G. and Green, S. (2002), 'Product Development Tensions: Exploring Contrasting Styles of Project Management', *Academy of Management Journal*, 45(3), 546–64.

Lewis, W.M. (2000), 'Exploring Paradox: Toward a More Comprehensive Guide', *Academy of Management Review*, 25(6), 760–76.

Lipnack, J. and Stamps, J. (1997), *Virtual Teams*, New York: John Wiley and Sons, Inc.

Locke, K. (2001), *Grounded Theory in Management Research*, Thousand Oaks, CA: Sage.

Luhmann, N. (1979), *Trust and Power*, Chichester, UK: John Wiley and Sons.

Maccoby, M. (1996), 'Resolving the Leadership Paradox: The Doctor's Dialogue', *Research Technology Management*, 39(3), 57–9.

MacIntye, A. (1985), *After Virtue*, 2nd edn., London: Duckworth.

Mainichi Shimbun (1997), 'Sign Language Interpreting and Videophones at Five Police Boxes in Tokyo', 3 June, 13.

Malone, T. and Crowston, K. (1994), 'The Interdisciplinary Study of Coordination', *ACM Computer Surveys*, 26, March, 87–119.

Mangham, I. (1995), 'MacIntyre and the Manager', *Organization*, 2(2), 181–204.

March, J. (1991), 'Exploration and Exploitation in Organizational Learning', *Organization Science*, 2(1), 71–87.

Markides, C. (1995), *Diversification, Re-focusing and Economic Performance*, Cambridge, MA: MIT Press.

Markides, C. (1997), 'Strategic Innovation', *Sloan Management Review*, 38(2), 9–23.

Markides, C. (1998), 'Strategic Innovation in Established Companies', *Sloan Management Review*, 39(3), 31–42.

Markides, C. (1999), *All the Right Moves: A Guide to Crafting Breakthrough Strategy*, Boston, MA: Harvard Business School Press.

Marquardt, M.J. (2000), 'Action Learning and Leadership', *The Learning Organization*, 7(5), 233–40.

Marshall, C. and Rossman, G. (1989), *Designing Qualitative Research*, London: Sage.

Martines, L. and Kambil, A. (1999), 'Looking Back and Thinking Ahead: Effects of Prior Success on Managers' Interpretations of New Information Technologies', *Academy of Management Journal*, 42, 652–61.

Marx, K. (1930), *Critique of Political Economy*, New York: Dutton.

Marx, K. (1967), *Writing of Young Marx on Philosophy and Society*, New York: Dutton.

Maturana, H.R. and Varela, J.F. (1998), *The Tree of Knowledge: The Biological Roots of Human Understanding*, revised edn, Boston, MA: Shambhala Publications.

McCall, G.J. and Simmons, J.L. (1969), 'The nature of Participant Observation', in McCall, G.J. and Simmons, J.L. (eds), *Issues in Participant Observation: A Text and Reader*, Reading, MA: Addison-Wesley, 1–5.

McTaggart, J.M., Konters, P.W. and Mankins, M.C. (1994), *The Value Imperative*, New York: The Free Press.

Mezias, J., Grinyer, P. and Guth, W.D. (2001), 'Changing Collective Cognition: A Process Model for Strategic Change', *Long Range Planning*, 34(1), 71–96.

Miles, M.B. and Huberman, A.M. (1984), *Qualitative Data Analysis*, Beverly Hills, CA: Sage.

Mintzberg, H. (1973), *The Nature of Managerial Work*, New York: Harper and Row.

Mintzberg, H. (1978), 'Patterns in Strategy Formation', *Management Science*, 24, 934–48.

Mintzberg, H. (1987), 'The Strategy Concepts I: Five Ps for Strategy', in Caroll, G.R. and Vogel, D. (eds), *Organizational Approaches to Strategy*, Cambridge, MA: Ballinger.

Mintzberg, H., Ahlstrand, B. and Lampel, J. (1998), *Strategy Safari: A Guided Tour Through the Wilds of Strategic Management*, New York: The Tree Press.

Mintzberg, H., Raisinghani, D. and Theoret, A. (1976), 'The Structure of "Unstructured" Decision Processes', *Administrative Science Quarterly*, 21(2), 246–75.

Mintzberg, H. and Walters, J. (1985), 'Of Strategies Deliberate and Emergent', *Strategic Management Journal*, 6, 257–72.

Mizukoshi, N. (2002), *Century of Innovation: I* (in Japanese), Tokyo: NHK Publications.

Morgan, G. (1981), 'The Systematic Metaphor and its Implications for Organizational Analysis', *Organization Studies*, 2, 23–44.

Mulligan, T. (1987), 'The Two Cultures in Business Education', *Academy of Management Review*, 5(3), 491–500.

Nadler, D.A., Shaw, R.B. and Walton, A.E. (eds) (1995), *Discontinuous Change: Leading Organizational Transformation*, San Francisco, CA: Jossey-Bass.

Nadler, D.A. and Tushman, M.L. (1989), 'Organizational Framebending: Principles for Managing Reorientation', *Academy of Management Executive*, 3, 194–202.

Nahapiet, J. and Ghoshal, S. (1998), 'Social Capital, Intellectual Capital, and the Creation of Value in Firms', *Academy of Management Review*, 23(2), 242–66.

Narayanan, V.K. and Fahey, L. (1982), 'The Micro-politics of Strategy Formulation', *Academy of Management Review*, 7(1), 25–34.

Natsuno (2000) *i-mode Strategy* (in Japanese), Tokyo: Nikkei BP.

Nelson, R.P. and Winter, S.G. (1982), *An Evolutionary Theory of Economic Change*, Cambridge, MA: Belknap Press.

Nihon Keizai Shimbun (1995), 'Joint Development between NTT and a US Firm (Low-Cost Videoconferencing)', 9 May, 10.

Nihon Keizai Shimbun (1996), 'NTT and US Firm in Joint Development (a PC-Based Conferencing System that Breaks the "200,000 Barrier")', 5 February, 10.

Nihon Keizai Shimbun (1997a), 'NTT Creates a New Company (Remote Videoconferencing – in Partnership with 16 Other Companies)', 16 April, 8.

Nihon Keizai Shimbun (1997b), 'Introduction to Sign Language Support System', 6 March, 12.

Nihon Keizai Shimbun (1998a), 'Live Hookup over Network', 16 June, 8.

Nihon Keizai Shimbun (1998b), 'Government Services by Videophone: Installation in Every Household in Katsuraomura, Fukushima Prefecture', 12 February, 38.

Nihon Keizai Shimbun (1998c), 'Kirin Holds a Videoconference Spanning all its Offices', 6 August, 10.

Nihon Keizai Shimbun (1998d), 'Using Videoconferencing to Present Public Lectures (Sponsored by NTT and Mitsubishi Sogo Kenkyusho) – on the Theme of Venture Businesses and Regional Industry', 7 August, 10.

Nihon Kogyo Shimbun (1996), 'NTT Releases DOS/V-Compatible Version', 3 October, 3.

Nihon Kogyo Shimbun (1998a), 'Vitalizing Mountain Villages by Videophone: A Response to the Aging of Depopulated Areas', 25 February, 8.

Nihon Kogyo Shimbun (1998b), 'Shugakusha Cram School: Remote Schooling Via Videophone: Linking 23 Classrooms in Tokyo and Nationwide', 4 February, 6.

Nihon Kogyo Shimbun (1998c), 'No-Inventory Used Car Sales Via Videophone (Gulliver International Inc.)', 4 March, 6.

Nikkan Kogyo Shimbun (1998), 'Group Interviews Via Videophone (Dentsu Research Inc.)', 10 June, 7.

Nikkan Kogyo Shimbun (1999a), 'Tokin Installs a Videoconferencing System that Links its Domestic and Overseas Locations', 19 February, 7.

Nikkan Kogyo Shimbun (1999b), 'Tanabe Seiyaku Directs its Efforts toward Computerizing Sales (Links 50 Locations via Videoconference)', 19 February, 7.

Nikkan Kogyo Shimbun (2000), 'NTT Phoenix Offers Videoconferencing and Sharing of Materials', 9 February, 5.

Nikkei Ryutsu Shimbun (1997), 'Videoconferencing Network Links 56 Access Points: Faster Information Flow at Reduced Cost', 23 October, 3.

Nikkei Sangyo Shimbun (1996), 'Videoconferencing System: NTT promotes low-price terminal', 3 September, 1.

Nikkei Sangyo Shimbun (1997a), 'Videoconferencing System: Renders PC Nowhere to Go (NTT)', 29 January, 8.

Nikkei Sangyo Shimbun (1997b), 'Video Conference-Based Linguistic Research', 1 July, 2.

Nikkei Sangyo Shimbun (1997c), 'Anabuki Construction Installs a Videoconferencing System in all its Sales Locations, Putting the Company in Close Contact with Rural Areas', 25 June, 3.

Nikkei Sangyo Shimbun (1997c), 'Videoconferencing PC Terminal: System Extension Version from NTT', 18 September, 8.

Nikkei Sangyo Shimbun (1998a), 'TV Conference Hookup Network: President Delivers Boisterous New Year's Address (NTT Phoenix Communication Network)', 1 January, 3.

Nikkei Sangyo Shimbun (1998b), 'NTT Phoenix TV Conference Split onto 8 Screens', 1 September, 8.

Nikkei Sangyo Shimbun (1999), 'Home Delivery of Medicine via Videophone: Doctors in Katsuraomura, Fukushima Prefecture Making Remote Diagnoses', 14 April, 8.

Nikkei Sangyo Shimbun (2000), 'Participants View Videoconferencing Materials Simultaneously (NTT Phoenix)', 15 February, 2.

Nisbett, R. (2003), *The Geography of Thought*, New York: The Free Press.

Nohria, N. and Ghoshal, S. (1997), *The Differentiated Network: Organizing Multinational Corporations for Value Creation*, San Francisco, CA: Jossey-Bass.

Nonaka, I. (1991), 'The Knowledge-Creating Company', *Harvard Business Review*, 9, November–December, 96–104.

Nonaka, I. (1994), 'A Dynamic Theory of Organizational Knowledge Creation', *Organization Science*, 5(1), 14–37.

Nonaka, I. and Konno, N. (1998), 'The Concept of "Ba": Building a Foundation for Knowledge Creation', *California Management Review*, 40, 40–54.

Nonaka, I. and Takeuchi, H. (1995), *The Knowledge-Creating Company*, New York: Oxford University Press.

Nonaka, I. and Toyama, R. (2002), 'A Firm as a Dialectical Being: Towards a Dynamic Theory of a Firm', *Industrial and Corporate Change*, 11(5), 995–1009.

Nonaka, I. and Toyama, R. (2003), 'The Knowledge-Creating Theory Revisited: Knowledge Creation as a Synthesizing Process', *Knowledge Management Research and Practice*, 1(1), 2–10.

Nonaka, I. and Toyama, R. (2005), 'Strategy-as-Phronesis (in Japanese)', *Hitotsubashi Business Review*, Winter, 88–103.

Nonaka, I., Toyama, R. and Konno, N. (2000), '"Ba" and Leadership: A Unified Model of Dynamic Knowledge Creation', *Long Range Planning*, 33, 5–34.

Normann, R. (1977), *Management for Growth*, New York: Wiley.

NTT DoCoMo Technical Journal (1999), 'Feature Article on i-mode Service (in Japanese)', 7(2).

Nutt, P.C. and Backoff, R.W. (1997), 'Organizational Transformation', *Journal of Management Inquiry*, 6, 235–54.

Ohira, H. Kodama, M. and Yoshimoto, M. (2003a), 'The Development and Impact on Business of the World's First Live Video Streaming Distribution Platform for 3G Mobile Videophone Terminals', *International Journal of Electric Business*, 1(1), 94–105.

Ohira, H., Kodama, M. and Yoshimoto, M. (2003b), 'A World First Development of a Multipoint Videophone System over 3G–324M Protocol', *International Journal of Mobile Communications*, 1(3), 264–72.

Ohmae, K. (2004), 'The Business Professionalism (in Japanese)', *Diamond Harvard Business Review*, August, 38–46.

O'Reilly III, C. and Pfeffer, J. (2000), *Hidden Value: How Great Companies Achieve Extraordinary Results with Ordinary People*, Boston, MA: Harvard Business School.

O'Reilly III, C. and Tushman, M. (2004), 'The Ambidextrous Organization', *Harvard Business Review*, 82, April, 74–82.

Orlikowski, W.J. (2000), 'Using Technology and Constituting Structures: a Practice Lens for Studying Technology in Organizations', *Organization Science*, 11(4), 404–28.

Orlikowski, W.J. (2002), 'Knowing in Practice: Enacting a Collective Capability in Distributed Organizing', *Organization Science*, 13(3), 249–73.

Orr, J. (1996), *Talking about Machines: An Ethnography of a Modern Job*, Ithaca, NY: ILP Press.

Orton, J.D. and Weick, K.E. (1990), 'Loosely Coupled Systems: A Reconceptualization', *Academy of Management Review*, 15(2), 203–23.

Osterlof, M. and Frey, B. (2000), 'Motivation, Knowledge Transfer, and Organizational Forms', *Organization Science*, 11(3), 538–50.

Pan, S.L. and Scarbrough, H. (1998) 'A Socio-Technical View of Knowledge-Sharing at Buckman Laboratories', *Journal of Knowledge Management*, 2(1), 63–4.

Pascale, R.T. (1985), 'The Paradox of Corporate Culture: Reconciling Ourselves to Socialization', *California Management Review*, 27(3), 26–40.

Pascale, R.T. (1990), *Managing on the Edge: How the Smartest Companies Use Conflict to Stay Ahead*, New York: Simon and Schuster.

Paul, J., Costley, L., Howell, P. and Dorfman, W. (2002), 'The Mutability of Charisma in Leadership Research', *Management Decision*, 40(1), 192–7.

Pawlowski, S.D., and Robey, D. (2004), 'Bridging User Organizations: Knowledge Brokering and the Work of Information Technology Professionals', *MIS Quarterly*, 28(4), 645–72.

Peng, K. and Akutsu, S. (2001), 'A Mentality Theory of Knowledge Creation and Transfer: Why Some Smart People Resist New Ideas and Some Don't', in Nonaka, I. and Teece, D. (eds), *Managing Industrial Knowledge: Creation, Transfer and Utilization*, London: Sage Publications, 105–23.

Peng, K. and Nisbett, R.E. (1999), 'Culture Dialectics, and Reasoning about Contradiction', *American Psychologist*, 54, 741–54.

Pettigrew, A.M. (1977), 'Strategy Formulation as a Political Process', *International Studies of Management and Organization*, 7(2), 78–87.

Pettigrew, A.M. (1985), *The Awakening Giant*, Oxford: Basil Blackwell.

Pettigrew, A.M. (1990), 'Longitudinal Field Research on Change: Theory and Practice', *Organization Science*, 1(1), 267–92.

Pettigrew, A.M. (2000), *The Innovating Organization*, London: Sage Publications.

Pettigrew, A.(2003), 'Strategy as Process, Power and Change', in Cummings, S. and Wilson, D. (eds), *Images of Strategy*, London: Blackwell.

Politis, J.D. (2001), 'The Relationship of Various Leadership Styles to Knowledge Management', *Leadership and Organizational Development Journal*, 22(8), 354–64.

Popper, M. and Lipshitz, R. (2000), 'Installing Mechanisms and Instilling Values: The Role of Leaders in Organizational Learning', *The Learning Organization*, 7(3), 135–45.

Porter, M. (1980), *Competitive Strategy: Techniques for Analyzing Industries and Competitors*, New York: Free Press.

Porter, M. (1985), *Competitive Advantage*, New York: Free Press.

Powell, W. and Brantley, P. (1992), 'Competitive Cooperation in Biotechnology: Learning Through Networks?', in Noria, N. and Eccles, R.G. (eds), *Network and Organizations: Structure, Form and Action*, Boston, MA: Harvard Business School, 366–94.

Powell, W., Koput, K. and Smith-Doerr, L. (1996), 'Inter-Organizational Collaboration and the Locus of Innovation: Networks of Learning in Biotechnology', *Administrative Science Quarterly*, 41, 116–46.

Prahalad, C.K. and Doz, Y. (1987), *The Multinational Mission: Balancing Local Demands and Global Vision*, New York: Free Press.

Prahalad, C.K. and Hamel, G. (1990), 'The Core Competence of the Corporation', *Harvard Business Review*, 68, 79–91.

Prahalad, C.K. and Ramaswamy, V. (2000), 'Co-opting Customer Competence', *Harvard Business Review*, 78(1), 79–87.

Prahalad, C.K. and Ramaswamy, V. (2004), *The Future of Competition: Co-Creating Unique Value With Customers*, Boston, MA: Harvard Business School Press.

Priem, R. and Butler, J.E. (2001), 'Is the Resource-Based 'View' a Useful Perspective for Strategic Management Research?', *Academy of Management Review*, 26(1), 22–40.

Proctor, T., Tan, K.H. and Fuse, K. (2004), 'Cracking the Incremental Paradigm of Japanese Creativity', *Creativity and Innovation Management*, 13(4), 207–15.

Quinn, J.B., Anderson, P. and Finkelstein, S. (1996), 'Managing Professional Intellect: Making the Most of the Best', *Harvard Business Review*, March–April, 71–80.

Quinn, R.E. and Cameron, K.S. (eds) (1988), *Paradox and Transformation: Toward a Theory of Change in Organization and Management*, Cambridge, MA: Ballinger.

Reimann, B.C. (1989), *Managing for Value*, Oxford: Basil Blackwell.

Ring, S. and Van de Ven, A. (1994), 'Developmental process of cooperative interorganizational relationships', *Academy of Management Review*, 23(3), 393–404.

Robbins, S.P. (1974), *Managing Organizational Conflict: A Non-traditional Approach*, Englewood Cliffs, NJ: Prentice Hall.

Romanelli, E. and Tushman, M.L. (1994) 'Organizational Transformation as Punctuated Equilibrium: An Empirical Test', *Academy of Management Journal*, 3, 1141–66.

Rond, M. and Bouchikhi, H. (2004), 'On the Dialectics of Strategic Alliances', *Organization Science*, 15(1), 56–69.

Rosenberg, N. (1982), *Inside the Black Box: Technology and Economics*, Cambridge: Cambridge University Press.

Rosenkopf, L. and Tushman, M. (1994), 'The Co-Evolution of Technology and Organizations', in Baum, J. and Singh, J. (eds), *Evolutionary Dynamics of Organizations*, Oxford: Oxford University Press.

Rosenkopf, L. and Tushman, M. (1998), 'The Coevolution of Community Networks and Technology: Lessons from the Flight Simulation Industry', *Industrial and Corporate Change*, 7(6), 311–46.

Rousseau, D., Sitkin, S., Burt, R. and Camerer, C. (1998), 'Not so Different After All: A Cross-Discipline View of Trust', *Academy of Management Review*, 23(3), 393–404.

Rumelt, R. (1974), *Strategy, Structure and Profitability*, Boston, MA: Harvard Business School Press.

Ryle, G. (1949), *The Concept of Mind*, London, UK: Hutchinson.

Sadler, P. (2001), Leadership and Organizational Learning, in Dierkes, M. *et al.* (eds) *Handbook of Organizational Learning and Knowledge*, Oxford: Oxford University Press, 415–42.

Sama-Fredricks, D. (2003), 'Strategizing as Lived Experience and Strategists: Everyday Efforts to Shape Strategic Direction', *Journal of Management Studies*, 40(1), 141–74.

Sanchez, R. and Mahoney, T. (1996), 'Modularity, Flexibility, and Knowledge Management in Product and Organizational Design', *Strategic Management Journal*, 17(winter special issue), 63–76.

Sawhney, M. and Prandelli, E. (2000), 'Communities of Creation: Managing Distributed Innovation in Turbulent Markets', *California Management Review*, 42, 24–54.

Schelling, T.C. (1978), *Micromotives and Macrobehavior*, New York: W.W. Norton and Co.

Schon, A. (1987), *Educating the Reflective Practitioner*, San Francisco: Jossey-Bass.

Schon, D.A. (1983), *The Reflective Practitioner*, New York: Basic Book.

Schutz, A. (1932), *Der sinnhafte Aufbau der sozialen Welt*, Berlin: Springer.

Seifter, H. and Economy, P. (2001), *Leadership Ensemble: Lessons in Collaborative Management from the World's Only Conductorless Orchestra*, New York: Times Books.

Seo, M. and Douglas Creed, W. (2002), 'Institutional Contradictions, Praxis, and Institutional Change: A Dialectical Perspective', *Academy of Management Review*, 27(2), 222–47.

Shannon, C. and Weaver, W. (1949), *The Mathematical Theory of Communications*. Urbana: University of Illinois Press.

Shone, D.A. (1983), *The Reflective Practitioner: How Professionals Think in Action*, New York: Basic Books.

Siggelkow, N. (2001), 'Change in the Presence of Fit: The Rise, the Fall and the Renaissance of Liz Claiborne', *Academy of Management Journal*, 44(4), 838–57.

Silvermann, D. (2000), *Doing Qualitative Research*. Thousand Oaks, CA: Sage.

Simon, H.A. (1969), *The Architecture of Complexity: Hierarchic Systems, The Science of the Artificial*, 3rd edn, Cambridge, MA: MIT Press.

Simon, H.A. (1976), *Administrative Behavior*, 3rd edn, New York: Free Press.

Sitkin, S., Rousseau, D., Burt, R. and Camerer, C. (eds) (1998), 'Special Topics Forum on Trust in and between Organizations', *Academy of Management Review*, 23(3).

Sloan, A. (1963), *My Years with General Motors*, London: Sidgwick and Jackson.

Spears, L. (1995), *Reflections on Leadership*, New York: Wiley.

Spender, J.C. (1990), *Industry Recipes: An Enquiry into the Nature and Sources of Managerial Judgement*, Oxford: Basil Blackwell.

Spender, J.C. (1992), 'Knowledge Management: Putting your Technology Strategy on Track', in Khalil, T.M. and Bayraktar, B.A. (eds), *Management of Technology*, 3, Norcross, GA: Industrial Engineering and Management Press, 404–13.

Spender, J.C. (1996a), 'Making Knowledge the Basis of a Dynamic Theory of the Firm', *Strategic Management Journal*, 17(1), 45–62.

Spender, J.C. (1996b), 'Organizational Knowledge, Learning and Memory: Three Concepts in Search of a Theory', *Journal of Organizational Change*, 9(1), 63–78.

Spradley, J.P. (1979), '*The Ethnographic Interview*', New York, Holt, Rinehart & Winston.

Stalk, G., Evans, P. and Schulman, L.E. (1992), 'Competing on Capabilities: The New Rules of Corporate Strategy', *Harvard Business Review*, March–April, 57–69.

Star, S.L. (1989), 'The Structure of Ill-Structured Solutions: Boundary Objects and Heterogeneous Distributed Problem Solving', in Huhns, M. and Gasser, I.L. (eds), *Readings in Distributed Artificial Intelligence*, Menlo Park, CA: Morgan Kaufman.

Starbuck, W.H. (1992), 'Learning by Knowledge-Intensive Firms', *Journal of Management Studies*, 29(3), 713–40.

Stein, B. and Kanter, R.M. (1980), 'Building the Parallel Organization: Toward Mechanisms for Quality of Work Life', *Journal of Applied Behavioral Science*, 16(1), 371–88.

Stepanek, M. (2000), 'Spread the Knowhow', *BusinessWeek*, 23 October, www.businessweek.com/2000/00_43/b3704051.htm, 27 July 2006.

Stewart, T. (1997), *Intellectual Capital: The New Wealth of Organizations*, New York: Doubleday.

Storck, J. and Patricia, A. (2000), 'Knowledge Diffusion through Strategic Communities', *Sloan Management Review*, 41, 63–74.

Strauss, A.K. (1987), *Qualitative Analysis for Social Scientists*. New York: Cambridge University Press.

Strauss, A.K. and Corbin, J. (1990), *Basics of Qualitative Research: Grounded Theory Procedures and Techniques*, Newbury Park, CA: Sage Publications.

Suchman, L.A. (1987), *Plans and Situated Action: The Problem of Human Machine Communication*, Cambridge, UK: Cambridge University Press.

Teece, D.J. (1982), 'Towards an Economic Theory of the Multiproduct Firm', *Journal of Economic Behavior and Organization*, 3(1), 39–63.

Teece, D.J. (1987), 'Conclusion', in Teece, D.J. (ed.) *The Competitive Challenge: Strategies for Industrial Innovation and Renewal*, New York: Harper and Row Publishers.

Teece, D.J. (1998), 'Capturing Value from Knowledge Assets', *California Management Review*, 40(3), 55–76.

Teece, D.J., Pisano, G. and Shuen, A. (1997), 'Dynamic Capabilities and Strategic Management', *Strategic Management Journal*, 18(3), 509–33.

Thompson, J.D. (1967), *Organizations in Action*, New York: McGraw Hill.

Tichy, N.M. with Cohen, E. (1997), *The Leadership Engine: How Winning Companies Build Leaders at Every Level*, New York: HarperCollins.

Tichy, N.M. and Devanna, M. (1986), *The Transformational Leader*, Chichester: Wiley.

Toffler, A. (1990), *Powershift: Knowledge, Wealth and Violence at the Edge of the 21st Century*, New York: Bantam Books.

Toulmin, S. (1990), *Cosmopolis: The Hidden Agenda of Modernity*, Chicago: The University of Chicago Press.

Tracy, L. (1989), *The Living Organization: Systems of Behavior*, Westport, CT: Greenwood Publishing Group, Inc.

Trowt-Bayard, T. and Wilcox, J. (1997), *Videoconferencing and Interactive Multimedia: The Whole Picture*, New York: Flatiron Publishing Inc.

Tsoukas, H. (1996), 'The firm as a distributed knowledge system: A constructionist approach', *Strategic Management Journal*, 17(1), 11–25.

Tsoukas, H. (1997), 'Forms of Knowledge and Forms of Life in Organizational Contexts', in China, R. (ed.), *The Realm of Organization*, London: Routledge.

Tsoukas, H. and Cummings, S. (1997), 'Marginalization and Recovery: The Emergence of Aristotelian Themes in Organization Studies', *Organization Studies*, 18(4), 655–83.

Tsushin Kogyo Shimbun (1999b), 'NTT's New Phoenix Mini Video Phone Shows Brisk Sales', 13 September, 1.

Turnbull, P.W. and Valla, J.-P. (1986), *Strategies for International Industrial Marketing: The Management of Customer Relationships in European Industrial Markets*, London: Croom Helm.

Tushman, M.L. (1977), 'Special Boundary Roles in the Innovation Process', *Administrative Science Quarterly*, 22, 587–605.

Tushman, M. and Nadler, D. (1978), 'Information Processing as an Integrating Concept in Organizational Design', *Academy of Management Review*, 3(3), 613–24.

Tushman, M.L. and O'Reilly, C.A. (1997), *Winning Through Innovation*, Cambridge, MA: Harvard Business School Press.

Tushman, M. and Romanelli, E. (1985), 'Organizational Evolution: A Metamorphosis Model of Convergence and Reorientation', *Research in Organizational Behavior*, 7(2), 171–222.

Ulrich, H. and Probst, G.J.B. (1984), *Self-Organization and Management of Social Systems*, Berlin: Springer Verlag.

Van de Ven, A.H. and Poole, M.S. (1988), 'Paradoxical Requirements for a Theory of Change', in Quinn, R.E. and Cameron, K.S. (eds), *Paradox and Transformation: Toward a Theory of Change in Organization and Management*, Cambridge, MA: Ballinger, 19–63.

Van de Ven, A.H. and Poole, M.S. (1995), 'Explaining Development and Change in Organizations', *Academy of Management Review*, 20(5), 510–40.

Van Maanen, J.V. (1979), 'The Fact of Fiction in Organizational Ethnography', *Administrative Science Quarterly*, 24, 539–50.

Vangen, S. and Huxham, C. (2003), 'Nurturing Collaborative Relations, Building Trust in Interorganizational Collaboration', *The Journal of Applied Behavioral Science*, 39(1), 5–31.

Vansina, L., Taillieu, T. and Schruijer, S. (1998), '"Managing" Multiparty Issues: Learning from Experience', in Woodman, R. and Pasmore, W. (eds), *Research in Organizational Change and Development*, 11, Greenwich, CT: JAI, 159–81.

Volberda, H.W. and Elfring, T. (2001), *Rethinking Strategy*, London: Sage.

Von Hippel, E. (1997), 'Successful and Failing Internal Corporate Ventures: An Empirical Analysis', *Industrial Marketing Management*, 6, 163–74.

Walsh, J.P. (1995), 'Managerial and Organizational Cognition: Notes from a Trip down Memory Lane', *Organization Science*, 6(3), 280–321.

Walton, R.E. and McKersie, R.B. (1965), *A Behavioral Theory of Labor Negotiations: An Analysis of a Social Interaction System*, New York: McGraw Hill.

Watkins, K. and Marsick, V. (1993), *Sculpting the Learning Organization*, San Francisco: Jossey-Bass Inc.

Watts, J. (2003), *Six Degrees: The Science of a Connected Age*, New York: W.W. Norton and Company.

Watts, J. and Strogatz, S. (1998), 'Collective Dynamics of "Small-World" Networks', *Nature*, 393(4), 440–42.

Webb, A. (1991), 'Coordination: A Problem in Public Sector Management', *Policy and Politics*, 19(4), 229–41.

Weber, M. (1924/1947), *The Theory of Social and Economic Organization*, vol. II, translated by A.H. Henderson and T. Parsons, New York: Free Press.

Weick, C.W. (2004), *Out of Context: A Creative Approach to Strategic Management*, Mason, OH: South-Western.

Weick, K.E. (1976), 'Educational Organizations as Loosely Coupled Systems', *Administrative Science Quarterly*, 21, 1–19.

Weick, K.E. (1979), *The Social Psychology of Organizing*, 2nd edn, Reading, MA: Addison-Wesley.

Weick, K.E. (1982), Management of Organizational Change among Loosely Coupled Elements, in Goodman, P.S. (ed.), *Change in Organizations*, San Francisco, CA: Jossey-Bass, 375–408.

Weick, K.E. (1987), 'Substitutes for Corporate Strategy', in Teece, D.J. (ed.), *The Competitive Challenge: Strategies for Industrial Innovation and Renewal*, New York: Harper and Row Publishers.

Weick, K.E. (1989), 'Theory Construction as Disciplined Imagination', *Academy of Management Review*, 14(4), 516–31.

Weick, K E. (1995), Sensemaking *in Organizations*, London: Sage.

Weick, K.E. and Browning, L. (1986), 'Argument and Narration in Organizational Communication', *Journal of Management*, 12(2), 243–59.

Weick, K.E and Roberts, H. (1993), 'Collective Mind in Organizations: Heedful Interrelating on Flight Decks', *Administrative Science Quarterly*, 38(1), 357–81.

Weiss, J. and Hughes, J. (2005), 'What Collaboration? Accept – and Actively Manage – Conflict', *Harvard Business Review*, 83(3), 139–45.

Welch, J. with Welch, S. (2005), *Winning*, New York: Harper Business.

Wenger, E.C. (1998), *Community of Practice: Learning, Meaning and Identity*, Cambridge: Cambridge University Press.

Wenger, E.C. (2000), 'Communities of Practice: The Organizational Frontier', *Harvard Business Review*, 78(1), 139–45.

Wenger, E., McDermott, R. and Snyder, W.M. (2002), *Cultivating Communities of Practice*, Boston, MA: Harvard Business School Press.

Wernerfelt, B. (1984), 'A Resource-Based View of the Firm', *Strategic Management Journal*, 5, 171–80.

Westley, F. and Vredenburg, H. (1991), 'Strategic Bridging: The Collaboration between Environmentalists and Business in the Marketing of Green Products', *Journal of Applied Behavioral Science*, 27(2), 65–90.

Whittington, R. (1996), 'Strategy as Practice', *Long Range Planning*, 29(5), 731–5.

Whittington, R. (2003), 'The Work of Strategizing and Organizing for a Practice Perspective', *Strategic Organization*, 1(1), 117–25.

Whittington, R. (2004), 'Strategy after Modernism: Recovering Practice', *European Management Review*, 1(1), 62–8.

Williamson, O.E. (1975), *Markets and Hierarchies: Analysis and Antitrust Implications*, New York: Free Press.

Williamson, O.E. (1981), 'The Economics of Organizations: The Transaction Cost Approach', *American Journal of Sociology*, 87(3), 548–57.

Williamson, O.E. (1985), *The Economic Institutions of Capitalism*, New York: Free Press.

Williamson, O.E. (1991), 'Comparative economic organization: The analysis of discrete structural alternatives', *Administrative Science Quarterly*, 36(2), 269–96.

Wood, D.J. and Gray, B. (1991), Toward a Comprehensive Theory of Collaboration, *Journal of Applied Behavioral Sciences*, 27(2), 139–63.

Wudunn, S. (1999), 'Japan Bets on a Wired World to Win Back Its Global Niche', *The New York Times*, 30 August, 1.

Yanow, D. (2000), *Conducting Interpretive Policy Analysis*, Thousand Oaks, Sage.

Yin, R.K. (1994), *Case Study Research: Design and Methods*, 2nd edn, London: Sage.

Yomiuri Shimbun (1998a), 'Online Karaoke At Home with Latest Songs', 19 May, 11.

Yomiuri Shimbun (1998b), 'Live Marriage Service Hookup Across the Pacific', 16 June, 8.

Yu, T.F. (2003), 'A Subjective Approach to Strategic Management', *Managerial and Decision Economics*, 24(4), 335–45.

Index